Private Tucker's Boer War Diary

Private Tucker's Boer War Diary

THE TRANSVAAL WAR OF
1899, 1900, 1901 & 1902
WITH THE NATAL FIELD FORCES

COMPILED & DESIGNED BY
PAMELA TODD & DAVID FORDHAM

ELM TREE BOOKS · LONDON

**TO
ANN**

First published in Great Britain 1980
by Elm Tree Books/Hamish Hamilton Ltd
Garden House 57–59 Long Acre London WC2E 9JZ

Copyright © 1980 by Pamela Todd and David Fordham

Book design by David Fordham

British Library Cataloguing in Publication Data

Todd, Pamela
   Private Tucker's Boer War diary.
   1. South African War, 1899–1902
   I. Title   II. Fordham, David
   968'.204   DT930
   ISBN 0-241-10272-3

Photoset and printed in Great Britain by
BAS Printers Limited, Over Wallop, Hampshire

Contents

Acknowledgements

We would like to thank everyone who has helped us with the book. We are especially grateful to Professor Denis Judd; Roger Houghton, Connie Austen Smith and Peter Kilborn at Elm Tree Books; Susan Jeffreys, the *Punch* Librarian; the British Library; Colonel J. Baker and Tom Craze of the Royal Green Jackets Museum, Winchester; George and Ann Fordham; and to Marion Harding and the staff of the National Army Museum. We would also like to thank Mr. Spark for producing the maps.

The following have been good enough to give us permission to quote from copyright works: Faber and Faber Limited—Deney's Reitz's *Commando*; The Estate of the late Rudyard Kipling; *Punch*; Cassell Limited—Frederick Treves' *The Tale of a Field Hospital*; The Hamlyn Publishing Group Limited—Winston Churchill's *Frontiers and War*. J. B. Atkins is quoted by kind permission of the *Manchester Guardian* and G. W. Steevens by kind permission of the *Daily Mail*.

PT & DF

Books Consulted

Amery, L. S. (Editor): *The Times History of the War in South Africa (Vols I–V) (1900–4)*; Arthur, Sir G.: *Not Worth Reading (1938)*; Arthur, Sir G.: *Life of Lord Kitchener (1920)*; Atkins, J. B.: *The Relief of Ladysmith (1900)*; Battersby, H. F. P.: *In The Web of War (1900)*; Billington, R. C.: *A Mule-Driver at the Front (1900)*; *Black and White*; Bovill, J. H.: *Natives Under the Transvaal Flag (1900)*; Bron, A.: *Diary of a Nurse in South Africa (1901)*; Churchill, W. S.: *Frontiers and War (1962)*; Cunliffe, Sir F. H. E: *History of the Boer War (2 Vols) (1901)*; Dickson, W. K. L.: *The Biograph in Battle (1901)*; Doyle, Sir A. Conan: *The War in South Africa (1902)*; Doyle, Sir A. Conan: *The Great Boer War (1903)*; Fremantle, Sir F. E.: *Impressions of a Doctor in Khaki (1901)*; Fuller, J. F. C.: *The Last of the Gentleman's Wars (1937)*; Gardner, B.: *The Lion's Cage (1969)*; Gardner, B.: *Mafeking: A Victorian Legend (1966)*; Grant, M. H.: *History of the War in South Africa (1906) (2 Vols)*; Haggard, Sir H. Rider: *The Last Boer War (1899)*; Hobhouse, Emily: *Camps of Women and Children in the Cape (1901)*; Hobhouse, Emily: *The Brunt of The War and Where it Fell (1902)*; Hobson, J. A.: *The War in South Africa (1900)*; Holt, E.: *The Boer War (1958)*; *Illustrated London News*; Judd, D.: *The Boer War (1977)*; Kruger, R.: *Goodbye Dolly Gray (1959)*; Lane, Margaret: *Edgar Wallace (1939)*; Lyttelton, Hon. Sir. N. G.: *Eighty years (1927)*; Melville, C. H.: *Life of General the Rt. Hon Sir Redvers Buller (2 Vols) (1923)*; Milne, J.: *The Epistles of Atkins (1902)*; Pemberton, W. Baring: *Battles of the Boer War (1964)*; *Pen Pictures of the War by Men at The Front (1900)*; *Punch*; Reitz, D.: *Commando (1929)*; *Sphere*; Symons, J.: *Buller's Campaign (1963)*; Treves, Sir F.: *The Tale of a Field Hospital (1912)*; Unger, F. W.: *With 'Bobs' and Kruger (1901)*; Wallace, R. H. E.: *Unofficial Despatches (1901)*; Wet, C. R. De: *Three Years' War (1902)*; Wilson, H. W.: *With the Flag to Pretoria (4 Vols) (1901)*

Picture Credits

The photographs and illustrations in this book are reproduced by kind permission of the following. The corresponding letter of the alphabet can be found after each individual caption, indicating the source of the illustration.

Photographs

A   The National Army Museum
B   Punch
C   With the Flag to Pretoria
D   The Illustrated London News Picture Library
E   The Imperial War Museum
F   Guerilla War
G   War Pictures
H   The Royal Green Jackets Museum, Winchester
J   Orbis Picture Library
K   Robert Hunt Library
L   The Royal Photographic Society
M   Sphere Magazine
N   The Postcard Collection of Toni and Valmai Holt
O   The Radio Times Hulton Picture Library
P   Babty and Co
R   The Review of Reviews
S   Kevin MacDonnell
T   John Topham Picture Library
V   The Maritime Museum, Greenwich
W   Popperfoto
Z   Stanley Gibbons

The two volumes of Guerilla War *were kindly lent by Tonie and Valmai Holt*

Glossary

Afrikaner: one descended from settlers of Dutch, Huguenot, Flemish or German stock, and living in South Africa
Boer: British term used to describe the Afrikaners; true meaning 'farmer'
Donga: dip or depression in the terrain
Dorp: town, village
Drift: ford across a river
Kaffir: strictly a particular tribe, but used as a general term for all natives in South Africa. Later became a term of abuse
Kopje: small hill
Kraal: African settlement or stock enclosure
Laager: encampment
Landdrost: magistrate
Nek: mountain pass or break in the hills
Outspan: to unyoke oxen from wagon
Spruit: stream, small river
Veldt: the earth, countryside
Vrou: wife, woman

A scene from the Battle of Majuba 1881.
(A)

Chronology

A brief chronological list of the contributory and main events which led up to the Anglo-Boer War of 1899–1902.

1652 Cape Town captured by Jan van Biebeeck, a Dutch ship's surgeon, on behalf of the Council of Seventeen, the ruling body of the Dutch East India Company
1683 Natal first visited by the British
1795 British force captures Cape Town
1825 Stephanus Paulus Johannes Kruger born in Cape Colony on 10 October
1836 Joseph Chamberlain born
1837 The Great Trek. Hundreds of Dutch farmers take their families to the remote parts of Natal, Orange Free States and the southern Transvaal in a search for freedom from British domination
1837 Hendrik Potgieter defeats the Matabele tribe, led by Mzilikazi, and claims the Transvaal
1845 Natal annexed by Britain
1848 Orange Free States annexed by Britain under the title of Orange River Sovereignty
1852 Sand River Convention recognizes the independence of the Transvaal, creating the South African Republic
1854 Bloemfontein Convention recognizes the independence of the Orange Free States, creating the second Boer Republic
1869 First sensational discovery of diamonds at Kimberley
1870 Cecil John Rhodes arrives in South Africa
1877 Transvaal annexed by Britain
1878 President Paul Kruger visits London with a petition, in an attempt to regain independence for the Transvaal peacefully
1879 British forces fight against the Zulu tribes, led by Chief Cetewayo
1880/1 1st Anglo-Boer War
1881 Battle of Majuba
1881 W. E. Gladstone's government restores the Transvaal's independence at the Pretoria Convention
1886/7 Huge gold deposits found in Johannesburg
1895 Joseph Chamberlain becomes Colonial Secretary and adopts a policy of 'aggressive Imperialism'
1895 Cecil Rhodes becomes Prime Minister of the self-governing Cape Colony
1895 Cecil Rhodes attempts unsuccessfully to overthrow the South African Republic. Jameson Raid
1897 Sir Alfred Milner elected as new High Commissioner and Governor of the Cape
1899 Bloemfontein talks break down
1899 Boers deliver a warlike ultimatum on 9 October
1899 Boers invade the Cape Colony on 12 October

Tucker and His Diary

Private Tucker's Boer War Diary was found in the traditional attic. A shabby account book, it is written in fading inks and, in some places, only in pencil. There are no bloodstains on the book! The existence of such a war-time diary, written by a young, simply-educated private, is rare and for that reason we have decided to keep the diary intact. We have included all the entries, even if they are small and perhaps repetitious, as these reflect, more honestly than any brief explanation could, the later crushing regularity of the routine for the lower ranks once the glory of full scale battles had been replaced by the guerilla tactics which the Boers were forced to adopt.

Little is now known about Frederick Tucker. The only surviving photograph of him, reproduced here and on the cover, was taken after the Boer War and shows a more experienced soldier than the young man of twenty-four who travelled to South Africa. He was born in 1875. The son of a lifeboatman, he was deserted by his mother during infancy. His childhood spent with an aged grandmother in Kent was harsh, his schooling was scarce and, by the time he was fourteen, he had enlisted in the army. He served in the Boer War and in the First World War, working between wars in the same gasworks where, as a cold and hungry child, he had scavenged for fuel. His diary, written during the three-year period of the war, serves a dual purpose. Not only does it sincerely record the daily life of a private soldier at the front—his fears, diet, triumphs, frustrations and, finally, the sheer, stifling monotony—it also provides a valuable insight into the activities, prejudices and attitudes of the late Victorian era.

Private Tucker (left) poses for the family album photograph, and (below) Tucker's notice to join the Army issued at the beginning of October 1899.

Introduction: Causes of Conflict

Johannes Paulus Kruger was born near Colesburg, Cape Colony, in 1825. As a boy of twelve he travelled with his family on the Great Trek. They settled first in Natal, and then in 1842 crossed the Vaal and settled in Rustenburg. Kruger was appointed Deputy Field Cornet under the Boer commando system when he was only seventeen and Field Cornet ten years later. He was obstinately religious and read nothing but the bible—newspaper reports of the war had to be read out to him—however there were rumours that he and his government were corrupt. His notoriously cruel attitude towards African natives and the fact that he turned a blind eye to 'presents' supported these rumours and underlined his hypocritical nature.

His dour expression and whiskered face quickly became familiar and delighted caricaturists the world over. (C)

The complicated and convoluted motives behind Private Tucker's Anglo Boer War of 1899 to 1902 stretch back to the Great Trek of the late 1830s when the Dutch settlers first settled in the Transvaal and the Orange Free State, away from the British domination they had come to despise. However, within forty years the Transvaal found itself in a precarious financial situation and threatened by Cetewayo, the chief of the Zulus, with a massive native war. Using the native war as a pretext, Lord Carnarvon, the Conservative Government's Colonial Secretary and avowed Empire builder, sent Sir Theophilus Shepstone to the Transvaal with authority to annex it to the British Crown. Carnarvon saw this as the first step towards confederation, believing that if one of the Boer republics came under the British flag, the other would willingly follow. For four months, Shepstone probed the problem diplomatically, using 'champagne and sherry' techniques. Then, on 12 April, 1877, he issued a proclamation annexing the Transvaal. The Boers were promised their own government, their own laws and their own legislature. President Burgers issued a formal protest, Cetewayo sent his warriors home, Shepstone became administrator of the new government and found 12s and 6d in the Treasury, and Lord Carnarvon chalked up a new colony to the British Empire without shedding a single drop of blood. (Although two years later it fell to the British to quell the Zulu uprising.)

Not all the burghers were happy about the new situation, however, and Paul Kruger, leader of the anti-annexation party, travelled twice to London, armed with petitions, to remind Carnarvon of his still unfulfilled pledge for Boer self-government. The Conservatives showed no interest in the Boer grievances and when, in 1880, Gladstone and the Liberal Party came to power, the Boers looked forward to the promised improvements. Gladstone had, undoubtedly, supported and championed the Boer cause before the election, but the Transvaal was rich in mineral deposits and he was not urged to forfeit this source of wealth. Far from improving, the Boer situation worsened and they soon realized that they would have to act or forever remain under British domination. Exhibiting their characteristic fighting spirit, they rose in rebellion in December 1880 and delivered a series of crushing defeats on the outnumbered British forces stationed in South Africa. Of these, the Battle of Majuba was the most disastrous and eighteen years later the British troops were to charge into battle shouting, 'Remember Majuba!' At the Pretoria Convention in 1881, Britain awarded the Transvaal its independence but, by claiming suzerainty, continued to hold the reins.

In 1886 gold was discovered in the Witwatersrand area. Johannesburg rapidly grew to become a huge cosmopolitan city, bustling with 50,000 Europeans (Uitlanders) and almost 100,000 black miners. The majority of the Uitlanders were British. They financed the booming gold industry with British capital and employed British technological skills.

Kruger, wary of their growing strength and financial power, refused to grant the Uitlanders the vote unless they had lived in the Transvaal for fourteen years. Having successfully excluded them from playing any part in the running of the country, he proceeded, with effortless legerdemain, to monopolize the dynamite industry and tax them relentlessly. The friction caused by Kruger's refusal to 'hand my country over to strangers' was not the sole cause of the second war. More discontent was fuelled by Cecil Rhodes, diamond millionaire, Prime Minister of the Cape Colony and defender of the Uitlanders' cause, who had plans for a northward expansion right through Transvaal. Add to this the unpopular shadow of the British claim to suzerainty and the bomb was complete. Of course, the fuse had still to be lit, which was where Dr Leander Starr Jameson, a close friend of Cecil Rhodes, stepped forward. A hot-headed braggart, he had assembled an armed force just across the Transvaal border ostensibly to protect 'the thousands of unarmed men, women and children of our race at the mercy of well-armed Boers', and, on Sunday 29 December, 1895, he set off to 'kick the Boers all around the Transvaal'. In fact, the opposite occurred. The Raid was a shambles, Jameson was imprisoned, Rhodes' political career was in ruins, and Joseph Chamberlain, the British Colonial Secretary, was quick to disassociate himself and the Conservative and Unionist Government from any responsibility.

The German Emperor, Wilhelm II, sent a telegram to Kruger congratulating him on having preserved his independence

General Sir George Colley's men reconnoitering the impressive heights of Majuba. The battle, fought on 26 February, 1881, proved a humiliating failure for the British. Colley did not live to bear the blame; he was among those who died during the battle. (A)

Alfred Austin, the Poet Laureate, rushed into print after the Jameson Raid with a neat piece of propaganda entitled 'Jameson's Ride'.

There are girls in the gold-reef city,
There are mothers and children too!
And they cry, 'Hurry up, for pity!'
So what can a brave man do?

Pretoria before the outbreak of war. The wagons in the foreground belong to the country Boers, who, four times a year, travelled to Pretoria for Nachtmaal (Holy Communion). They brought their wives and children and camped out on the church square for a week, taking time off from their prayers to visit the town's shops and stock up for the next three months. (C)

'ALL THE COMFORTS OF A HOME!'
John Bull (Inspector of Transvaal School).
'Look here, Mr. Kruger! I've just received
this complaint from the boys. Perhaps you'll
kindly inform me what it means?'
Mr. Kruger (Headmaster). 'Complaints,
Mr. Bull! I've heard no complaints! Why,
they're as happy as the day is long!'

When the Uitlanders petitioned the Queen
with their grievances, Kruger was finally
compelled to acknowledge their cause and he
met several times with Alfred Milner,
although he was still far from prepared to
make any concessions. (B)

"ALL THE COMFORTS OF A HOME!"

Joseph Chamberlain was also a favourite of
the caricaturists. He wore his hair close cut
and his monocle proudly. As a young man he
had made enough money from the profits of
his Birmingham screw factory to enable him
to devote himself to public life at the young
age of thirty-eight. He entered Parliament
as a Radical Liberal, became President of
the Board of Trade, broke with Gladstone
over the Irish Home Rule question and
became a leader of the Liberal Unionist
party, who eventually joined in coalition with
Lord Salisbury and the Conservatives. He
became Colonial Secretary in 1895 and was
an ardent Imperialist. (F)

QUERY
Is it Kruger or Krüger?
The point's truly knotty.
It may be the latter
When Kruger is dotty

'without appealing for the help of friendly powers' – a scarcely veiled hint that Germany would have taken Kruger's side in the event of trouble for which Queen Victoria felt obliged to reprimand her grandson.

The Raid served to strengthen anti-British feeling and threw a new light on Kruger as the strong man of Afrikaner nationalism. Kruger had little time, however, to linger in the limelight. He was busy spending a quarter of his state revenue on arms. When Sir Harry Escombe, the Prime Minister of Natal, questioned him on such extensive re-arming, Kruger shrugged off his concern, explaining that he needed the arms for fighting 'kaffirs and such-like objects'.

Kruger, a stoically devout man, could almost be taken as the embodiment of the Boer character. He described his rudimentary education himself when he said: 'I have not had much schooling in the ordinary acceptation of the term. When I was ten years old I had to begin fighting for my life in my country and since then I have always been busy. That has been my only schooling.' He had a strict, uncompromising attitude towards other religions; felt that Kaffirs were 'not men, but mere creatures with no more soul than a monkey has'; and was widely reported to have

MORAL SUASION.

THE SMILE THAT FAILED.

A Boer family of sharpshooters from Johannesburg. As a burgher was entitled to choose his own commando, large families or groups of friends found it easy to remain together.
   Deneys Reitz, one of five brothers, described how his commando operated in his book, Commando:
   'We divided ourselves into corporalships by a kind of selective process, friends from the same Government department or from the same part of the town pooling their resources in the way of cooking utensils, etc., and in this manner creating separate little groups that in course of time came to be recognised as military units.' (D)

opened a Jewish synagogue with the words: 'In the name of the Lord Jesus Christ I declare this building open.'

In 1897, Sir Alfred Milner was appointed as the new High Commissioner for South Africa and Governor of the Cape. Within a year, during which the Uitlanders had petitioned the Queen with their grievances, he felt sure that a war with the Transvaal was unavoidable. In May, 1899, he met Kruger at Bloemfontein, the capital of the Orange Free State, to discuss the Uitlander question, but the conference broke down and Milner described Kruger as 'dribbling our reforms like water from an old squeezed sponge'. In a telegram to Chamberlain, he wrote, 'it seems a paradox, but it is true that the only effective way of protecting our subjects is to help them to cease to be our subjects.'

Uitlanders leaving Johannesburg in haste at the first hint of war. (D)

Private Views: Mostly Unpopular.
(by Mr. Punch's Vagrant.)

TRANSVAAL QUESTIONS.

Is England Suzerain or not, Sir?
Is Mr. Krüger bond or free?
Does Alfred Milner know what's what Sir?
How stands the case of Joseph C.?
Is every plan, when we prepare it,
Serenely just, profoundly right?
Is black as black as men declare it,
Or just a darker shade of white?

The Uitlander would fain renounce us;
He pines to be a Transvaal Boer.
Shall Uncle Krüger always bounce us
By closing every open door?
Our remedy for wrongs so grievous
Is just to make Oom Paul allow,
These British citizens to leave us,
And help to milk the Transvaal cow.

It's joyous to be urged to slaughter
On Sunday; but when Monday comes
The wine of threats is thinned with water;
Furled are the flags and hushed the drums.
Next day our peacefulness we smother;
We mean to give old Krüger fits,
And make the Dutchman be our brother
By shooting every Boer to bits.

On Wednesday we don't quite like it;
We might *make war, but what's the use?*
A nail's all right if you can strike it,
But if you miss it, it's the deuce.
Besides, the Boers much lead have brought
them;
They're armed and ready for the fray—
Ask Jameson, who went out and fought
them,
And Mr. Rhodes who stayed away.

But Thursday's terrors, who shall state 'em?
That morn the bellicose D.T.
Puts forth its private ultimatum
And every Jingo shouts with glee.
That pink and patriotic journal,
The Globe, makes evening fiery red
By calling down for flames infernal
To scorch the crown of Krüger's head.

Then Friday finds us pale and breathless;
The strain was much too tense to last;
Oom Paul, it may be, isn't deathless;
We'll wait until his days are past.
On Saturday we range from raging
Down to the Westminster Gazette,
Which bids us, while we're slowly aging,
Pause calmly—well, we're pausing yet.

Boer commandos entraining for the front.
They were called to war in person by the
local magistrate. (D)

Neither these sentiments nor the deadlock which had been reached pleased the Prime Minister, Lord Salisbury. 'We have to act,' he wrote to Lord Lansdowne, Secretary for War, 'upon a moral field prepared for us by him (Milner) and his jingo supporters. And therefore I see before us the necessity for considerable military effort—and all for a people whom we despise, and for territory which will bring no profit and no power to England.' How many Uitlanders would have accepted the franchise at the cost of fully adopting Transvaal nationality and becoming liable to fight for the Republic on commando service? It appears that no one bothered to find out.

The fuse had been lit. In September, while Joseph Chamberlain argued eloquently that Britain's supremacy in South Africa and her existence as a great power in the world, and not the franchise, were the issues at stake, thousands of Uitlanders left Johannesburg by every available train and burghers steadily enrolled in their commando units.

On 9 October, 1899, the Boers played right into Chamberlain and Milner's hands. They delivered a stiff, warlike ultimatum demanding that Britain withdraw all her troops from the

borders of the Transvaal and send any reinforcements back immediately. If, after forty-eight hours, Britain had not agreed to their terms, they would consider themselves at war.

On 12 October, the Boers invaded the Cape Colony.

By making the first move, Kruger quashed many of the qualms some British people might have had about entering into war with a small country many thousands of miles away and for a tiny percentage of British citizens who were apparently anxious to discard their citizenship. Instead, the British public were roused into a patriotic fervour. Jingoistic verse, popular in the Victorian age, whipped up more enthusiasm, but Rudyard Kipling reflected the other side of war in this poem:

General Sir Redvers Buller was born in 1839. He had served bravely in China and in various native wars in South Africa. But his eleven year period in the War Office was said to have 'softened him up' a little and he was known to drink large quantities of champagne. (C)

When you've shouted 'Rule Britannia', when you've sung
                      'God Save the Queen',
  When you've finished killing Kruger with your mouth,
Will you kindly drop a shilling in my little tambourine
  For a gentleman in khaki ordered South?
He's an absent-minded beggar, and his weaknesses are great—
  But we and Paul must take him as we find him—
He is out on active service, wiping something off a slate—
  And he's left a lot of little things behind him!
Duke's son—cook's son—son of a hundred Kings—
  (Fifty thousand horse and foot going to Table Bay!)
Each of 'em doing his country's work
  (And who's to look after their things?)
Pass the hat for your credit's sake,
  And pay—pay—pay.

And pay they did. Employers were offering half wages to the women and children whose breadwinners had been called away and enormous funds were found to support any widows and orphans.

A total British force of 50,000 men was despatched 6,000 miles overseas and the War Office, claiming that the defence force had been completely depleted, immediately pressed the Cabinet to implement a replacement policy.

Certainly at first it seemed that the war would be over by Christmas. The Boers were heavily outnumbered and British officers were confidently assured by Colonial settlers that their famous marksmanship had declined along with the numbers of big game in the country. This was nonsense. The Boers were a military people; a nation of rugged farmers who had fought protracted and severe battles against the native population to secure their country; who were trained from their youth to ride and shoot; and who were conscripted into the commando service at the age of sixteen (though there were many burghers under that age and also a fair proportion over sixty). In addition to the commando units, both the Transvaal and the Orange Free State (which was bound by treaty to the Transvaal and went immediately to Kruger's assistance) had professional artillery. In October, 1899, there were about 800 burghers in the Transvaal State Artillery and about 400 in the Orange Free State Artillery. Tucker and his comrades were going to have a fight on their hands which would last almost three years.

War fever ran high in Britain and in the Republics. The British troops were treated to special, regimental 'send-off' suppers, featuring such bizarre dishes as 'Mafeking Mutton', 'Transvaal Turnip', 'Cape Sauce', 'Pretoria Pheasant', 'Peace Pudding', and the inevitable 'Dutch Cheese'. In contrast, the Boers ate their last supper at home, en famille—often all the males, from grandfather down, were leaving for the front. Each Boer was expected to provide his own horse, rifle and provisions (biltong, strips of dried meat, and biscuits) for eight days, after which the government took over responsibility for feeding the commandos. The Boers were unpaid.

The British force consisted of: three infantry divisions of 30,000 men, one cavalry division of 5,500, 5,000 service corps troops and the rest were reserves. The War Office had seriously misjudged the necessity for mounted infantry to fight on the open veldts of South Africa. Only ten per cent of the force was mounted—such a ludicrously low figure that the Empire had to be combed at once for cavalry. Canada provided 1,000 expert horsemen, the New South Wales Lancers were called in and, from South Africa itself, came the Imperial Light Horse.

Chapter One:
On the Move

General Sir Redvers Buller, Commander of the British Expeditionary Force, left England on 14 October, 1899. He sailed on the Dunottar Castle *together with Winston Churchill, J. B. Atkins, both war correspondents, a nephew of President Kruger, and, for good measure, a film crew from the Biograph Cinema Company who were travelling to South Africa to make a film of the war.*

On 9 October, 1899, I received notice to rejoin the colours of the 1st Class Army Reserve. On 14 October I proceeded to Gosport and gave my papers in at the Rifle Depot meeting several old comrades. Everything seemed strange to me but I soon felt at home once again.

Reserve men enrolling at their regimental depot. 'Reserves' were short service men who had returned to civilian life but still received a modest payment in return for their readiness to rejoin their colours in the event of war.

Along with his call-up papers, each man received a railway warrant for the journey and a postal order for three shillings. (D)

Unlike the first Boer War of 1881, the British troops were no longer kitted out with 'red-coats', a much lamented fact by the Boers, who were looking forward to the easy targets made by these distinctive red tunics.

Just before he sailed, Private Tucker was hastily refitted with a more appropriate khaki uniform.

Khaki is a canvas-like fabric which retains the heat in winter and yet remains cool in summer. It was used originally in India. The name is derived from the Persian word for dust, which it resembles precisely in colour.

15th October 1899

Passed by the Medical Officer and immediately after drew my kit and equipment. In the afternoon about fifty of us proceeded to Fort Brockhurst.

16th October 1899

In the morning did four hours aiming drill and then in the afternoon went to Browndown and commenced a short course of musketry. After firing, marched back to Fort Brockhurst.

17th October 1899

Did nothing in the morning but about four o'clock in the afternoon, two hundred of us, all reservists, marched to Stokes Bay Pier and crossed over the water to Ryde, where we entrained for Newport. We arrived at Newport at seven o'clock in the evening and were met by the band of the 1st Battalion and a large crowd of people who gave us a good cheering on arrival. The band played us up to Albany Barracks, Parkhurst. Crowds of people lined the streets of the town and along the road to the Barracks, they cheered loudly as we marched between them. On arrival at Parkhurst, we were taken at once to our quarters and I spent a jolly evening with all my old comrades.

18th October 1899

Another medical inspection. In the evening another large party of reservists arrived.

19th October 1899

The reservists of our Battalion do four hours drill each day. We were supplied with some kit for the field.

22nd October 1899

Church Parade service was held this morning in the Garrison Church. The Chaplain, the Reverend A. W. Milroy, gave us a farewell address.

23rd October 1899

The usual drills.

24th October 1899

The Battalion paraded at 10.00 a.m. and several photographs of us were taken.

Mobilization.
'His regiment didn't need to send to find him.' (C)

The glowing enthusiasm which welcomed Private Tucker and the 1st Class Army Reserves at Newport was typical throughout the country. The nation, aflame with patriotism, delved deep into its pocket as the streets echoed to the tramp of marching boots and the refrain:

> *Goodbye Dolly I must leave you,*
> *Though it breaks my heart to go*
> *Something tells me I am needed,*
> *At the front to fight the foe,*
> *See the soldier boys are marching,*
> *And I can no longer stay—*
> *Hark! I hear the bugle calling,*
> *Goodbye Dolly Gray.*

Private Tucker's khaki kit consisted of: 1 serge suit (serge frock and pants), 2 pairs of puttees, 2 flannel shirts, 4 pairs of socks, 2 pairs of boots and laces, 1 pair of cork socks, 2 pairs of drawers, 2 vests, 2 flannel body belts, 1 pair of braces, 1 haversack, 1 bandolier, 1 waterbottle, 1 felt hat, 1 overcoat, 1 pocket filter, 1 tin vaseline dubbin, 1 pocket knife and lanyard and 1 cake of soap.

Repeatedly washed, slept in and fired at, the uniform soon took on a shabby appearance. Towards the end of the war, the discrepancies between the burghers and the British troops had become much less marked, as the British adopted the wide-brimmed felt hats favoured by the Boers, and the Boers, out of necessity, wore khaki uniforms stripped from prisoners.

Private Tucker carried a Lee-Enfield rifle of .303 inch calibre, with a detachable magazine holding ten cartridges, each of which had to be inserted singly. These weapons were thought to 'thoroughly satisfy modern requirements' but, as the Boer War was essentially a mounted war, they had to be shortened to serve as carbines for the mounted infantry, and this considerably reduced their accuracy.

The Boers, on the other hand, were mostly mounted and had the double advantage of speed and clip-loading German Mausers of .275 inch calibre. (C)

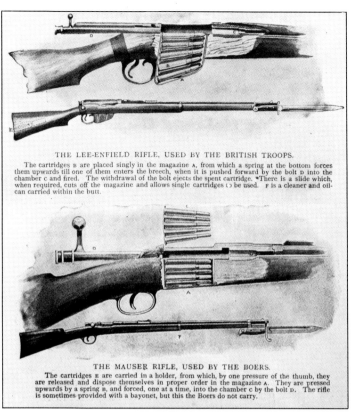

THE LEE-ENFIELD RIFLE, USED BY THE BRITISH TROOPS.

The cartridges B are placed singly in the magazine A, from which a spring at the bottom forces them upwards till one of them enters the breech, when it is pushed forward by the bolt D into the chamber C and fired. The withdrawal of the bolt ejects the spent cartridge. There is a slide which, when required, cuts off the magazine and allows single cartridges to be used. F is a cleaner and oil-can carried within the butt.

THE MAUSER RIFLE, USED BY THE BOERS.

The cartridges E are carried in a holder, from which, by one pressure of the thumb, they are released and dispose themselves in proper order in the magazine A. They are pressed upwards by a spring B, and forced, one at a time, into the chamber C by the bolt D. The rifle is sometimes provided with a bayonet, but this the Boers do not carry.

'TO THOSE IT MAY CONCERN'
Jack Tar. 'Good luck, mate! You're goin' to do the job on land. If there's anything wanted at sea—against other parties—I'm on!'

A typically reassuring patriotic cartoon, stressing once again the might of the Empire. (B)

Fighting men, intoxicated by the attention of the nation and the bottles of spirits thrust upon them by admiring citizens, reeled as they bade unhappy farewells to their families. However, once at sea, the men were peaceful and content, secure in the belief that the war was not expected to last more than a few months.

25th October 1899

We spent today and 26 and 27, drilling and preparing for our departure.

28th October 1899

The Battalion paraded at 6.30 a.m. in preparation for the march to Cowes. A large crowd from all parts of the island assembled at Parkhurst Barracks to see us off. At about 7.00 a.m. the Battalion marched forward headed by the Isle of Wight Rifle Volunteers' Regimental Band. The greater part of the crowd followed us to Cowes. The streets were gaily decorated with flags and bunting, proclaiming such mottos as: 'Remember Majuba', 'Good Luck', 'God Speed', and 'Bon Voyage'.

It was a grand sight and will long be remembered. The Mayor of Newport was at Cowes to bid us farewell. The Rifle Brigade were great favourites and had made many friends on the island.

About 8.30 a.m. we boarded two steamers and crossed over to Southampton, the cheers were magnificent as we left Cowes. On arrival at Southampton we embarked on the *S.S German* of the Union Line. The Duke of Connaught, Lord Bingham and several

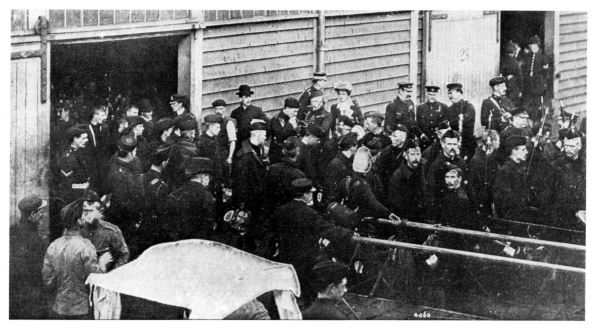

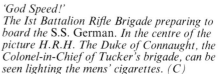

ex-officers of the Rifle Brigade were there and inspected the Battalion. There was an immense number of people on the jetty. A cornet player made the scene more cheerful by playing lively airs and patriotic songs such as: *Soldiers of the Queen* and *Au Revoir*. At 2.00 p.m. we were towed out, everyone cheering like mad, both on the ship and on the pier. And so for the second time I leave the shores of Old England. I can only say ours was a grand send off: a very pretty and touching scene.

It was a very good voyage out, the food supplied to us was much better than that supplied to troops on ordinary troop ships and there was singing and dancing which was greatly enjoyed by both the troops and the passengers.

'God Speed!'
The 1st Battalion Rifle Brigade preparing to board the S.S. German. In the centre of the picture H.R.H. The Duke of Connaught, the Colonel-in-Chief of Tucker's brigade, can be seen lighting the mens' cigarettes. (C)

Singing and dancing were not the only entertainments available to Private Tucker on board ship. The long, monotonous voyage was broken up by bouts of beer drinking and long, inexhaustible games of 'ouse' (later known as Housey Housey*) while the officers drank whiskey and dabbled with whist, poker, baccarat and bridge. The more energetic played quoits and organized wheelbarrow and potato races.*

Drunkenness was not particularly prevalent during the voyage, although there were occasional scenes of misconduct from some of the men, who were suffering from unhappiness and home-sickness.

'Bon Voyage!'
The enthusiastic cheers from the quayside at Southampton were rivalled only by those from the decks of the S.S. German *as she sailed. (C)*

General Buller landed at Capetown on 31 October, 1899, and was enthusiastically greeted—unlike General Sir George White who was in deep disgrace after the fiasco of the previous day at Nicolson's Nek, when a thousand British soldiers, under his command, had been taken prisoner. Following 'Mournful Monday', as the day was later dubbed, White was forced back on Ladysmith and it soon became evident that General Joubert, an old and cautious Boer leader, planned to besiege the town. General Buller's first task was to relieve the beleaguered garrison, which he knew would involve his men in bitter conflict.

During the six week voyage the men had ample time to become reacquainted with one another and relax before being pitched into battle. (D)

The voyage was covered and protected at three stages by the Royal Navy's Channel Squadron. Firstly, eight battleships followed their manoeuvres at Gibraltar, then three cruisers, Furious, Pactolus, and Pelorus, covered the troop ships from Gibraltar to the Canaries where the Diadem and the Niobe took over. The rumour of a Boer privateer had been causing havoc among the fleet. The Niobe followed the activities of the suspicious cruiser while the transport boats steamed in darkness and altered their courses by a route of one hundred miles further west until the unidentified stranger disappeared.

5th November 1899

Arrived at Teneriffe, one of the Canary Group and a rather attractive place. The ship docked there for several hours for coaling and water so we were able to buy plenty of fruit from the natives who flocked around the ship in their small boats.

Buying from bum-boys.
British ships in Teneriffe harbour were immediately surrounded by small trading craft, laden with fresh fruit, exotic birds and basket chairs. (E)

The hills on the island looked very picturesque with their snow-clad tops contrasting with the lightly coloured houses—a sight well worth seeing. The inhabitants are a mixed race, mostly Spanish.

16th November 1899

Our next port of call was St. Helena, a bare and desolate looking place with very high mountains. There we took on water and

While Tucker was at sea, events were unfolding in South Africa. In the besieged town of Kimberley, seventy Boer shells had fallen in one day, 7 November, 1899. Luckily, they were of such inferior quality that they had succeeded only in wounding a cooking pot. The fragments of the luckless victim were promptly put up for auction and the larger limbs went for as much as two pounds.

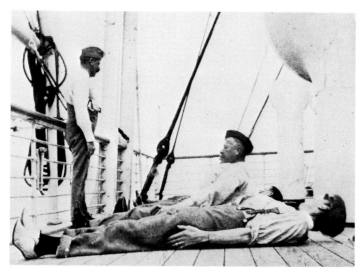

On 9 November, 1899, Private Tucker toasted the Prince of Wales at sea. In Ladysmith, despite the oppressive heavy rains, the men's spirits remained high and they celebrated the Prince's birthday with a 21 gun salute. The Boers, not wishing to be left out, responded with rather less felicitous shell and shrapnel fire.

The only casualties at sea were a quantity of horses, lost when the transport ship Ismore *sank off St. Helena's Bay. Not a single soldier lost his life at sea.*

Battling against boredom. Men exercising on board ship. (A)

landed a few passengers and mail. I took the opportunity to send a letter home myself. Only the officers and sergeants were allowed ashore. A few troops are stationed there: a West Indian Regiment and a few artillery. However, we couldn't see the town as it lies between two hills.

The depressing news of the capture of the Gloucesters and Dublin Fusiliers, caused by the stampeding of mules, was reported to us and we were all glad to get to sea again.

Nothing of particular importance took place so I have not kept an account of our daily life on board ship, suffice to say we arrived at Capetown on 20 November, 1899, having been at sea for twenty-two days, twenty-two and a half hours.

Armchair generals offered ample advice throughout the war. This picture reflects on the possible results of adopting all their proposals simultaneously.

In fact, the horses had little, if any, exercise but floating targets were employed for firing practice and the men had an opportunity to relieve the tedium of the voyage by firing off rounds of old, out-dated ammunition. (G)

The S.S. Nubia *was to return to Table Bay, re-fitted for service as a stationary hospital. (A)*

The dividing line between rank and file was rarely more firmly pronounced than during the Boer War. The British officers, for instance, toasted the Prince's health with champagne—the troops raised their glasses filled with stout. Their insistence on rank distinction was, however, to prove fatal. Each officer made a point of striding gallantly into battle sporting a gleaming set of buttons on his uniform and a magnificently polished sword, thereby advertising himself and his importance to every Boer marksman. The Boers, not wishing to seem impolite, accepted the officers insistent offer and within ten days (between 10 and 20 November) the commissioned ranks of the British Army had been severely depleted.

The operation to despatch the troops to South Africa was conducted at a leisurely pace and many valuable days were lost in the first few months of the war amassing the various food and transportation requirements.

The Sumatra *carried 1,200 troops to Capetown and fed them on:*
6,000 lb of preserved meat
14 sides of salt beef   21 barrels of port
2,500 lb of preserved potatoes
400 lb of compressed vegetables
670 lb of salt   100 lb of mustard
60 lb of pepper   150 gallons of vinegar
100 lb of pickles   1,250 lb of rice
1,300 lb of split peas   6,000 lb of sugar
140 barrels of flour   336 lb of suet
900 lb of raisins   1,300 lb of coffee
113 lb of chocolate   1,300 lb of treacle
4,520 lb of oatmeal   10,800 lb of biscuits

Hardly a balanced diet. In addition to these government rations, the ship's canteen stocked up on corned beef, ginger-biscuits, bloater paste, brawn, butter, cheese, tinned haddock, herring, lobster, mackerel, jams, marmalades, sausages, potted meats, condensed milk, blacking, laces, soap and tobacco which they made available to the troops at additional cost.

20th November 1899

We had expected to land and go straight up country but instead we received orders to proceed to Durban and take part in the relief of Ladysmith. We were not able to see much of Capetown by daylight as we were anchored far out in Table Bay, and in the evening when we were towed into the docks all hands were busy transferring our baggage and stores from the *S.S German* on to the hired transport ship, *S.S. Nubia*, which was to take us on to Durban. We were working nearly all night and part of the next day.

21st November 1899

Towards evening we left Capetown for Durban. We all felt the change of ships very much. The food was not so good nor so plentiful and the space on deck for troops was very limited, but, mercifully, the voyage was a short one.

Dinner time on board a transport ship. Mealtimes were cramped but jovial. (C)

25th November 1899

We arrived at Durban and immediately disembarked. Durban trains were waiting on a siding for us; they were ordinary goods trucks and were fitted up with more regard to space than to comfort. The people of Durban treated us with great kindness, posting our letters and giving us plenty of tobacco pipes, cigarettes and fruit. We all felt we should like to have seen more of their pretty town. As we left the inhabitants came out and greatly cheered us. They continued to wave their handkerchiefs long after we had passed them.

The railway is a marvel of engineering, sometimes running close to very high precipices and making such quick curves it almost takes one's breath away, especially when running down the steep inclines. The countryside, through which it winds, is very hilly, from the high peaks one could see the marvellous scenery stretched below. Game is very plentiful: deer in abundance. At several places along the line we saw immense quantities of arum lilies growing wild.

The natives and European residents threw plenty of banners into our trucks as we passed and the natives greatly amused us with their war dances and acting as only niggers can.

KRÜGER'S VISION.

On arrival at each station there were huge cauldrons of hot tea waiting for us, prepared by the Europeans and for which everyone was thankful. The ladies and children were very anxious to have our cap badges and we all gave them freely.

We stepped down at Pietermaritzburg and ate our dinner on the platform: bully beef and potatoes. Several ladies gave us writing paper, envelopes, tobacco pipes, cigarettes and lemonade. We thoroughly enjoyed all the attention. We had travelled a total distance of seventy-one miles from Durban to Pietermaritzburg.

After waiting on the platform until 5.00 p.m. we were told that

The colonists of Durban in staunchly British Natal, greeted the British soldiers not only with enthusiasm, but also with pineapples, cigars, pillows, ladies' visiting cards and promises to send off anything which might be needed 'on demand'.

The British policy concerning African natives differed vastly to that of the Boers. As a young man, Paul Kruger had taken part in raids on Kaffir kraals and had helped to round up hundreds of slaves. Although considered brave by his own people, he had built up such a resentment among the Kaffirs that he had been obliged to carry a rifle with him wherever he went.

In the latter part of the war, when most of the country had been devastated, the Boers were dependent to a large extent on Kaffirs supplying them with food and forage.

In Britain the response to a proposal to set up a support fund for widows and fatherless families was enormous; women sent their rings and children their pennies; The Princess of Wales, heralded as the 'Princess of Pity' by an ecstatic press, was head of the Red Cross Society and raised, with the aid of Lady Randolph Churchill and other Americans living in London, a fund to finance the hospital ship, Maine; Lady White collected money to furnish soldiers at the front with Christmas presents. Everywhere generosity abounded.

KRUGER'S VISION
'What, will the thin red line stretch out to the crack of doom?—Mabeth, Act IV., Scene 1.
The notion that Kruger and the Boers could be frightened by sheer numbers was popular among the Jingoists. (B)

Pietermaritzburg, named originally after two Boer leaders, Pieter Retief and Gert Maritz, was the centre of government in Natal. Approximately half of the 20,000 population were white and the town boasted a museum, town hall, library, legislative council buildings, as well as a smattering of churches, hotels, clubs and banks.

Major-General the Hon. Neville Gerald Lyttelton had been in the army for almost thirty-five years, ever since leaving Eton. (C)

General Sir Francis Clery was, indeed, a well-known tactician. His standard book on the subject had been translated into four languages.

Mooi River, dismissed so casually by Private Tucker, had been the stage for an exciting confrontation between 3,000 Boers and 5,000 British only days before, on 22 November. Although the British had been forced to retreat, the Boers, too, unnerved by the show of strength, had considered it prudent to withdraw.

Hailstones as big as eggs were reported to have fallen, indeed, two or three men had been wounded by them. More conventional weapons had accounted for eleven dead and sixty-seven British soldiers wounded.

The 1st Rifle Brigade crossing a spruit on their march to Willow Grange. The blazing heat made one private soldier wish he had 'his body in a pool and his head in a public house'. (H)

we were not to go on that night, so we took our baggage to a place provided for it and then marched to the camping ground—two miles from the station. Then we had to wait for our canvas in the rain and as it did not arrive until 9.30 p.m. we were forced to pitch camp in the dark and eventually settled down for a night's rest.

When we woke next morning, we were rather surprised to find a lot of natives outside the tents selling butter, eggs, milk, fruit, vegetables and stuff for the troops. To my mind the natives did fairly well out of us, making good profits as the men were only too pleased to buy *anything*!

We stayed at Pietermaritzburg for one week, parading and mounting attacks on imaginary foes around the surrounding kopjes. The rainy season had set in as we soon discovered to our discomfort: every evening it rained. We were not allowed to visit the town without a pass and only five were issued each night to men of my company. One evening I secured one and managed to see a great deal of the town, which was extremely attractive and a great many Europeans have settled there.

2nd December 1899

We received the order to proceed to Mooi River to join our brigade. We travelled by rail. Our brigade consists of:

2nd Scottish Rifles; 3rd King's Royal Rifles; 1st Durham Light Infantry; 1st Battalion Rifle Brigade.

and is commanded by General Lyttelton. The General and his staff are mostly Rifle Brigade officers and are, therefore, well known to most of us. Our brigade number is the 4th Brigade and we belong to the 2nd Division commanded by General Clery, the well-known tactician.

Mooi River is rather a barren place, it has a station and station master's house, also a hotel and that is all there is of the town. We were disappointed as we had hoped to see quite a large town.

4th December 1899

We were on outpost duty that night and caught three spies trying to pass through our lines.

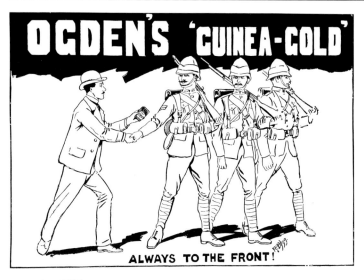

OGDEN'S 'GUINEA-GOLD'

ALWAYS TO THE FRONT!

Advertisers were quick to recognize the financial gains to be made from exploiting the war and the British troops were loyally sent packing with everything from hair-restorer to cigarettes. (D)

5th December 1899

We marched to Willow Grange, a distance of ten miles. I find the marching very hard as it is very dusty and hot, and the country is very hilly.

6th December 1899

We marched on to Estcourt.

7th December 1899

We marched on to Frere and joined our division making the total strength up to about 22,000. Here the usual routine of camp life is gone through. The chief amusement of the troops is football. One thing to be admired about British soldiers is they will not be denied sport, and if a football is to be found they will have it.

The trains at Frere.
Frere, a crucial rail link, was the site of one of the largest British camps. The men were housed in rows of tents, although General Buller took up his quarters in the station master's house.
The week before, the Boers had succeeded in destroying an iron bridge and had torn up some of the rails, but their damage, and the delay, had been slight.
One railway truck was fitted with the signalling apparatus from H.M.S. Forte *and flashed nightly messages to the besieged town of Ladysmith. (J)*

Chapter Two:
Colenso and The Events of Black Week

In England, Kipling had just refused a Knighthood on the grounds that it would hamper his work. He was soon to arrive in South Africa himself.

This drawing by war artist, R. Caton Woodville, clearly illustrates the transport difficulties during the long and arduous march from Frere to Chieveley. Many ox wagons came to grief in the fierce currents or on the stony beds of the Tugela River. (K)

The first battle in the trilogy of Black Week was Stormberg—brief and doomed to failure from the start. General Gatacre marched 3,000 train-weary troops through the night over difficult terrain until finally, misled by their guides, they were fired upon from the hills by Boers. Six hundred men were left behind in the ensuing retreat and taken prisoner.

General Methuen's share in Black Week was more dramatic. With a strong force of 13,000 men, he set out to relieve Kimberley, but first he had to cross the Magersfontein hills where Generals De la Rey and Cronje lay in wait with 8,500 men, artfully entrenched not on the slopes as usual, but 200 yards before them.

For two hours Methuen bombarded the slopes five miles distant, until he was convinced the Boer defence had crumbled. Then, under cover of darkness and through a driving storm, he despatched Major-General Wauchope and the Highlanders. The men never reached Magersfontein. As they stumbled through the mud towards the dim outline of the hill they were mown down by invisible Boer fire. Upwards of 1,000 men were killed, wounded or captured.

13th December 1899

We marched to Chieveley, a distance of eight miles. After pitching camp we viewed the Boer positions.

14th December 1899

We watched our naval 4.7 guns shelling nearly all day but the Boers refused to return a single shell. In the evening we were told what was to be done on the next day and many a message was passed from comrade to comrade to be sent home in the event of falling in the fight. War is a terrible affair; one can never say when his last moment has come.

The Battle of Colenso

The Battle of Colenso was the third contribution to a series of disasters which began with General Sir William Gatacre's ignominious reverse at Stormberg and was speedily followed by General Lord Methuen's inglorious defeat at Magersfontein.

England, numbed by this double dose of bad news, looked to General Redvers Buller, the Commander-in-Chief, who was marching through Natal with a formidable force of over 20,000 men, to relieve the besieged town of Ladysmith. Between Buller and General White in Ladysmith, lay the deep, swift Tugela river and a force of 8,000 Boers led by General Louis Botha.

Buller's only map, a crude farm survey with no contours and a scale of one inch to the mile, was inadequate in the extreme. Using this as his guide, he devised a three-pronged attack plan, intending to cross the Tugela at Colenso and march uphill to Ladysmith, as General White, co-ordinating his main force of men in the Ladysmith garrison, attacked the Boers from the rear. The plan misfired from the very outset. General White was expecting Buller's attack to commence on the 17 December, but for reasons now obscured by time and Buller's own denials, the attack was brought forward two days. (It was widely reported that Ladysmith was riddled with spies which could account for Buller's secrecy.)

Gatacre, a strict disciplinarian and intensely energetic man, was known among his soldiers as 'back-acher'.

The British Government spent a meagre £11,000 per annum on maintaining an Intelligence Division. The insignificance of that sum does not, however, excuse the inaccuracy of the maps—there had been a British garrison in the district for two generations.

'Saki' (H. H. Munro) of the Westminster Gazette *laid the blame at the feet of Lord Lansdowne, Secretary for War. He portrayed him as the White Knight in one of his 'Alice in Westminster' sketches. 'The fewer places,' explained the Knight, 'your army moves to, the fewer maps you have to prepare. And we hadn't prepared very many.'*

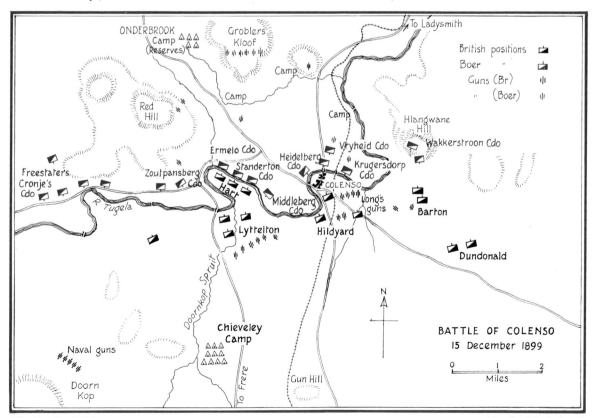

The Battle of Colenso

Map by Mr A. Spark

The town of Ladysmith had been under siege since the end of October. The townspeople and the defenders suffered more from physical discomfort than actual danger. The Boers bombarded the town relentlessly with their big guns but after the first fortnight the casualties consisted only of one civilian, two natives, a horse, two mules, a wagon and about half a dozen houses.

Louis Botha was born in Natal in 1864. Before the war, he had been a successful farmer living in the Transvaal. He spoke fluent English and became well respected by both his adversaries and his fellow countrymen, who elected him Commandant-General in 1900 following the death of Joubert. (A)

The first intimation White had of the change of plans was the distant rumble of Buller's field guns bombarding the Boer trenches from long range. This impressive show of strength succeeded only in announcing to the Boers the imminent attack.

Louis Botha, a wily Boer general, had entrenched his 8,000 burghers along a ten mile stretch of kopjes opposite the Tugela. His plan, and the placement of his guns, was based on sound strategy. Having first booby-trapped the bed of the Tugela with barbed wire, he ordered his men to remain silent, which they did, refusing to return a single shot during the two day bombardment. The numerical strength of the British force coupled with the legendary reputation of Buller, had had a debilitating effect on the morale of the burghers and, initially, Botha had difficulty in keeping them together.

At dawn on the 15 December, Buller began his advance. On the left, he despatched General Hart's Irish Brigade (consisting of: 1st Connaught Rangers, 1st & 2nd Royal Dublin Fusiliers, 1st Royal Inniskilling Fusiliers and 1st Borderers) with orders to cross the Tugela. Misled by a Kaffir guide, Hart's brigade found themselves caught in a loop of the river, treacherously exposed on three sides to Boer fire. Even though there was no place to ford the river, Hart urged his men, in tight-packed formation, forward. Within forty minutes, 400 of them lay dead or wounded. Buller watched Hart's bloody failure from Naval Gun Hill. He rode across to Major-General Lyttelton and ordered him to support Hart, saying: 'Hart has got himself into the devil of a mess down there: get him out of it as best you can.' Lyttelton's reinforcements, however, arrived too late and he found many of the Irish Brigade falling back, wounded and exhausted. The plan had failed dismally; even with the combined force, they were unable to advance any further.

Colonel Lord Dundonald's mounted brigade were having no more luck on the right. They had made an abortive attempt to capture Hlangwane Hill, the key position for an attack on Colenso, and Buller, underestimating the importance of the hill, had refused to send reinforcements.

The naval 4.7 guns in action at Colenso. The carriages were specially adapted for the field by Captain Percy Scott. (D)

R. Caton Woodville.

The main thrust of the attack was to have come from the centre where Colonel C. J. Long, in charge of the artillery, had been ordered to support the infantry attack to be made by General Hildyard and the 2nd Brigade. Instead of supporting the main infantry force, he blundered ahead with twelve field and six naval guns, not halting until he was within 600 yards of the river and a mile in front of the main force. He lined up his twelve guns with a strict precision and was preparing to fire when a single shot rang out from the opposite bank. It was immediately followed by a burst of fire, which fortunately went too high, but eventually forced the British gunners to fall back to a donga 400 yards to the rear. Colonel Long, shot through the arm and liver, was urged to abandon the guns, but he stubbornly refused, shouting above the roar, 'Abandon, be damned! We never abandon guns!' The Boers, who used smokeless powder which made it difficult to gauge their position, were virtually invisible to the British gunners throughout the battle. Buller rode up and ordered his aide-de-camp to call for volunteers to retrieve the twelve unmanned guns. Among the men who eagerly answered the call was Lieutenant the Hon. Fred Roberts, the only son of Field-Marshal Lord Roberts. With the others, he galloped across the 400 yards of open veldt and within moments was struck by three bullets and mortally wounded. Through the hail of bullets, the rest of the rescue party managed to bring back two of the guns and there then followed a succession of daring attempts to recover the wounded Roberts and the remaining ten guns.

Loss of the guns at Colenso.
Five years after the war, Lord Roberts surveyed the battlefield on which his only son had lost his life, and to a friend he declared: 'It was murder, sheer murder.' (D)

In December, 1899, Winston Churchill outlined the problems in South Africa. His article in the Morning Post *made an appeal to England's horsemen. 'The individual Boer,' he wrote, 'mounted, in a suitable country is worth four or five regular soldiers. The power of modern rifles is so tremendous that frontal attacks must often be repulsed. The extraordinary mobility of the enemy protects his flanks. The only way of treating them is either to get men equal in character and intelligence as riflemen, or, failing the individual, huge masses of troops. It would be much cheaper in the end to send more than is necessary. There is plenty of work here for a quarter of a million men, and South Africa is well worth the cost in blood and money. Are the gentlemen of England all fox-hunting? Why not an English Light Horse? For the sake of our manhood, our devoted Colonists, and our dead soldiers, we must persevere with the war.'*

Dismayed by defeat and demoralized by his wound, Buller heliographed to White in Ladysmith: 'As it appears certain that I cannot relieve Ladysmith for another month, and even then only by means of protracted siege operations . . . . you will burn your ciphers, destroy your guns, fire away your ammunition, and make the best terms possible with the general of the besieging forces, after giving me time to fortify myself on the Tugela.'

Later Buller maintained that the message had been misinterpreted, what he had meant was should White feel obliged to surrender, he would take the responsibility upon himself. Buller's intricate denials and the neat way he shrugged off any blame, usually depositing it on some other, less fortunate general, bewildered the British public and prompted 'Saki' (H. H. Munro) of the Westminster Gazette *to write the following poem:*

> *I sent a message to White*
> *To tell him—if you* must, *you might*
> *But then, I said you p'raps might not*
> *(The weather was* extremely *hot)*
> *This query, too, I spatchock-slid,*
> *How would you do it, if you did?*
> *I did not know, I rather thought—*
> *And then I wondered if I ought.*

First aid to the wounded. The Army Medical Corps at work under heavy fire at Colenso. (C)

Buller, like Churchill, had at last registered the need for mounted men and he requested a force of 8,000 to be despatched at once. After Black Week a patriotic fever had swept Britain and a volunteer force of Imperial Yeomanry was soon assembled.

If Buller's reputation as a military tactician was foundering, his popularity among his men was still in evidence. He kept his men's well-being very much in mind and consulted his medical officers before every battle, deciding where field hospitals should be set up and giving them rough estimates of possible casualties.

During this show of gallantry, Buller sat coolly on his horse tucking into sandwiches well within the range of the Boer fire. Indeed, a fragment of shell bruised his ribs although he mentioned it to no one. Four Victoria Crosses were won: Roberts' was awarded posthumously.

At the same time, Hildyard's infantry force were making short rushes across the open veldt, taking as much cover as they could behind anthills, and had managed to cross the river. The Queen's Regiment had actually entered the village of Colenso and had driven the Boers back from their front trenches. But, by then, Buller had lost his nerve. His wound, the long hours spent on horseback in the hot sun, and the impossible bravery of the volunteers attempting to rescue the lost guns, combined to crush his spirit and he gave the order for a full withdrawal. The guns he abandoned with their breech blocks intact.

On the continent the events of Black Week fanned a wave of anti-British feeling, while in England the British public were appalled as they watched the chinks appear in the armour of their military machine. The culmination of humiliating defeats prompted the Government to remove Buller from his command and they replaced him with the bereaved Field-Marshal Lord Roberts of Kandahar, then sixty-seven. Major-General Lord Kitchener was appointed as his Chief of Staff. The combination of these two powerful personalities was to prove an effective one for Britain, but until they could land in South Africa to put right 'a big business badly begun' (to quote Kitchener), Buller was still in charge and was to lead his men into several more infructuous attempts to relieve Ladysmith.

15th December 1899

The never to be forgotten Battle of Colenso.

At daybreak we struck camp and paraded to attack the village of Colenso and the long line of adjoining hills. The order of battle was, to my judgement, as follows:

The naval guns in the centre. One infantry brigade under General Hildyard on the right and one on the left under General Hart. One brigade (ours) in the centre under General Lyttelton to support either the right or left brigade. The field artillery and naval 12-pounders were to work in conjunction with each other and to pay special attention to Fort Wylie. The general idea appeared to be, as far I could judge, to make a demonstration of the left and to force the right. Our naval guns opened fire on Fort Wylie and for a long time did not get any reply. As soon as General Hart's Irish Brigade moved forward in quarter columns toward the banks of the Tugela, the Boers sent their first shell into his closed ranks and took twelve men off one section and then it seemed as if all hell had been let loose. Mauser, rifle, pom-pom, Maxim big guns and I don't know what else rang out until the air seemed alive with iron and lead. The Irish Brigade retired at the double but soon advanced again in open order with the intention of crossing the river at the ford but they could not find the right place to cross. The wily Boers had forseen this movement and had dammed the river making it unfordable. Several men attempted to swim across but a shell fell amongst them and they all lost their lives, either by the blast or they were drowned. The Boers had also laid barbed wire entanglements in the bed of the river. All the time there was a terrific roar of musketry from both sides.

15 December was a scorchingly hot day in South Africa, without wind or cloud. In contrast the whole of England was blanketed in bitterley cold fog.

A Vickers-Maxim automatic gun ('pom-pom') in firing position. (C)

The view across the Tugela River as seen from Fort Wylie. This picture was taken before the bridge was destroyed. (A)

From the British side, a sketch plan, made on the spot, of the positioning of forces on the field during the Battle of Colenso. And a Boer's eye view (lower right) of the field of battle as seen from their entrenchments. (D) (A)

Meanwhile, Hildyard's brigade, on the right, were well advanced towards Colenso railway station and the village, while we received orders to support the Irish Brigade, led by General Hart, who we could see were falling fast. My regiment at once extended in one long line, each man six paces from the other, and advanced towards the firing line. I have never seen a regiment extend and move forward in such good order as ours did that day; if they had been doing the same movement at ordinary peace manoeuvres it could not have been done better. No-one seemed to take the least notice of the shot and shells that were falling amongst us, every one was cracking jokes and making as much fun as they could. Luckily for us, few of the Boer shells exploded or our losses would have been much more severe. We reached the Irish Brigade and five companies of the Battalion lay down under cover of a small ridge while the other three companies ('A', 'B', 'D') went forward and took cover very close

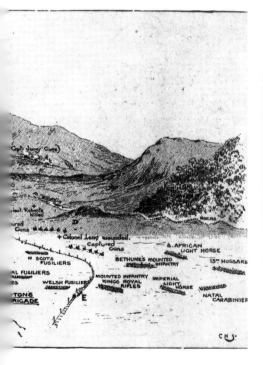

to the Tugela. Just at this time the Irish Brigade began to retire, which meant that we came in for all the shot and shell the Boers had to spare: which was considerable. Pretty soon we had the stretchers at work amongst us. Had their shells been properly fired I don't think I should have been able to write this diary. They fell within a few feet, showering us with clouds of dirt and a shrapnel burst just over our heads, the pieces falling over our bodies like acorns from a tree. It was a very trying time and I think it is impossible to write of one's feelings when under fire for the first time as we were. I lit my pipe and smoked almost the whole time I was there. My Captain, who was next to me, lit a cigarette and began to write, I did the same. Not one of my

Dash of the Dublins across the Tugela. The Irish Brigade were famed for their bravery. (C)

Among the volunteer stretcher bearers was a young lawyer named Gandhi. He was then a member of the Natal Indian Congress, founded in 1885, and within twenty years he was to become one of its leaders.

The stretcher bearers, who were unpaid volunteers, had various nicknames, among them 'body-snatchers', 'catch-em-alive-ohs', and 'pick-me-ups'.

Digging in. British troops had to glean what scanty cover they could from clumps of bushes and anthills. They might have to spend the whole day lying flat in the scorching sun. (K)

The fierce heat made the agony all the worse for the wounded, though they bore the pain stoically. A fourteen-year-old bugler, John Dunne, who had had his left arm shattered, was later praised in a typical patriotic verse popular at the time:

> *What shall we give my little Bugelar,*
> *What for the bugle you lost at Tugelar?*
> *Give me another! that I may go*
> *To the front and return them blow for blow.*

Boys could enlist into the British Army at fourteen for a period of twelve years. Their pay began at 8d a day and rose to 1/1d on promotion to drummer.

Tucker's impression that Colonel Long's men had been shot down and their guns put out of action was not quite correct. It was true that he had considerably overshot his mark and was well within the Boers' range when they opened fire, but fortunately they fired high at first and the British gunners managed to maintain their fire until their ammunition ran out. Then they retired to a donga in the rear, to await both fresh supplies and their infantry escort. The guns were quite unscathed. Of the eighty-four officers and men, only eight were killed and about fifteen wounded. However, Buller's snap decision at 10.00 a.m. to withdraw all his men—despite the fact that three quarters of his infantry and half his mounted men had not fired a single shot—kept them from returning to their posts.

General Clery, surrounded by his staff, views the Boer positions at Colenso through his field glasses. (A)

Private Tucker writes that eleven field guns were lost, when, in fact, the correct number was only ten, although ten field guns comprised nearly half of Buller's total artillery.

At Windsor Castle the Queen dismissed any ideas of a British defeat. 'There is no depression in this house,' she told her visitors. 'We are not interested in the possibilities of defeat. They do not exist.'

regiment was hit by shells, although several were hit by Mauser bullets. The daring and bravery of the Irish Brigade is beyond description. Even though they had been ordered to retire, they absolutely refused and others, catching sight of us, came and joined our forces saying, 'Come on boys, let's go up with the Rifles!'

I have only one fault to find with the Irish—but perhaps it is a good one—they are too reckless as regards taking cover. They expose themselves too much and thus more lives are lost than is necessary. In fighting an enemy like the Boer, in his native cover, this is madness. The wounded were a sad sight, some were hit in five or six places but they bore the pain quite cheerfully.

Just about this time, Barton and Hildyard's brigades had actually forced their way into the station at Colenso but Colonel Long, who was in charge of the artillery, got too close. He took two batteries of artillery, without their infantry escort, within 1,500 yards of Fort Wylie and not more than 600 yards away from the Boer rifle pits. His object was, obviously, to get within a more effective range but his men and horses were shot down and very soon all his guns were out of action. Several attempts were made to save them; Lieutentant Roberts lost his life in the first

attempt and several others distinguished themselves. In the end, eleven were lost and Colonel Long was severely wounded. It is the general opinion that this loss of guns lost us the day, for it precipitated the order for a general retirement. We held the ground while the remainder slowly fell back. When our turn came, we rose from the ground with a keen bitterness in our hearts but comforted by the thought that our turn would come some day. As we stood up to retire the Boers caught sight of us once more and renewed their rifle fire, but they could not hurry us and we retired even better than in the advance, leisurely and without the slightest hurry. Indeed anyone meeting us would have thought that it had been a victory for us, instead of the reverse.

Despite wounding several of our men as we retired, the Boers were not fools enough to follow us. We formed up, just as we had

Waiting their turn. Only one quarter of Buller's impressive force was active during the Battle of Colenso, while the remainder looked anxiously and impotently on. (A)

started nine long hours before, and marched back to our camping ground to pitch camp as if nothing had happened. We tried to eat but the bully beef was not very tempting. We were all feeling a bit done up for it had been an exceptionally hot day and one I shall never forget as long as I live.

Bringing in the wounded. The Natal Field Force was equipped with hooded stretchers to protect the wounded from the fierce sun.

With casualties of over a thousand, doctors at the front were severely overworked; one, who treated 249 men, listed their injuries: in the head, 19; face, 7; neck, 3; back and spine, 20; upper extremity, 76; lower extremity, 118; other wounds, 6. All except eight of the wounds were caused by Mauser bullets which left a very clear hole that readily healed. (J)

After Colenso.
A group of soldiers slaking their thirst around a military water cart. On the right of the picture, Indian stretcher bearers carrying one of the wounded to the field hospital. (D)

16th December 1899

Birthday!

I woke up greatly refreshed after my sleep and ready for another go. We were told that an armistice had been requested, and granted, for twenty-four hours. Various rumours of yesterday's fighting and the number of our casualties were circulating. Some very good stories were told, some droll, others sad and a lot of unhappy faces were to be seen: men who had lost a brother or chum. Our total casualties were about 1,097; the Irish Brigade losing the most. The number in our regiment was slight. The Boer losses are generally supposed to be heavier than ours but one can

Private Tucker's birthday coincided with an important and sacred date in the turbulent history of the Boers. On 16 December, 1838, 470 trekkers had beaten off an attack by 10,000 Zulus, killing 3,000 without loss to themselves. The site of the battle, the Ncome River, was renamed Blood River, and each year the Boers gave solemn thanks to God for His protection.

A Hospital train. Fitted out with iron bedsteads and staffed with female nurses and doctors, these trains carried the wounded from the battlefield to the hospital ships anchored off Table Bay. Many European hotels offered to take in the wounded men. (C)

scarce credit it, considering their impregnable positions, their splendid entrenchments and our exposed advance over two miles of open plain without a vestige of cover. As we advanced we had to find our own range, whereas they had all the ground marked out like a rifle range and had only to watch the ground we passed over, sight their rifles accordingly, and let drive. Not only that but when we were within the deadly distance of 300 yards from them, we were checked by the river and its barbed wire entanglements. So it is hard to believe that they lost as heavily as is being reported.

During the evening we received orders to strike camp and prepare for moving. The reason for this sudden move was soon evident: the Boers had been placing guns on the hills overlooking our camping ground. By doing so they had broken the laws of the armistice, and coupled with the scarcity of water, our general thought it safer to move.

At twelve midnight we paraded but did not move off until 3.30 a.m. (We amused ourselves by watching the eclipse of the moon.) The Rifle Brigade were rearguard and had to wait patiently until the long train of bullock wagons, mules and horses had moved off. We were not told where we were going but eventually we found ourselves back in Frere. The Boers' disappointment on not finding our camp still standing for them to fire into, must have been very acute, for they must have worked pretty hard to get their guns up the hill.

The British casualties had been heavy: upwards of 1,000 officers and men had been killed, wounded or taken prisoner. Private Tucker had found the exaggerated reports of the Boer losses difficult to believe, but would he have found the truth any easier to swallow? The Boers had lost less than forty men. General Lyttelton, who had been in the thick of the action, confessed that he hadn't seen a single Boer all day.

During the twenty-four-hour armistice the British buried their dead, many of whom had been stripped of their uniforms by the Boers, who were desperately short of clothing. Those wounded who found themselves uncomfortably close to the Boer front lines were given water, kindly treated and allowed to be carried off by the stretcher bearers, although they were, naturally, divested of all their arms and equipment first. The Boers took only the slightly wounded officers as prisoners.

Against the background of the wrecked Frere bridge, British soldiers bathing in the Little Tugela. (A)

Buller, at sixty, had an impressive war record. He had been awarded the Victoria Cross for saving four men's lives during the Zulu War and he had the reputation of always being at the centre of the action; but what he lacked, foremost, was the strength of his own convictions. He would launch a plan, waver from his first intentions, deliberate, hesitate and change his mind until, finally, he was forced to concede defeat.

At Frere we found that only two brigades had returned: ours and the Irish. The others had taken up a position a safe distance from the Boer guns, though they were still close by. None of us felt very lively on the march that morning as we felt we were marching the *wrong* way and I feel sure a great many of us were thinking of those who had fallen in the fight.

After our camp was pitched and we had breakfasted, we fell to criticizing General Buller's latest move. The general opinion arrived at was: that we were going to try another road to Ladysmith; that the General knew what he was about; and that we should eventually get there, even if we had to lose half our men to do it. After a good day's rest, ending with a game of football in the evening, the Battle of Colenso was almost forgotten and the next fight eagerly looked forward to. At night we were cruelly reminded that it was still the rainy season; at 11.00 p.m. a severe thunder storm broke upon us and, as we were not prepared for such an event—no trenches had been dug around our tents to carry off the water and our camp was situated on the slope—so we soon had the water running through our tent,

When called to give evidence before the Royal Commission after the war, Buller recklessly claimed: 'I never attacked on the fifteenth at all. I have been accused of having done so and it has been said that every military man condemned the execution of that attack. But I made no attack, I stopped at the very earliest moment in the morning.'

Of course he had attacked on the fifteenth, Tucker's diary is innocent proof of that. It was unfortunate that a man of Buller's stature could not let sleeping dogs lie. However, from the very beginning of the war he had made it quite plain to the Cabinet that he did not feel himself to be the right man for the job of Commander-in-Chief. In a letter home, he wrote rather languidly, 'Ever since I have been here I have been like a man who with a long day's work before him overslept himself and so was late for everything all day.'

On learning the Cabinet's decision to replace him with Field-Marshal Lord Roberts, Buller—who had been nicknamed 'the ferryman' by a humorist because of his frequent crossings and recrossings of the Tugela—sent an official reply saying: 'Lord Lansdowne is kind enough to suggest that the decision may be distasteful to me, but I trust that any decision intended for the interests of the Empire will always be acceptable to me.'

MARK TAPLEY ATKINS
Officer (going his rounds after a night of heavy rain). 'Well, did you find the ground very wet last night?'
Tommy. 'Oh no, Sir. Our blankets soaked up all the rain!' (B)

MARK TAPLEY ATKINS.

soaking our kits and ourselves. The rain continued to pour down all through the night and we sat, covered in mud and rain, like drowned rats. A more miserable night one can scarce imagine. I think only one man in my tent slept that night and he rolled himself up in his wet blanket and made the best of it. We were relieved when the sun came up to warm us and dry our blankets and clothing. However, we gradually got used to such weather and sleeping in our wet clothing was thought nothing of.

Nothing of particular importance took place during our stay at Frere. Our chief amusement was bathing and washing our clothing in the Little Tugela. We played football most evenings.

One landmark of great interest to us all, was the scene of the armoured train disaster which occurred on 15 November. A visit to it and the graves of those who were killed was considered an item not to be missed. The grave itself was a work of art from a soldier's point of view—the lettering was done in a rather novel

On 19 December, 1899, the British destroyed the Colenso road bridge in an attempt to trap any Boers who had crossed over to the south side of the Tugela. Had the British intelligence reports been a little better informed, they would have known of the existence of another bridge, north of Hlangwane, of which the Boers were making good use.

Dublin Fusiliers clambering into the armoured train at Estcourt. Later, when the train was derailed, these men fell into Boer hands. (L)

The scene of 'the armoured train disaster', which Private Tucker visited with such conscientious, soldierly interest, had caused much thrilled and horrified concern in England, and had brought Winston Churchill, the £250-a-month war correspondent for the Morning Post, *into public prominence.*

The train had been used by General Wolfe-Murray as a reconnaissance vehicle, (cavalry scouts would have been better suited to this espionage work but none were available). Each day it had travelled north from Estcourt through Frere and Chieveley, armed with 150 men, and had noted the Boer placements.

On 15 November, 1899, the Boers blocked the line with boulders and ambushed the train near Chieveley. Churchill and a party of men leapt down and attempted to clear the line while those men who could packed themselves on to the engine and tender—the armoured wagons had been derailed. The engine alone chugged back to Estcourt. Seventy men were left behind and were promptly taken prisoner by the Boers. They were sent to Pretoria. Later, Churchill was to hit the headlines once more when he escaped and made a perilous journey back to the British lines on foot and travelling in coal trucks.

Inside the armoured train. These open-topped, heavily manned, trains were used for reconnaissance purposes but the men nick-named them 'death-traps'. (J)

The grave of the Dublin Fusiliers and the Durham Light Infantry. (A)

Britain's defeats during Black Week were greeted with spiteful glee on the continent. For months afterwards, German and French newspapers were peppered with anti-British caricatures, some of which proved so obscene that they had to be banned.

There were now ten field batteries in Natal, and Sir Charles Warren had just arrived with 7,000 reinforcements and a reconnaissance balloon—a far cry from the fighter 'planes of the First World War.

manner—the letters were formed with empty cartridge cases cemented together, they were the same ones used by the heroes who defended the train. The grave looked very neat, stones had been cut and placed around the sides forming a square. The top was flat and cemented all over. The cases forming the inscription were tightly and well placed. Those who are buried there belong to the Dublin Fusiliers and the Durham Light Infantry, and the grave was made by the men of the Border Regiment.

A little further along the line was another grave belonging to a Corporal of the Dublins who was wounded in the same affair. The story of his death was very sad: he was found with one leg just showing above the earth. The Boers had buried him, and when the grave was opened and the body examined, it was found that he had not died through his wounds but had been buried alive. A Kaffir, who witnessed the affair saw the earth that covered the poor fellow move for some time while the Boers stood by until all the movements had ceased. This horrible story I heard from good authority and all those who saw his lonely grave and heard the story vowed they would avenge this poor fellow's terrible death.

About every fourth day while we were at Frere, we were stationed on outpost duty on the surrounding hills. The rain made the duty none too pleasant, frequently we came off duty wet through to the skin, and we were often disturbed during the night duty by guns firing in the direction of Ladysmith and Chieveley.

Familiar Faces.
  Popular badges of Buller, Roberts and Kitchener. (A)

24th December 1899

Christmas Eve

We were on outpost and went out at 4.30 a.m. I passed a rather dull and uneventful day. My thoughts were with those at home with many wishes for their future welfare and happiness. About nine o'clock in the evening we were treated to another one of those South African thunderstorms which continued nearly all night. Christmas day was not a very happy one for us. We had

Meanwhile, back in England, Saturday, 23 December saw London decked out in bunting and bursting with appreciative crowds, who had turned out to cheer their diminutive, white-haired hero, 'Bobs'.
  Field-Marshal Lord Roberts sailed on the Dunottar Castle, the same ship that had carried Buller to South Africa. He was joined at Gibraltar by Kitchener.

"COMPLIMENTS OF THE SEASON."

'Fat, Sir!' Law bless ye, no, Sir! It's Christmas presents from 'ome, Sir. Cardigan jackets, flannin' hunder-wear, hall-wool socks, an' cetterar. Got 'em hall on. Bullet-proof today, Sir!'
  Christmas at the front, in the middle of a sweltering South African summer, presented itself in the form of lovingly knitted balaclavas and socks. (B)

Father Christmas. 'Confound you, Mister President, you've quite spoiled my show this year.' (B)

As Churchill bade farewell to 'a century of wrong' and wrote hopefully, 'Perhaps 1900 is to mark the beginning of a century of good luck and good sense in British policy in South Africa,' lesser minds were debating whether 1900 was really the first year of the twentieth century or the last of the nineteenth. The argument was finally settled by the Astromoner Royal, who decided that the twentieth century would begin on 1 January, 1901.

'Bobs' turn to take a crack at the obstinate head of Kruger while Buller and Kitchener stand back to watch. (G)

Mess'rs Lyons sent 10,000 Xmas puddings to the front, and eventually every soldier received the Queen's gift of a small tin of chocolates bound in red, white and blue ribbon with her portrait on it.

The cacophony of heavy artillery, which Tucker and the 30,000 other soldiers of the surrounding British army could hear coming from Ladysmith, was the result of a continuous assault which the Boers had begun at 2.00 a.m. It was a black, stormy day and during the rare periods of sunshine, anxious messages were heliographed from Ladysmith: '9.00 a.m. Enemy attacked Caesar's Camp at 2.45 this morning in considerable force. Enemy everywhere repulsed, but fighting still continues.' '11.00 a.m. Attack continues and enemy has been reinforced from south.'
   Two brigades were sent from nearby Chieveley to attack the Boers at Colenso, but the uncertainty was maintained during the whole day as despairing messages filtered through the black clouds:
'12.45 p.m. Have beaten enemy off at present, but they are still round me in great numbers, especially to south, and I think renewed attack very probable.
'3.15 p.m. Attack renewed. Very hard pressed.' Then a terrific storm broke, thunder and lightning raged and the surrounding forces were left in suspense until the next day, when they learnt that the Boers had been repulsed, but not without severe British losses.

dinner at five o'clock in the evening, the usual camp stew, only it appeared to us worse than usual and I think most of it was thrown in the refuse pit. Those who cared for beer were given two pints each and drank each other's health.

1st January 1900

New Year
We received the Xmas puddings sent out to us by Mess'rs Lyons.

6th January 1900

We could plainly hear the reports of guns around Ladysmith. Later on we heard of the severe fighting that had taken place there today.

   Nothing occurred worthy of note until 10 January, when we struck camp to march to Springfield. We paraded at 4.30 p.m. but did not march away until 7.30 p.m., the moving off of baggage causing the delay. The first two hours' marching were very good and then yet another of those storms came upon us, soaking us through and making the road very muddy and slippery. Marching was anything but pleasant. We kept on until midnight and then bivouacked for the night, lying on the wet ground in our sodden clothes. However, this did not stop us from

The baggage train on the move. (A)

snatching a few hours sleep even though we had nothing to cover us and consequently we woke up very sore, stiff and shivering with the cold. We had no rations with us so the 'Dubs' invited us to a breakfast of hot tea, bully beef and biscuits, which soon put life in us again. I am sure the whole of my regiment appreciated this act of generosity and kindness on the part of the Dublins and will not forget it in a hurry.

11th January 1900

We paraded at 8.30 a.m. and continued our march. At noon we halted by a stream and had dinner, a rest, a good wash, and felt greatly refreshed. At 4.00 p.m. we fell in and marched on until we crossed a river, after which we bivouacked for the night.

Paraded again next morning at 4.00 a.m. and marched for three hours, arriving at Spearman's Hill, where General Buller, himself, compliments our brigade on its marching. From the outpost we can see the Boers busy making their trenches on the hills opposite, across the Tugela, however, our position here is immensely strong.

The following is an extract from general orders by General Sir Redvers Buller:

Sunday, 14 January, 1900

The field force is now advancing to the relief of Ladysmith where, surrounded by superior forces, our comrades have gallantly defended themselves for the last ten weeks. The General Commander knows that every one in the force feels as he does. We must be successful, we shall be stoutly opposed by a clever and unscrupulous enemy, let no man allow himself to be deceived

War correspondents were attached to the column and this is how G. W. Steevens of the Daily Mail *described the conditions: '. . . the soldiers' legs seemed to be embedded in a serpentine cast of clay, while their boots could only be inferred from the huge balls of stratified mud around their feet. The mud was of various colours—red, yellow, black, brown—and the mens' puttees were somewhere in the middle of this mass of heavy, sticky soil.'*

J. B. Atkins, the Manchester Guardian's *correspondent, wrote graphically: 'The hills seemed to melt down like tallow under heat; the rain beat the earth into liquid, and the thick, earthy liquid ran down in terraced cascades . . . From Estcourt to Frere the division waded, sliding, sucking, pumping, gurgling through the mud: the horses floundered or tobogganed with all four feet together; the wagons lurched ankle-deep into heavy sloughs and had to be dragged out with trebled teams of oxen.'*

THE SULLIED WHITE FLAG
John Bull. 'If you abuse that flag, I won't answer for my men.'
  Rumours of the unsportsmanlike tactics were filtering back and outraging the British public. (B)

A remarkable feature of Buller's columns was the string of hundreds of wagons packed with supplies, tents and provisions. The wagons were pulled by teams of sixteen oxen, or ten mules, and were guided by two native drivers. Progress was interminably slow as oxen could only travel twelve miles in a day. Also, it was necessary to carry fodder for the animals and this increased the amount of supplies. Churchill is quoted as saying: 'The vast amount of baggage this army takes with it on the march hampers its movements and utterly precludes all possibility of surprising the enemy. I have never before seen even officers accommodated with tents on service, though both the Indian frontier and the Sudan lie under a hotter sun than South Africa. But here to-day, within striking distance of a mobile enemy whom we wished to circumvent, every private soldier has canvas shelter, and the other arrangements are on an equally elaborate scale. The consequence is that the roads are crowded, drifts are blocked, marching troops are delayed, and all rapidity of movement is out of the question. Meanwhile the enemy completes the fortification of his positions and the cost of capturing them rises. It is poor economy to let a soldier live well for three days at the price of killing him on the fourth.'
  As for the Boers, they travelled light, carrying only a few strips of biltong, biscuits, 200 rounds of ammunition and their rifles.

THE SULLIED WHITE FLAG.

by them. If a white flag is displayed it means nothing unless the force displaying it halts, throws down their arms and holds up their hands at the same time. If they get a chance the enemy will try to mislead us by false words of command and false bugle sounds; every one must guard against being deceived by such conduct. Above all, if anyone is surprised by a sudden volley at close quarters, let there be no hesitation, do not turn from it, but rush at it, that is the road to victory and safety, a retreat is fatal. The one thing the enemy cannot stand is our being at close quarters with him. We are fighting for the health and safety of our comrades, we are fighting in defence of our flag against an enemy who has forced war on us for the worst and lowest of motives, by Treachery, Conspiracy and Deceit. Let us bear ourselves as our cause deserves.

At these words from our general, which showed how much he, like us, felt for our besieged comrades and how much he had the cause we were fighting for at heart, we felt doubly determined to

Buller was kept informed of the Boers' movements on Spion Kop and the surrounding mountains by means of heliographed messages from Ladysmith.

make our next venture a fight to the finish. The bad luck we had had at Colenso surely couldn't last forever and we had great hopes for the next engagement.

The scenery from our position was splendid, the river winding between the two positions—Boers and ours—looked deceptively pretty and Spearman's Hill was densely wooded down one side with very lush trees. We could also see Potgieter's Drift.

Following the flags at home. There was an even larger map outside the offices of the Illustrated London News *in the Strand which attracted avid crowds. (D)*

Tucker's 'splendid' position provided him with a view of the Tugela as it curved and doubled back, producing two tongues of land enclosed by the river. From these tongues, on the north side, an undulating plain rose gently to the mountains where the Boers could be seen entrenching themselves. The most dominant peak in the panorama was Spion Kop, its steepest side facing the British position and leading to a flat-topped, grassy summit.

Beyond the Drakensberg range could be seen the dim outlines of the Biggarsberg, then the hills near Elandslaagte, and beyond this screen, the unseen town of Ladysmith.

Makeshift mess. Rifle Brigade officers relaxing below Spearman's Hill. (H)

Chapter Three:
If At First You Don't Succeed

Warren had now amassed provisions for seventeen days and was ready to march to Trichardt's Drift, Tucker, with the rest of Lyttelton's brigade, was part of a plan to mislead the Boers by a show of force into believing that the main attack would come from Potgieter's Drift. We now know that the Boers were convinced by this feint and quickly moved their commandos into a strong defensive position.

16th January 1900

On Tuesday we received sudden orders that our brigade, General Lyttelton's, was to move in closer to the enemy position by crossing the Tugela at Potgieter's Drift.

The British column stuttering to a start. In the background the reconnaissance balloon looms large, advertising the movements of the column to the Boers. Although preposterously well supplied and equipped, Warren somehow neglected to provide the small force that stormed Spion Kop with sufficient water, ammunition or field telegraphs. (E)

The Tugela River, when in flood, varied in width from between 100 to 300 feet and travelled at a rate of ten miles an hour. Even when the stream was low, attempts to cross were made treacherous by hidden rocks and boulders. Wagons, especially, came to grief during the crossing.

At 2.30 p.m. we moved off in columns, with my regiment, 1st Royal Rifle Brigade, leading. Just before marching off, the Bishop of Natal read prayers and gave us a short address, asking us to prepare for the unknown world. This gave us the idea we were in for severe fighting. We moved over the hill and opened out into skirmishing order as we approached the river. The water was about four feet deep at the place we forded. The current was

Potgieter's Drift, named after the early Boer hero, Hendrik Potgieter, who defeated Mzilikazi and the Matabele tribe in 1837. (A)

A recruitment poster. (M)

rapid, making it very difficult to walk forward but the crossing was eventually accomplished, with a good deal of laughter, caused mostly by some poor luckless fellow slipping on a smooth stone and making a sudden dive under. As each company crossed, it moved forward once more in skirmishing order to occupy a low range of kopjes which lay in front of the Boer positions at Brakfontein. We occupied these without encountering any resistance; the Boers, evidently thinking it not worth while to interfere, treated our advance with contempt.

At about 9.00 p.m. an officer and one hundred men went out to within 1,000 yards of the Boer trenches and commenced firing, the idea, obviously, was to draw the Boer fire and so expose their position but they would not answer. The Boers remained stubborn and would not fire a single shot. The men returned grumbling because they had not been shot at! We lay down on the bare hard rocks of the kopjes in our wet clothing and attempted to sleep but rain came on and poured in torrents all night. So, wet, cold and rather hungry we passed another tiring night, with the single comfort of having been the first regiment to cross the Tugela—an honour indeed. Each man carried two days

The Boers refusal to exchange shots with the British at Potgieter's Drift was characteristic of their military strategy so far seen in the Natal campaign. They preferred to wait for a frontal attack, meanwhile extending their right flank further west to prevent it being turned.

It seems mighty churlish to contradict Tucker when he is so wet and exhausted, but the weight of evidence does point to the Scottish Rifles and the Durham Light Infantry as having been the first regiments across the Tugela.

Killing two birds with one stone. Two British soldiers strip off and cross the river. (A)

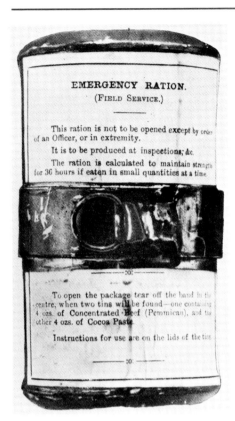

rations with him on leaving Spearman's Hill but unfortunately these had become very wet during the river crossing. The biscuits, however, really improved by the soaking as it made them softer, but no fires were allowed so we could not make tea to warm us until the morning.

17th January 1900

We stood to arms at 4.30 a.m. and, shortly after, a howitzer battery that had crossed over during the night, opened fire, the naval guns also joined in from Spearman's Hill and the shelling continued all day. We were greatly interested by the firing of the howitzer battery, who were sending shells into trenches they could not see. The guns stood unlimbered behind the hill, an officer, standing on top of the hill, gave distance and elevation; watching closely we could see the shells going through the air like cricket balls and on reaching their destination a huge column of earth and green smoke could be seen. These guns fire Lyddite.

Emergency rations were issued to every soldier and had to be produced at inspections. The cylinder contained two four-ounce tins, one of concentrated beef, the other, cocoa paste. Either could be eaten dry or boiled for an hour to make a nourishing drink of beef tea or liquid cocoa. (C)

The 5-inch howitzer was designed to fire shells into the air from an elevation of forty-five degrees. This meant the shells would fall well within the Boer defences.

The howitzers shelled the Boers from Tucker's position every day. J. B. Atkins, war correspondent for the Manchester Guardian, described the scene: 'The hills crashed with guns and rattled with musketry. At a little distance you might have supposed that the resonant noises came from some haunted mountain, for the hills looked sleepy, and peaceful, and deserted, and there seemed to be no reason for all these strange sounds—the bark of field guns, the crackle of musketry, the rapping of Vickers-Maxims, and the tat-tat-tat-tat-tat-tat of Maxims.' (A) (C)

The hill we occupied was called Mount Alice but we rechristened it Maconochie Hill as Maconochie Army rations were so often issued to us.

Each day the guns continued to shell the Ladysmith Road where the Boers are reported to have trenches four miles long. The balloon section was with us and gave us very useful information. Demonstrations were made each day by us and the Scottish Rifles. On one occasion, the Boers opened fired with a pom-pom and their rifles, killing two and wounding nine of the King's Royal Rifles, who were also with us. Every day the guns continued but we could not make a real attack until Sir Charles Warren, who was working on our left position, had got closer to us.

The hill occupied by the 1st Rifle Brigade was not Mount Alice (which is situated on the other side of the Tugela) but One Tree Hill. When one considers how poor the generals' maps were, it becomes easy to understand Tucker's mistake.

One of the daily demonstrations Tucker talks of was made on 18 January by the Scottish Rifles, the 3rd King's Royal Rifles and Tucker's brigade. The troops advanced in a convex line, supported by the artillery. Yellow and green plumes of smoke rose from points along the eastern face of Spion Kop where the lyddite shells had struck, but the Boers refused to return the fire. From the air the balloonists could see the Boers lining their trenches; obstinate, resolute.

Meanwhile, at Trichardt's Drift the troops under Warren's command were becoming very restless. They had suffered a loss of thirty-four dead, 293 wounded and two missing during the sporadic skirmishes and abortive attacks. Many of the force were bivouacked on bare mountain slopes; the days were scorching, the nights were bitterly cold, the townspeople of Ladysmith were starving and still Warren delayed. On 19 January he sent a message from the 'Left Flank' to Buller explaining that he needed two or three more days 'to adopt some special arrangements' and added, 'I will send in for further supplies and report progress.'

Bastion Hill had been taken by Dundonald and the front line had been advanced as far as Three Tree Hill but the men were weary and constantly exposed to shell fire, Buller insisted that Warren should 'withdraw or assault'. Warren chose to storm Spion Kop.

Directing the advance on Potgieter's Drift from a balloon.

Twenty military balloons were sent out to South Africa. Each held 11,000 cubic feet of gas. The wickerwork basket was fitted out with telegraphic apparatus and carried two passengers. The Boers, believing that the balloons would be used to drop explosives, tried vainly to bring them to the ground with shell fire. (C)

The Battle of Spion Kop

Churchill watched the mighty column floundering through the torrents of rain, and wrote: 'It was not possible to stand unmoved and watch the ceaseless living stream—miles of stern-looking men, marching in fours so quickly that they often had to run to keep up, of artillery, ammunition columns, supply columns, baggage, slaughter-cattle, thirty great pontoons, white-hooded, red-crossed ambulance wagons, all the accessories of an army hurrying forward under cover of night—and before them a guiding star, the red gleam of war.'

Once more we are indebted to J. B. Atkins' sharp ear and ready pen for noting down this laconic criticism:
'What are we waiting 'ere for? Why don't we go on?' asked one private soldier of another.
'Don't yer know?'
'No,' said the first man.
'To give the Boers time to build up their trenches and fetch up their guns. Fair—ain't it?'

The Battle of Spion Kop was one of the bloodiest, most terrible and most futile battles of the whole war. It served, more so than any other campaign, to illustrate the inadequacies of British generalship.

Sir Charles Warren, a confident and notoriously irascible general, had joined Buller bringing reinforcements, which swelled the ranks to 30,000 men, and a dormant commission appointing him Commander-in-Chief in the event of Buller's death or disablement. The column, consisting of 650 ox wagons, 24,000 infantry, 2,600 mounted troops, eight field batteries and ten naval guns, stretched seventeen miles. Buller set up his camp on Mount Alice where he could oversee the proceedings and handed the command over to Warren. This curious course of action on the part of Buller can perhaps be explained by his resentment of Warren coupled with the fact that he was marking time until Roberts and Kitchener arrived.

The original plan to reach Ladysmith by Potgieter's Drift was abandoned and, instead, Warren marched west during the night of 16 January, with the intention of crossing the Tugela ten miles up river at Trichardt's Drift. He left his camp standing and gave orders that bugles were to be sounded as usual, in an ingenuous attempt to dupe the Boers into believing that his men were still

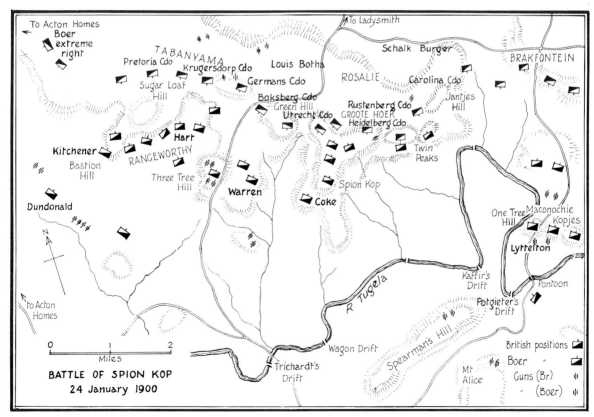

The Battle of Spion Kop

Map by Mr A. Spark

encamped there. Lyttelton, eager to consolidate the deception, sent his men (including Tucker) across the Tugela at Potgieter's Drift and made a night attack on a small group of hillocks. They dislodged the Boers and renamed One Tree Hill, 'Machonochie Kopje'.

Lyttelton's attack convinced the Boers that Buller was about to make a full attack across Potgieter's Drift and accordingly they hastened to reinforce Brakfontein which lay directly behind it.

Meanwhile, Warren, instead of taking immediate advantage of Lyttelton's decoy and advancing at once, calmly waited twenty-six hours while his precious baggage train crossed the Tugela. The whole advantage of the gruelling night march, Lyttelton's feint, and the element of surprise was lost.

Colonel Dundonald, exasperated by Warren's inactivity and out-dated preoccupation with the baggage, set off north independently. Warren flew into a fury and sent him a reprimanding message ordering him to send back the cavalry to protect the oxen, although, at that time, there were no Boers in the vicinity. Warren would have done better to have issued his men with two days' rations and sent them on ahead, leaving the baggage to follow leisurely. However, Dundonald dutifully sent back the Royals' and pressed on to Acton Homes with the remainder of his men. They ambushed a party of 250 Boers and succeeded in capturing or killing about fifty of them with a loss of only three British soldiers.

Instead of reinforcing Dundonald's bold advance, Warren waited the whole day before sending for him and complaining ungraciously that the role of the cavalry was to protect the baggage and not to 'indulge in semi-independent antics'.

While Warren vacillated, the Boers extended their western flank and dug themselves in. Buller, watching from Mount Alice, thought Warren's operations 'aimless and irresolute'. Nevertheless, he heliographed to White in Ladysmith that all was going well and victory was certain.

Despite the fact that a balloon unit was available to him, Warren failed to reconnoitre the area and, on 20 January, sent his artillery forward. The men advanced towards, and gained, the first crest only to find that the terrain was composed of undulations and the Boers were immovably dug in 1,000 yards away behind a second crest. Dundonald managed to charge Bastion Hill with the South African Light Horse and capture it, but Warren chose only to bombard the enemy from long range for two days, on the principle that it would demoralize them sufficiently for his men to 'finish them off with the bayonet'. In the light of events that were to follow his boasts were pathetically inaccurate.

Warren was incurring continuous casualties and getting nowhere. Buller urged him to 'withdraw or assault' and eventually he decided to take Spion Kop, a conical shaped mountain rising 1,470 feet. No one knew the terrain, and maps, when they existed, were crude and inadequate.

At 7.30 p.m. on 23 January, General Woodgate amassed a small force of 1,800 men of the Lancashire Fusiliers (six companies from the Royal Lancasters and two from the South

An unexploded, 50 lb lyddite shell which was fired from a British naval gun during the Battle of Spion Kop.
The finder had it suitably engraved and presented it to President Kruger. (C)

Wide gaps in the training of the British troops quickly became apparent during the action. A squadron of South African Light Horse—familiar with the country—held a kopje all day under heavy fire and by taking careful cover they did not lose a single man. Close by, two companies of British regulars held a hill under a similar fire and, neglecting cover, lost twenty men.

Major-General Woodgate was born in 1845 and died at 10.00 a.m. on 24 January, 1900, while supervising the attack on Spion Kop. Struck in the eye, he was carried off the field, murmuring, 'Let me alone! Let me alone!'

Lt. Colonel Thorneycroft was in command of the Mounted Infantry in South Africa. He had had previous experience of the country during the Zulu War of 1879 and the 1st Boer War fought in 1881.

Lancashire), a company of Royal Engineers and 200 dismounted men from Thorneycroft's Mounted Infantry. Each man carried a rifle and 150 rounds of ammunition. The password was Waterloo.

The men set off through a light drizzle under cover of darkness, advancing silently over grass, then rocks until the path began to steepen. The climb took seven gruelling hours, during which the men were urged not to make a sound. At the summit they surprised a small picket of Boers who quickly fled. Down below, Warren heard a faint cheer go up. The tiny force occupying the hill had no field telegraph linking them with headquarters, no oil for the signal lamps, very few heliograph operators or flag signallers and, either through exhaustion or lack of initiative in the officers, they failed to entrench themselves properly during the few remaining hours of darkness they had.

The German impression of how the Boers beat the British at Spion Kop is shown on this postcard from Berlin. (N)

Am Spionkop.
Chor der Buren:
Mang uns mang is keiner mang
Der nich mang uns mang gehört.

GRUSS VOM KRIEGSSCHAUPLATZ

Churchill climbed to the top of Spion Kop to ascertain the true facts for himself. 'Streams of wounded,' he wrote, 'met us and obstructed our path. Men were staggering along alone, or supported by comrades, or crawling on hands and knees, or carried on stretchers. Corpses lay here and there. . . There was, moreover, a small but steady leakage of unwounded men of all corps. Some of these cursed and swore. Others were utterly exhausted, and fell on the hill-side in stupor. Others, again, seemed drunk, though they had no liquor. Scores were sleeping heavily. . . We were so profoundly impressed by the spectacle and situation that we resolved to go and tell Sir Charles Warren what we had seen. . . One thing was quite clear—unless good and efficient cover could be made during the night, and unless guns could be dragged to the summit of the hill to match the Boer artillery, the infantry could not, perhaps would not, endure another day. The human machine will not stand certain strains for long.'

As the mist lifted the men realized with despair that they had not reached the true summit and that they shared the sloping plateau with the Boers who were being steadily reinforced by Botha under cover of the mist. The battle lasted eleven hours. The Boers were entrenched in perfect positions and poured a murderous fire into the British ranks. The two front lines were so close at some points that the opposing forces wrestled in hand to hand combat. Soon the men were able to build barricades from the dead bodies which were piling copiously up around them. Behind this gruesome cover and under a scorching sun, they put up a desperate resistance. Many officers were dead and the men suffered from lack of direction and lack of water. Confusion and panic reigned on the congested summit as Warren sent reinforcements and Buller persisted in interfering with vague advice. General Woodgate was struck through the eye and Warren appointed Thorneycroft to command but neglected to tell Crofton, who had correctly assumed command as next in superiority. Some men even began to surrender but Thorneycroft ran up shouting, waving his arms and his gun and ordered them back.

From below, J. B. Atkins, war correspondent for the *Manchester Guardian* followed the action: 'I saw three shells strike a certain trench within a minute, each struck it full in the face, and the brown dust rose and drifted away with the white smoke. The trench was toothed against the sky like a saw—made, I supposed, of sharp rocks built into a rampart. Another shell struck it, and then—heavens!—the trench rose up and moved forward. The trench was men; the teeth against the sky were men. They ran forward bending their bodies into a curve, as men do when they run under a heavy fire; they looked like a cornfield with a heavy wind sweeping over it from behind ... They flickered up, fleeted rapidly and silently across the sky, and flickered down into the rocks without the appearance of either a substantial beginning or end to the movement.'

Waiting for Tommy Atkins. In the shade of the Vierkleur, *two Boers on Spion Kop. (C)*

The King's Royal Rifles marching towards Spion Kop. (A)

Lyttelton, on his own initiative, sent the King's Royal Rifles to storm the eastern face of Spion Kop. The Boers began to fall back before them and they succeeded in gaining the summit but were unwittingly shelled by their own artillery from Warren's camp on Three Tree Hill. They were recalled.

As daylight faded, Thorneycroft found himself in disputed command with no further orders from Warren; his myriad wounded were tormented with thirst and his force was severely depleted. He had no idea what was happening elsewhere. Under cover of darkness he resolved to evacuate the hill, justifying his action to an incredulous Churchill, who had struggled up the hill to see what was happening for himself, with the words: 'Better six battalions safely off the hill than a mop-up in the morning.'

Simultaneously, the Boers were departing on the other face. When the Boers returned to collect their dead, just before dawn, they were amazed to find the hill deserted and reclaimed it at once.

At dawn on the following day, 25 January, the unwittingly triumphant Boers were greeted only by dead or wounded. 'In some of the trenches and parts of the kopje where the fire was hottest,' wrote a Boer correspondent, 'bodies were actually entangled, as if the dying men had clutched each other in the death struggle, the spirit of battle in their souls as they sped from earth. On all sides were mute evidence of the desperate nature of the battle. Dozens of stones were spattered with blood, and empty Lee-Metford shells lay about everywhere by the bucketful, testifying that the English had spent an enormous amount of ammunition. Many cartridge belts were found entirely empty.'

During the night of 23 January the comparatively small force of 1,800 men under General Woodgate's command had scaled Spion Kop and reached the summit: shrouded in impenetrable blackness and a thick wet mist.

Before silently setting out, Thorneycroft had addressed his Mounted Infantry with the following words: 'We are about to attack Spion Kop. Make no noise. It's bayonet work only. No shots are to be fired. No smoking. No talking. Keep in close touch with one another. The honour of the Regiment is in your hands. I can trust you all to do your duty.'

By 24 January, 1900, the British force in South Africa totalled 180,000, which outnumbered the entire Boer population.

Following 'the red gleam of war'. Warren's lengthy column on the move toward Spion Kop. (K)

24th January 1900

The Battle of Spion Kop.

Long before daybreak we paraded and advanced to within a few hundred yards of the Boer position, which we were to take as soon as Sir Charles Warren gave us the signal that he had taken the hills he was fighting for. Our guns were constantly shelling the Boer trenches and we were lying within easy rifle range: a move designed to compel the Boers to stay put and so relieve the pressure on Sir Charles Warren's force. We lay there nearly all day, the heat was terrific, and we knew by the sound of heavy firing nearby, that a very severe fight was taking place. Meanwhile, two regiments of our brigade, the 2nd Scottish Rifles and the 3rd King's Royal Rifles, had climbed up the almost inaccessible heights of Spion Kop, on the reverse side. The heavy firing was still going on on the other side and they had almost gained the top before the Boers discovered them. As soon as they were sighted, the Boers opened a heavy fire, our men rushed forward and took the trenches but all for nothing for they were ordered to retire just as they had gained the position and really got the Boers beaten. But retire they must—although much against their will.

Only two regiments remained on the north side of the Tugela, us and the Durham Light Infantry. It was rumoured that our casualties were as high as 1,500.

Very little firing took place for several days after the Spion

A view of the Boer positions on Spion Kop. In the early stages of the war the Boers proved themselves far more adept at taking cover than the British, although the discrepancies, through necessity, evened out. (A)

An army surgeon, Frederick Treves, described the condition of the wounded on the summit: 'The men were much exhausted by the hardships they had undergone. In many instances they had not had their clothes off for a week or ten days. They had slept in the open without any great-coats, and had been reduced to the minimum in the matter of rations. The nights were cold, and there was on nearly every night a heavy dew. Fortunately, there was little or no rain. The want of sleep and the long waiting upon the hill had told upon them severely. There is no doubt also that the incessant shell fire must have proved a terrible strain. Some of the men, although severely wounded, were found asleep upon their stretchers when brought in. Many were absolutely exhausted and worn out independently of their wounds. In spite of all their hardships, the wounded men behaved as splendidly as they always have done. They never complained. They were quite touching in their unselfishness and in their anxiety 'not to give trouble'. One poor fellow had been shot in the face by a piece of shell, which had carried away his left eye, the left upper jaw with the corresponding part of the cheek, and had left a hideous cavity at the bottom of which his tongue was exposed. He had been lying hours on the hill. He was unable to speak, and as soon as he was landed at the hospital he made signs that he wanted to write. Pencil and paper were given him, and it was supposed he wished to ask for something, but he merely wrote, 'Did we win?' No one had the heart to tell him the truth.'

Kop affair. We still remained on Mount Alice, lying in the hot sun all day and getting wet through and almost frozen solid at night, for we still had no blankets with us. We remained on the hills until 3 February, when we were relieved by the 5th Brigade and twelve batteries of artillery which had also arrived. We retired back across the Tugela, not sorry to leave our uncomfortable position, where, for three weeks, we had been exposed to all weathers without even the friendly shade of a tree. The hills were nothing but a mass of rocks, jagged and jutting, impossible to lie on, let alone sleep on.

3rd February 1900

We bivouacked at the foot of Spearman's Hill. Sunday, as well.

The following morning, the 243 dead British soldiers were buried on the hill where they had fallen. The 500 wounded men were brought down the hill; many died during the descent. The Boers wrapped their dead, estimated at about sixty, in blankets and carried them down the hill.

The Boer government practised propaganda to the extent of having ghoulish photographs of the British dead (which they erroneously estimated at over 1,000) circulated in the shops of Pretoria and Johannesburg. (A)

The Battle of Vaal Krantz

Roberts was as popular with the British public as Buller was with his well-fed troops. Yet his short stature and blindness in one eye would have exempted him from military life today. Kipling wrote affectionately:

> *There's a little red-faced man,*
>   *Which is Bobs,*
> *Rides the tallest 'orse 'e can—*
>   *Our Bobs.*
> *If it bucks or kicks or rears,*
>   *'E can sit for twenty years*
> *With a smile round both 'is ears—*
>   *Can't yer Bobs?*

The Boer commander, Ben Viljoen, a young editor of a pro-Kruger newspaper (although his own politics were pro-Joubert) was a stirring speaker and rallied his men with the cry 'God and the Mauser'.

Not all the commandos were farmers; many had left their jobs as lawyers and civil servants in the large towns of Johannesburg, Pretoria and Bloemfontein to fight against the British.

Ladysmith eluded Buller cruelly. Success seemed constantly just within grasp but continued to evade him. The defeats were debilitating both to the men and to his fast diminishing reputation. He decided to make another attack and, on 3 February, he declared that he had the key! This was a break in the range of hills to the right of his position on Spearman's Hill. He planned to seize Vaal Krantz on the left and Doorn Kop on the right and then march his mighty force through the centre.

The omens were good. Unbeknown to Buller, many of the burghers and their leaders—including Louis Botha—had granted themselves leave (as they were at liberty to do whenever they wished. One of the recompenses for not being paid, no doubt). There were only about 4,000 Boers, under the command of a young Transvaaler, Ben Viljoen, left on the hills compared to Buller's recently reinforced total of 20,000 troops. His artillery, too, had been supplemented and he could now boast seventy-eight serviceable guns.

The problem was that there was no natural ford across the river. However, the British army was equipped to handle this contingency and, at 7.00 a.m. on 5 February, the Royal Engineers threw two pontoon bridges across the Tugela. The first, at Potgieter's Drift, which threatened the Boer defences at

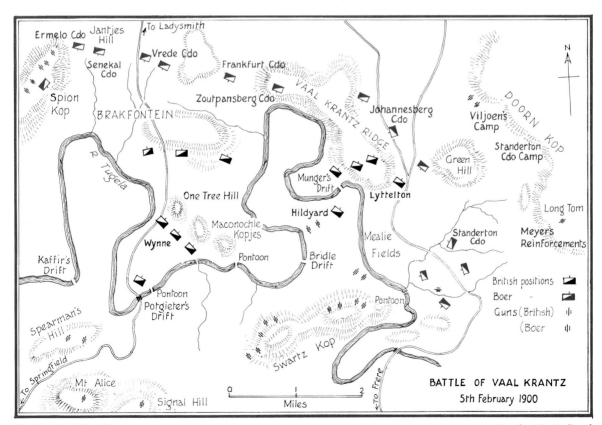

The Battle of Vaal Krantz   *Map by Mr A. Spark*

Brakfontein, was designed as an elaborate diversion. And, indeed, it worked well, save for the fact that more field batteries than planned crossed over. Some of them were needed for the genuine eastern attack and valuable time was lost in retrieving them. The eastern pontoon was completed in fifty minutes, but by then it was 2.00 p.m. and Ben Viljoen's suspicions had been aroused. The delay had given him time to reinforce Vaal Krantz and Tucker and his comrades were given a fierce reception as they crossed the hastily constructed pontoon and ran, bent double, across the vast open mealie field.

Tucker's brigade (the 1st Rifle Brigade) and the Durham Light Infantry managed to reach the foot of Vaal Krantz, routing the Boers at Munger's Farm on their way. However, something was not right. Lyttelton appealed to Buller for the rest of the force to follow, but Buller's nerve had once more given way. The fire from Doorn Kop to the west was heavier than he had anticipated and so he had decided to break off the attack and was detaining the Scottish Rifles and the 60th Rifles on the other side of the pontoon.

A furious and astounded Lyttelton pointed out that his men were already committed to the attack and, reluctantly, Buller allowed them to cross, but the cavalry and the force calculated to storm Doorn Kop were held back.

Nevertheless, Lyttelton led his attack and the men quickly drove the Boers from the southernmost ridge of Vaal Krantz. They held their position for the rest of the day, taking what scanty cover the loose rocks afforded, until night fell and they could entrench themselves properly.

While Tucker spent an anxious night in an exposed position on the side of Vaal Krantz, Buller spent the night in camp agonizing over his next step. Lyttelton entreated him to implement the whole of the plan he had orginally conceived and take Doorn Kop. In despair, Buller sent a telegram to Roberts, whose immediate answer to push on and relieve Ladysmith still didn't have the effect of galvanizing Buller into action.

At noon the following day Botha arrived and rallied his men, injecting them with a fresh enthusiasm. The commandos made a rush for the hill and for a split second it looked as if they would drive the British back, but half a battalion of the 60th Rifles rose, bayonets fixed, and charged them. They retreated. Buller had decided to do the same.

On 8 February he withdrew through Springfield—where Tucker bivouacked—back to his former base in Chieveley.

Protected by a stone sangar, a soldier sets his sights. (A)

The day before the battle, Buller sent this telegram to Roberts:
'Ladysmith is in a bad way; White keeps a stiff upper lip, but some of those under him are despondent; he calculates that he has now 7,000 effectives; his men are dying about eight or ten per day, and when he last gave me a statement, he had 2,400 in hospital; they are eating their horses, and have very little else. He expects to be attacked this week, and although he affects to be confident, I doubt if he really is. He has begged me to keep the enemy off him as much as I can and I can only do this by pegging away. I am going to have a try and get through the mountains here tomorrow.'

Buller attributed part of the blame for this latest defeat to White, who, he claimed peevishly, had not detained enough Boers around Ladysmith.

A bird's-eye view of Chieveley camp. It housed thousands of troops and stretched neatly across a vast area of the veldt. (D)

After the Spion Kop disaster Buller was in a period of limbo. His command was soon to be relieved by Roberts, who was now in South Africa and marching towards the Modder River with a strong force to relieve Kimberley, and yet he refused to be patient.

Pontoons are temporary bridges supported by floats. It was no mean feat to construct one during peace manoeuvres let alone under rifle fire, and it said much for the courage and determination of the Royal Engineers that, despite having eight of their number wounded, they were able to complete the bridge in under an hour.

The British troops dubbed the Boer 5·9-inch Creusot gun 'Long Tom' because it had a range of 10,000 yards.

Engineers at work constructing a pontoon bridge. The bridges were taken up after use, dismantled and carried in sections on ox wagons until needed again. (A)

5th February 1900

Battle of Vaal Krantz

We fell in at 6.30 a.m. knowing we were to attack yet another of those hills which the Boers know how to fortify so well. With the Durham Light Infantry, we formed the firing line supported by the other two regiments of our brigade. We marched for about three miles under Spearman's Hill and then halted for some time to allow the Engineers time to build a pontoon bridge for the crossing of the Tugela. Meanwhile, our guns kept up a heavy fire, and it was a treat to watch our artillery, who took up position on the open plain, fully exposed to the enemy's long range guns which throw one hundred pound shells compared to our field artillery 15-pound shells. Theirs carry 10,000 yards and ours 5,000 but nevertheless, our gunners kept up a brave fire. They could not reach the Boer Long Toms so they treated them with contempt and turned their fire instead on the Boer trenches. We could see that the attack was developing on the left front of us. The brigade who relieved us on Mount Alice were, with the aid of several battalions of artillery, making a false attack and had succeeded in drawing the Boer fire with their diversion. However, pom-pom, Mauser and big guns forced them to retire to a safer distance. The Engineers had succeeded in laying the bridge despite the heavy fire they were under and the stretchers were bringing back their wounded as we advanced. The Durhams led, crossing the bridge amidst a hail of Mauser and Maxim bullets—the Boers were firing for all they were worth. The first man of my regiment to step on the bridge was shot dead—hit in the head and the heart. We crossed over in single file at the double but even with this precaution several of our men were badly hit. Some excellent sprinting was done through air alive with bullets, like bees humming around. We formed up under the river bank, there

The naval guns crossing the pontoon over the Tugela River to begin the bombardment of Grobler's Kloof. (A)

were a lot of wounded men and the doctor was very busy. Almost immediately we left the bank of the river and found ourselves in a mealie field, where the Boers made it very lively for us with their big guns, rifle and pom-pom fire. (The men of my regiment have nick-named these mealie fields 'death-traps' as we are such exposed targets for the Boers as we pass through them.)

My regiment and the Durhams were still advancing in skirmishing order, no shot or shell could stop us that day and soon the foot of Vaal Krantz was reached, and, with fixed swords, we charged up the hill in the face of deadly shot and shell fire. When we reached the top we found only a few Boers remaining and these we took as prisoners. Very soon the whole of the regiment was on the hill and the men set to work at once building walls for protection as we were still under a very heavy cross fire from the front and the right. It was fortunate that we did this for as soon as our heads were shown above the wall a well aimed volley rang out. The Boers kept firing until it was quite dark, so it was not safe to move our casualties, which were very heavy—about eighty in the Rifle Brigade. A few Boers kept sniping all night while we strengthened our walls.

The Durham Light Infantry gaining the crest of Vaal Krantz. The Rifle Brigade were close behind in support. On the summit they found a few Boers who had survived the extensive bombardment; they were taken prisoner. (C)

LYDITE BOM ONTPLOFT JUIST VOOR ONZE KANONSCHANS
LYDITE-SHELL EXPLODING JUST IN FRONT OF CANNON

A lyddite shell exploding near a Boer cannon. These fifty pound shells, which the British howitzers fired, sent up plumes of green and yellow smoke and smashed the bodies of unfortunate targets into fragments scattered across an area of fifty feet or more. If the Boers had any time to bury their dead, these victims had to be collected by the shovelful: a sickening task. (A)

A Boer's view of the British Infantry advance. (O)

Buller hated the thought of sacrificing the lives of his men for the success of any battle. In the case of Vaal Krantz he firmly believed that he would forfeit at least 3,000 and even then there would be a strong chance of defeat. His men seemed to understand and appreciate his exaggerated concern for them and, although they grew more despondent with each retreat, they never blamed him and continued to follow him loyally.

Among the dead at Vaal Krantz appears the name of Private G. Mauser, ironically killed by a Boer Mauser rifle.

Theron's scouts, part of the Boer force besieging Ladysmith, keeping up a persistent sniping fire. (A)

At daybreak the Boers let us have it from all sides with their long range guns. Spion Kop sent us greetings with shells, and Groblers Kloof with its 8-inch gun, which came across with a noise like a traction engine. Their pom-poms, too, were very active and taken altogether we were having a very lively time,

lying on the side of the bare hill (Vaal Krantz) with no-one able to come to our assistance. The remainder of our troops were trapped on the other side of the river, unable to cross the open plain which lay between us because of the heavy Boer shell fire. We couldn't advance and wouldn't retire, so there we lay, as close to the ground as possible. We could not see a single Boer to aim at, only a trench about 1,000 yards in front of us which some of our men fired at just for the sake of something to do.

A great many men were wounded during the day while we waited, fully expecting some movement from the other troops, but none came. Twice the balloon went up and we were relieved

A contrasting account from the Boer trenches is provided by a Boer correspondent who wrote: 'Scattered about, crouching low among the boulders, and in the innumerable tiny ravines, the Boers, with the phelgm of their race, patiently endured the storm and waited for Tommy Atkins to come within rifle range. The boulders which covered them were shattered and splintered by the iron hail, but the Boers did not budge. It is really marvellous how the burghers manage to fight effectively while keeping so perfectly concealed. A wounded English officer, who was brought into the laager after the fight, told me that the men who carried him off the field were the first Boers he had seen. During the fight he had not caught a glimpse of a single man.'

The reconnaissance balloon Tucker watched was Mark II, the first having been damaged by shrapnel during Spion Kop week. The balloonist used a telephone to communicate any observations he might make to the generals below. When tested at Aldershot, the balloons had risen to 4,000 feet but the important fact that much of the area was already 3,500 feet above sea level had been overlooked. Thus the balloons were only able to rise another 500 feet, making them quite redundant in the more mountainous regions.

A Boer trench under fire. The Boers made thrifty use of their ammunition and were careful not to return the British fire unless compelled to. While a few men remained on guard, the others relaxed over their pipes and caught up on the news of the war. (P)

at 7.00 p.m. under cover of darkness by another brigade led by Colonel Kitchener of the West Yorks who told Colonel Billy Norcott that we had been greatly praised by General Buller for the way we had taken the hill. The Boers made one attempt to retake it but they were driven back in such a hurry that they left one hundred rifles and several dead and wounded behind them; they did not try that game again!

Frederick W. Kitchener, a younger brother of Lord Kitchener, had served under Roberts once before during the Afghan War of 1878–80.

Boers in battle. Experienced marksmen, the Boers sighted their guns with care and made every shot count. (A)

Bridging the gap. One of the pontoon bridges, used by the Rifle Brigade, which crossed the Tugela River. (H)

Having been relieved, we marched back under Spearman's Hill again to bivouack for the night. I was not sorry to be away from the incessant noise of shot and shell—we had been under fire for thirty hours. It goes without saying that I slept soundly that night despite being on the open veldt without any covers. I woke early next morning, cold, stiff and shivering, my clothes wet through with the heavy dew. We lay on the side of Spearman's Hill all day waiting for the order to attack the remainder of the Boer positions and, occasionally, getting a shell close to us. No orders came to advance, indeed, the balloon appeared to be the only thing at work with the exception of the guns! Night fell and we were ordered to go on picquet on the pontoon bridges, there we bivouacked. During the night the bridges were taken up (another pontoon bridge had been placed close by Vaal Krantz), and the hill which we had lost so many lives taking was evacuated. So all our hopes of relieving Ladysmith this way were scattered.

I shall never forget our retirement: the Boers tried to hurry us up with the huge shells from their 8-inch Long Tom. We passed Generals Buller, Clery and Lyttelton; Clery was on a stretcher and looked very sick, while Buller had disappointment written all over his face. 'Come on, Rifle Brigade, hurry up!' he said, as we passed him, for we were not hurrying very much, we were reluctant to leave what we had won. I think my regiment was the

British burying their dead on Vaal Krantz. (M)

With Ladysmith still starving and Buller repeating his retreats with much rehearsed practice, Punch *summed up the progress of the war in a poem purporting to come from Arthur Balfour, Leader of the House of Commons.*

> I think it would be almost wrong
> To say that we are going strong;
> Our recent triumphs, we confess,
> Fall short of absolute success.
>
> Things look, at first, a little blue:
> They almost nearly always do:
> I fail to notice, all the same,
> That anybody is to blame.
>
> Although I seldom see the news,
> I have my military views;
> And fortunately these agree
> With those of all the Ministry.
>
> I cannot honestly disguise
> That Krüger took us by surprise:
> Quite sure were we, or almost quite,
> The gentleman would never fight.
>
> We heard that he had got some guns,
> But only very little ones:
> We also heard of mounted forces,
> But never dreamed they rode on horses!

last to leave, for when we passed Spearman's Hill, we found nearly all our division had marched off. The 4th Brigade, we learned, were to march to Chieveley.

After marching for some time we camped in Springfield. This was the first time we had been under canvas since leaving Frere

The British losses—twenty-five killed, 344 wounded and five missing—were not considered heavy, but as no advance had been made they were more than enough. The Boers placed their losses as twenty-one killed and thirty-one wounded.

Boer graves, carefully fenced off with barbed wire. In the latter part of the war the Boers had little time for such elaborations. (A)

Some top surgeons were earning as much as
£100 a week, with a free, first class passage
to South Africa and back, and they certainly
earned it. Many of the field hospitals,
wagons and stretcher bearers were fired on
by the Boers during the course of the war,
which caused much outrage in Britain. But,
to be fair, the range of firing was often vast,
the red cross on the side of the wagon
scarcely discernible and the 'body-snatchers'
(as the Indian stretcher bearers were
known) hardly distinguishable from the
distant band of fighting men. It could hardly
have been an uplifting sight, however, to
watch newly bandaged men wounded again
as they rested.

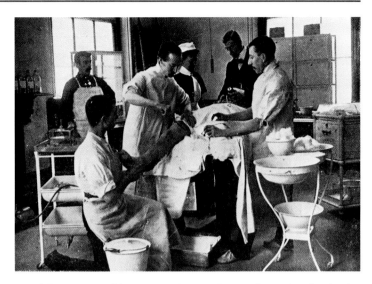

*Surgeons amputating a leg in a field
hospital. Hygiene was little understood then,
and they did not wear gloves or masks. (G)*

on 10 January and it was a welcome change from sleeping in the
open. Some of us had such luxuries as Quaker Oats, tins of cocoa,
etc., stowed away in tent bags and we were soon busy making fires
and cooking, each his own little mess tin full of whatever he
possessed. Speaking for myself, I thoroughly enjoyed a meal of
Quaker Oats followed by a good sleep without the expectation of
being woken by a sudden alarm or a screaming shell.

*Neville Lyttelton reports the following
conversation he had with Buller after the
Battle of Vaal Krantz in his book,* Eighty
Years:
*'I went to report to Buller who was at dinner.
He asked me what sort of time I had had, to
which I replied, 'Very bad; shot at day and
night from nearly all sides by an invisible
foe, against whom our fire was perfectly
innocuous.' 'Wait a bit,' he said, and came
out with a large jorum of champagne, the
most refreshing drink I ever had.'*

*All the comforts of home. The luxury and
variety of the tinned goods with which the
British soldier was supplied was incredible.
(A)*

On the following day we rested, passing the day bathing and
washing our underclothing—a thing they were very much in need
of!

10th February 1900

*On 10 February, while Tucker was preparing
to bed down under the stars, White was
anxiously scanning the horizon for signs of
battle, or, more optimistically, signs of
relief, for Buller had signalled to him that he
would make another bid that day. In the
event, it took five more days for Buller to
assemble his force, march it five miles and
settle on one of his myriad schemes.*

We struck camp, and marched seven miles towards Chieveley.
That night we bivouacked on the open veldt again for a few hours
sleep and early next morning we finished our march to Chieveley.
('A' Company on outpost.)

12th February 1900

We ate bread again for the first time since 14 January, and we did it full justice too, for it was a grand change from the hard biscuits.

The next day was spent in camp at Chieveley, the mail arrived and I was very pleased to receive some letters and papers from England.

14th February 1900

We struck camp and marched off for Hussar Hill and then the music started again, the Boers gave us plenty of rifle fire and we

Buller's plan was to take Cingolo and the Monte Christo ridge and so command the lower Hlangwane plateau, turn the Green Hill entrenchments and force the Boers to evacuate their position on Hlangwane Hill. From the summit of the hill he could then use his artillery to dominate the Colenso kopjes to the west, the hills in front of Pieter's Hill and the low ridges between the Tugela and the Klip. (The plan was not unlike one Dundonald had put forward before Colenso. Then, Buller had dismissed it out of hand.)

New Conciliatory Drill-Book for the British Army (Recommended and approved by the 'Stop-the-War' 'Peace-at-any-Price' Party.)
Pacifism did not suit the manly attitudes of the Victorian age and the anti-war campaigners were greeted with hoots of derision when they held their public meetings. (B)

Some 5,000 Boers had left for the Orange Free State to lend their weight to Cronje, who was opposing Roberts, leaving a force of between 15 to 20,000 commandos in the neighbourhood of Colenso and around Ladysmith. The 'Red Bull', as Buller had become known among the Boers, had 24,000 men and a fearsome array of artillery, which he positioned on and around Hussar Hill. The artillery bombarded Green Hill and Cingolo while the infantry, in open formation and covered by the unremitting shell fire, advanced.

A crowd clusters outside the offices of The Times of Natal *in Pietermaritzburg, waiting for the latest news which was posted outside. (D)*

While Tucker and his comrades were repeatedly hitting their heads against the Boer defences around Ladysmith, relief was at hand for another besieged town. Kimberley, the centre of Cecil Rhodes' diamond mining industry, had been under siege for four months. The townspeople were in danger of dying from malnutrition, or, more immediately, of being killed by a shrapnel burst from the Boer Long Tom; horse and mule flesh was practically their sole diet, although kittens were fetching black market prices of 5s 6d.

General Lord Methuen had tried and failed, it was now the turn of Lord Roberts. On the morning of 10 February, he set out with a combined force of 25,000 infantry and cavalry to cross the two rivers and 150 miles that lay between the Modder River Camp and Kimberley.

The cavalry, commanded by General French, succeeded in pushing back the Boers at every point and at each deserted laager they found supplies of food and abandoned ammunition.

Save for a daring raid, led by Christian de Wet, during which the Boers managed to capture or destroy almost 200 supply wagons, the Boer defences crumbled and French was able to march on to Kimberley and to the miraculously lavish welcoming dinner Rhodes had produced from a husbanded hoard of delicacies.

Portuguese Customs Officer. 'Anything to declare? Nothing contraband, *I hope?' Boer. 'Oh dear me. No!!'*

Ammunition arrived packed in innocent looking cases marked 'agricultural implements'. (B)

threw it right back at them. About 4.00 p.m. the howitzer battery, which we were escorting for the day, opened fire near us, and the Boers, who were firing at the battery, made it very uncomfortable for us. We were compelled to take more cover. The shelling continued nearly all night as it was a very moonlit night, and we were bivouacked near the guns so did not get much sleep.

Water was very scarce, we had to go about one and a half miles to the river bed, dig a hole in the sand and then wait for the water to spring through before we could get a drink. Even then it wasn't very good water, but it was much better than none at all.

We opened fire at eight next morning, the Boers only returned a few shells so at nine we moved forward, leaving Hussar Hill. We crept forward to another hill, named Inkwane, and occupied it at about 3.00 p.m. It was a fearfully hot day and we had little or no water with us but we took full advantage of a running stream which was close by.

"THE OPEN DOOR."

Every soldier at the front was sent a blue, red and gold tin box, containing chocolate from Queen Victoria, Three chocolate manufacturers, Frys, Cadburys and Rowntrees, supplied the 120,000 packets of chocolate. The Queen was anxious that only soldiers should receive her gift and so the number of tins was strictly limited and any extra ones were destroyed at her request. (A)

We started out again the following morning with an artillery force to make a reconnaissance, then returned and took up our positions on Inkwane again. At 8.00 p.m. we received the Queen's gift of chocolate which we had been anxiously waiting for. Such a cheer went up that the Boers must have thought we had taken leave of our senses and gone mad. That night I had a supper of chocolate, biscuits and water. After my meal I slept soundly with the chocolate box forming part of my pillow.

A primitive painting of the Heilbron commando's laager near Ladysmith. Drawn by W. du Toit, Junior for G. van Moerkerken G.O. (A)

Unharnessed artillery wagons wait behind Boer lines while the guns open fire. (A)

The tin chocolate boxes quickly became treasured objects and many were sent straight back to Britain again for safe keeping with their contents intact. It cost fourpence to register the box and a penny an ounce to send it home. Tucker saved himself about three days' pay by eating the chocolate first—a full box, with adequate wrapping, cost over five shillings to send.

An innocent looking biscuit box, filled with cartridges and smuggled into the Boer camp. (M)

At daybreak we were ready to make our attack, the artillery commenced firing at 5.30 a.m. and we advanced in attack formation. The Boers opened fire on us with all kinds of guns but didn't do much damage as we took advantage of all the cover we could possibly find until we got within their rifle range. Then we got it pretty hot, but, fortunately, their shooting was so bad that we did not lose many men and succeeded in staking a very good position. As it was almost dark by then, we bivouacked for the night. I finished my chocolate and felt satisfied with my day's work. The empty tin now became an object of interest, so I carefully wrapped it up and placed it in my haversack. I carried it during all the fighting my regiment was involved in until I had a chance to send it to England. I fear the box got a few knocks but it still remains the Queen's gift and much cherished.

18th February 1900

We advanced again at 5.30 a.m.

As soon as we moved off, the Boer guns started shelling but had little effect. It was their Mauser fire which did the most damage to our men today—several were hit. My regiment was in the firing line and advanced splendidly; some very spirited fighting took place. We had plenty of cover for skirmishing so we drove into their advance posts, getting quite close to their main position, or laager. The Boers fought so well that we had to fight hard for every inch of ground and when, at last, after several hours of sharp fighting, we drove them off their splendid position, we captured their camp, horses, stores and a quantity of ammunition. This was the Middelburg Commando and supposed to be *the* crack Commando of the Boer Army! However, to give honour where honour is due they fought terrifically well and gave us a hard day of it.

We began plundering immediately. Every man had a rug or blanket, all colours of the rainbow, clothes and boots; horses' saddles could be bought for a shilling or a packet of cigarettes.

Biltong being sliced with a carpenter's plane by a Boer cook. British soldiers pronounced the dried meat hard enough to be used for tent pegs. (D)

For the first time in the Tugela campaign, Buller pitched the whole of his force on to the Boer positions and, after so many deflating retreats, he had the satisfaction of watching the Boers flee across the Tugela.

Underclothing was needed most urgently and soon we were changing; worn-out khaki trousers were discarded, knee breeches or plaid trousers taking their place. General Lyttelton rode up and was greatly amused by us. General Buller also rode up and was loudly cheered. He was very pleased and said, 'The Rifle Brigade should not cheer me, it is me that should cheer you.' He mentioned us in his despatches, praising our 'stern fighting qualities and splendid dash'. Our casualties were: four killed, three officers and thirty men wounded. However, it was a very satisfactory day, for amongst the stores I found bread, brawn, tea, coffee, sugar and a bottle of brandy, along with plenty of cooking pots and kettles, all ready for use. At the first opportunity we were busy lighting a fire and we had something hot for supper. The several Boers we had captured were very thankful for the food we gave them even though it was taken from their own stores! However, they too had been fighting all day and I suppose they had had very little chance of getting anything to eat for they had been waiting for us to surrender, and

Deneys Reitz, a young burgher, described the retreat in his book, Commando*: 'At intervals the curtain lifted. . . To approach our men through that inferno was to court destruction, while not to try seemed like desertion. For a minute or two we debated and then, suddenly, the gunfire ceased, and for a space we caught the fierce rattle of Mauser rifles followed by British infantry swarming over the skyline, their bayonets flashing in the sun. Shouts and cries reached us, and we could see men desperately thrusting and clubbing. Then a rout of burghers broke back from the hill, streaming towards us in disorderly flight. The soldiers fired into them, bringing many down as they made blindly past us, not looking to right or left. We went too, for the troops, cheering loudly, came shooting and running down the slope. . . . The British had blasted a gap through which the victorious soldiery came pouring, and wherever we looked Boer horsemen, wagons and guns, went streaming to the rear in headlong retreat.'*

The Boers had bolted leaving behind a shambles of long-accumulated supplies and articles of dress, including some womens' clothing. All the wounded, including several young boys, were taken prisoner. Both British and Boer wounded were sent in trainloads to hospital ships, where they remained until well enough to return to their ranks or to be sent home. In the case of Boers, prisoners of war were sent to British colonies: Bermuda, Ceylon, St. Helena.

Informatie-Bureau van het Roode Kruis, Pretoria.

(IDENTITY DEPARTMENT OF THE TRANSVAAL BRANCH OF THE GENÈVE RED CROSS SOCIETY, PRETORIA)

BEWIJS VAN IDENTITEIT.

Proof of Identity. No 8845

In geval van dood of verwonding van houder dezes wordt men dringend verzocht deze kaart ingevuld op te zenden aan bovenstaand adres.

In case of bearer of this being killed or wounded, you are requested to send this card through the nearest Commanding Officer, or Responsible Official, to the Identity Department above mentioned.

Naam / Name }

Ouderdom / Age }

Woonplaats / adres familie Residence }

Commando }

Gesneuveld / Killed { Plaats / Locality Datum / Date }

Welke Verwonding / Nature of Wound }

Gewond / Wounded { Plaats / Locality Datum / Date }

The Identity Department of the Red Cross Society will forward to English authorities information about wounded English soldiers who might be made prisoners.

Telegraphic and Postal Address: Molengraaff, Pretoria.

A Boer identification card. These were issued by the Red Cross Society at Pretoria. (F)

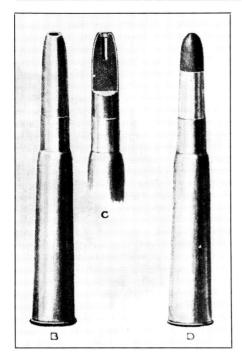

Explosive bullets had been formally forbidden during the war. They were fitted with a soft tip which expanded, or 'mushroomed', inside the body and left a gaping wound on exit. In peacetime, the Boers had used them to shoot big game, but shrapnel which carried dirt and stones into the wound could be just as deadly. The soft-nosed expanding bullet on the right is from a Boer camp and the 'dum-dum' on the left is a British issue. (C)

A Boer commandant. Each Boer provided his own horse and rifle. They were issued with no uniforms nor rewarded with any medals or decorations. (A)

The abrasive bombardment was vividly described in the Manchester Guardian *by J. B. Atkins: 'From Monte Christo a buttress or spur runs out; it is a hill of smooth sides (when you see them from a distance) and rich green grass. Green Hill it was named once. Red dashes, when trenches had been cut into the red earth, were the lineaments of its smooth face. Under one's gaze the unwrinkled face grew disfigured and pock-marked with the bursting shells. Soon one end was alight, and the grass fire steadily ate its way forward under a constant breeze. But all this day never a Boer stirred on Green Hill that I could see.'*

had not expected us to come the way we did; he also said that they did not think we fought on Sundays! I inspected their trenches and they were marvellous. In some places rocks had been blasted and they were perfectly shell proof, about six feet deep and strewn with ammunition. The bullets had been dipped in verdigrease and were green with poison. There were also a lot of soft-nosed and split bullets, made by Ely of London, in evidence. The boxes these cartridges were packed in were marked for sporting purposes. It occurs to me that that Ely firm must have thought the Boer Government went in for a lot of sport when they sent these deadly explosive bullets to this country. When a man is hit by one these bullets he is either killed or ruined for life, perhaps with the loss of a leg or an arm. I would rather be hit by six Mauser bullets than one of these explosive soft-nosed or flat top sort.

The name of the hill we have just taken is Cingolo. We passed through Monte Christo valley before we settled down for the night. The Boers sent us a few shells; one fell amongst a section of the company and the force of it knocked about a dozen men over to the ground. We were enormously surprised when we saw them all get to their feet again, quite unhurt. The shell had not exploded, but merely buried itself in the soft ground. After this affair we bivouacked for the night. The next morning our big guns were brought forward and opened a heavy fire, our brigade advanced but we didn't get very far because the Boers were returning our fire with their Maxim, Mauser and pom-poms. The Scottish Rifles and the King's Royal Rifles were in the firing line, with our regiment and the Durhams in support. Meanwhile,

another brigade had taken Hlangwane, a hill on the left of us. I suspect they had been unopposed, but nevertheless it was a good commanding position facing Colenso.

Our brigade retired after a wet miserable day to Cingolo. The Scottish continued bringing their wounded comrades in on stretchers. We hadn't pushed the Boers back a single inch all day which was very disappointing and we all vowed we would shift them on the morrow, as it was our turn for the firing line again.

I'm not sure if it is that our fellows have more dash when they go in, or whether they have more luck but I've always noticed that the 1st Rifle Brigade have never failed to take a position and once taken, we have never lost it again.

The last rush. Sensing their victory, the British infantry swept on, bayoneting the few Boers left defending Hlangwane Hill. (K)

That night, while Tucker was resting after the triumphs of the day, the Boers were saddling up and trekking away from Hlangwane Hill. Botha tried to rally them but the situation seemed hopeless and he telegraphed to Kruger that all was lost. Kruger, in a typical burst of religious fanaticism, replied: 'It seems to me as if your faith and that of your burghers has been replaced by unbelief. The moment that you cease to hold firm and fight in the name of the Lord, then you have unbelief in you; and the moment unbelief is present cowardice follows, and the moment that you turn your backs on the enemy then there remains no place for us to seek refuge, for in that case we should have ceased to trust the Lord. No, no, my brethren; let it not be so; let it not be so.' And he urged Botha to 'read this out to all officers and burghers, and my faith and prayer lie in my firm confidence that the Lord shall strengthen His people in their faith. Even if they have no earthly rock behind which to seek cover, they shall win on the open plain.'

Cartoon from *Le Matin*.]
[Paris.
WHY THE BOERS DO NOT REPLY WHEN BOMBARDED!

'Why the Boers do not reply when bombarded!' A cartoon from the French magazine, Le Matin. *(R)*

General Lyttelton had succeeded to the command of the 2nd Division after General Sir Francis Clery had been disabled by a fall from his horse.

In England the news of Buller's successes had caused much excitement; some reports even went so far as to state that Ladysmith had already been relieved, but White knew better.

By 20 February there were no Boers on the south side of the Tugela and Buller, characteristically, now decided to alter his line of advance. Instead of continuing around the Boer left, where they were weakest, he resolved to move by Colenso—the Boer centre.

A view of the scene from behind the Boer lines by a French war artist. In the face of fierce shell fire, the Boers kept up a gallant defence, however, they were losing their hold on the battle. (A)

About this time, some changes in commands had taken place; General Clery was on the sick list so General Lyttelton took command of the 2nd Division and our own Colonel Norcott was in command of the 4th Brigade. The command of the 1st Rifle Brigade was taken over by Lieutenant-Colonel Colville after his promotion from 4th Battalion as Colonel Norcott's term of command had expired.

20th February 1900

We paraded at 5.00 a.m. The Rifle Brigade formed the firing line and we were soon in action, pushing the Boers back gradually. We reached a farmhouse and made a big capture of ammunition, mostly soft-nosed .303s all made by the firm Ely. The Boers had loaded all the ammunition on a wagon in readiness for their retirement, but we were too quick for them. Having got the Boers moving we pressed them hard in spite of the heavy fire they were pouring into our ranks. We did not give them time to dig rifle pits but drove them back until they finally took up a safe position on the other side of the Tugela, not far from Retusa Hill. From this vantage point they fired at us for the remainder of the day with impunity—we could not cross as they had taken up the bridge behind them.

The Durhams were close by us and together we kept up sniping until it was too dark to see anything. Then we made ourselves as comfortable as possible under the circumstances, by making fires to warm us, and having some coffee before bivouacking for the night. However, we were not at all comfortable. The Boers would keep on sniping and I had a narrow escape. I was sitting by the fire, my rifle leaning against a bush in front of me, when a bullet skimmed close by my ear and struck the back sight of my rifle rendering it useless until it had passed through the hands of the armourers. After this, we thought it was safer to keep down, which we did and we slept soundly.

Early next morning our artillery and naval 4.7 guns were pounding away as usual and we kept up a heavy fire across the river all day. We had to risk our lives to get water from the river and several of our men were wounded getting it.

We were covering the right flank of our other brigade who were advancing by Colenso. By dint of our good work and that of the 4th Brigade in taking Cingolo, we had turned the enemy's left flank, causing them to evacuate the impregnable Colenso. It was a fine piece of work and the only possible way of reaching Ladysmith.

23rd February 1900

At 2.00 a.m. we paraded and marched in the darkness for about two miles to our left, crossing a pontoon bridge which had been laid while we kept the Boers amused higher up the river. After crossing, the music commenced again in real earnest, daylight was just breaking and the shot and shell began to fall around us pretty thick. Soon the stretchers were busy with candidates for the doctors' skill in bandaging.

We were escort to the howitzer battery which the Boers couldn't reach with their guns, so, instead, my regiment came in for a good deal of their attention—something we could have done well without! The Irish Brigade and our Rifle Reserve Battalion were in the firing line and were losing men fast. I saw many an old comrade of mine (late of the 1st Battalion) carried past me on the stretchers, but we pressed forward, despite the heavy casualties all around. We heard that the Irish Brigade had taken Pieter's Hill but had been driven off again with very heavy losses. This

Gradually, as they had not been pursued and Buller's progress was so slow, the burghers were persuaded to make a stand. Indeed, Botha was able to send Kruger the following favourable report:

21 February

Thanks to our Father the burghers already showed today that they had taken heart again, when they had such splendid shooting at the enemy with their Mausers at 300 yards range. As soon as the moon rises I will go along our whole position in order, if necessary, to encourage officers and burghers still further. . . With the help of the Lord, I expect that if only the spirit of the burghers keeps up as it did today the enemy will suffer a great reverse.

A compact line of Boers in their trenches, repulsing an English advance. (P)

As the British troops crossed the Tugela by pontoon bridge, the Boers delivered a counter-attack from the north bank. Among the wounded was General Wynne, the successor of General Woodgate, who had been shot through the eye at Spion Kop. Wynne's command was given to Lord Kitchener's younger brother, Frederick, of the West Yorkshire Regiment.

In the morning General Hart, commanding the Irish Brigade, launched an attack on Railway and Pieter's Hills. At one point, his men had to run in single file across a narrow, iron railway bridge, in full view of a storm of Boer fire. As the wounded men dropped from the bridge, the British artillery rained shells upon the hills, throwing up clouds of yellow dust. Although the Irish managed to get within a few hundred yards of the Boer positions, they were constantly held off by the steady Boer rifle fire and night found them building rough shelters on the lower slopes, determined to renew the attack in the morning.

For two days the Boers, outnumbered by five to one, kept up a brave rearguard action and caused many casualties among the British, who, having crossed the Tugela, now found themselves unable to advance.
    Wounded men were strewn between the two opposing lines and, once more, J. B. Atkins takes up the narrative: 'In the morning the wounded lay in the heat, and in the afternoon—which was perhaps better— in the rain. It was real South African rain, threshing off the whole top skin of the country: and when it had lasted half an hour the land was changed as a negative is developed under the chemicals; unsuspected roads gleamed on the brown hills where nothing had been before, the tracks and fibres were discovered and displayed as clearly as in ice which has begun to thaw. Wounded men, dripping bundles, were being carried to hospitals at the rear; the bearers themselves were small cascades of water.'

'LEAST SAID SOONEST MENDED.'
Master Campbell-Bannerman. 'Please, Sir, I know who did it.'
Dr. Bull (severely). 'Never mind who did it. Get to work and wipe it off between you.'
    Campbell-Bannerman, the fervently anti-war leader of the Liberal Party, is portrayed by Punch *as a classroom sneak, whose aim is solely to stir up more trouble. Chamberlain is shown lurking guiltily behind John Bull. (B)*

was not very encouraging and we were ordered to reinforce them. To do this, we had to go along the railway line some distance and then along the river bank. It was pitch dark, the enemy who were very close, kept sniping at us all the time as we made our way forward. That night will not be forgotten by us for a long time; what with the continual sniping, falling over rocks, and getting scratched by barbed wire, our night march was anything but pleasant. To make things worse the ammunition mules were along with us and the noise they made alerted the Boers, inviting many of their volleys. One mule fell into the river and everything on its back was lost—mule as well. Then we had to wait because two men went astray with all the ammunition mules and it was impossible to locate them that night because of the darkness. The Sergeant-Major who was in charge of them became very anxious, fearing they had been captured.

    The Boers are very artful: they had placed a whitewashed boat on the bank, lying on its side in the open, where they expected us to pass. We would have shown up clearly as marvellous targets and they would have been able to pot us off leisurely. Fortunately, we noticed it in time and passed by on the other

"LEAST SAID SOONEST MENDED."

side. We even found the Irish Brigade that night, after a lot of searching.

The fight recommenced the next morning but we let the Boers do most of the firing. We kept under cover as much as possible and only had to show a helmet to have a volley poured on it. By not returning the fire we must have made the Boers think they were doing a lot of damage, for at seven o'clock in the evening they decided to drive us from our position. The first we knew of their plan was a heavy fusilade of rifle fire from them, but they didn't get beyond our outposts; a few volleys and then the bayonet quickly made them change their minds about coming to close quarters with us. Instead, they drew off to their trenches and kept up a spiteful rifle fire nearly all night which kept us close to the ground. The ground was like mud after the rain and we were compelled to lie there with our swords fixed, shivering with cold and with bullets flying all around us all that night. Several men were wounded, but I'm surprised that there weren't more, as we had no cover whatsoever.

We were all relieved when daybreak came. At 7.00 a.m. we requested a twelve hour armistice to bury the dead and remove the wounded. We made the best of this short spell from action by cooking, and bathing in the Tugela. I even snatched some sleep.

We took up our positions again at 7.00 p.m., at about 9.30 p.m. we were surprised to hear them singing the 'Old Hundredth'. This reminded us that it was Sunday. The grand old hymn sounded so beautiful and seemed so strange that we could not resist standing up to listen. At the end, or rather just before the Amen had finished, we got what we least expected: a very heavy volley from their trenches which made us dive for cover! Only a minute

Signalling apparatus being positioned.
Searchlights were used during the night to flash messages, via low clouds, to the troops trapped inside Ladysmith. Heliographs operated when conditions were suitable during the day, otherwise there were carrier pigeons. (A)

The respite afforded by the armistice gave Buller time to devise a new plan. He decided to launch a three-pronged attack on Pieter's Hill and, as he shifted his army into position, Botha was prompted to write optimistically to Joubert: 'It is quite possible that the enemy is retiring again. Their wagons and tents, as well as their big guns, have already recrossed the river. Their infantry are still in the trenches, though some of them have already left. It is evident that their losses were heavy. By to-morrow morning we shall know for certain what the enemy's intention really is.'

During the armistice the two sides had come together, exchanging small talk and tobacco. Replying to a Boer, who had asked if the British were having a hard time, General Lyttelton said: 'Yes, I suppose so. But for us, of course, it is nothing. We are used to it and we are paid for it. This is the life we always lead.'
'Great God!' the man replied.

before we had been giving them credit for their religious ways and were even praising their singing and this was the way they returned our kindness for letting them have their service in peace! They kept up the sniping for a few hours but as we wouldn't waste a shot on them they got tired at this fun and only fired when they heard someone move; but they did not hit anyone.

A French war artist's romantic illustration of the Boer commandos singing hymns during the night. (P)

A commemorative handkerchief bearing a portrait of Sir Redvers Buller surrounded by loyal colonial regiments. (A)

26th February 1900

Monday was spent in sniping between the two outposts. Our troops were brought forward for the final advance at about seven in the evening. I went on outpost with my company and spent a lively night, building a wall—when safe to do so. Every time the

Buller's casualties arriving in Cape Town. If their wounds were not too serious, the men remained in hospital at Cape Town until they were fit enough to return to their regiments, but many were invalided home. (K)

Boers could see or hear us they gave us a volley and, naturally, we fell flat on the ground at once.

The weather was blistering hot all day and very cold, and often wet at night.

27th February 1900

Majuba Day.
We were told of Cronje's capture and such a cheer went up from everyone that the Boers must have thought us quite mad.

At about 10.00 a.m. we were relieved of outpost duty by the Connaught Rangers and were told that the 1st Rifle Brigade and the East Surrey Regiment had been selected from among all the troops on Fusila Hill for taking the Listire Kopje, or, as it is better known, Pieter's Hill. The honour was even greater, as the Irish Brigade, composed of such renowned regiments as the Dublins, Connaughts, Inniskillings and Borderers, had tried to take it on the 23 February. They had charged it three times and each time had been driven back with heavy losses. We all felt very proud, every man made up his mind to take the hill or die in the attempt and were were eager for the word to advance.

It didn't come until 12.00, when we formed up for the attack and lay low, allowing the big guns to do their work. A heavy artillery duel commenced and presently shell after shell fell amongst as as we lay, snatching a few mouthfuls of bully beef and biscuit. 'Never miss the opportunity of a snack,' is an old maxim of ours, and one which everyone on a campaign would do well to remember, for when going into action one never knows when one will get the chance of another meal.

The artillery continued their noisy duel until 3.00 p.m. while we endured the worst trial a fighting soldier can be subjected to, that is: waiting under fire without being able to return a shot. Anyone who has not experienced this sensation would hardly credit how trying it is to one's temper. Sometimes, we have had to wait like this for hours, never knowing when you may get one for

The confidence felt by the senior officers that Buller had, at last, hit upon a rational plan of attack, transmitted itself to the whole force. This, coupled with the news of Cronje's surrender, had the whole army literally straining at the leash.

General Cronje and Lord Roberts breakfasting after Paardeburg. (A)

On the very brink of battle we must leave Tucker for a moment and travel to the Orange Free State, where newsmen and photographers were poised to record a historic meeting.

On 27 February, General Cronje and his force of 4,000 burghers, surrendered to Lord Roberts. For ten days, since the fierce and bitter battle of Paardeberg, they had been under siege, surrounded by a force six times as strong as their own.

Inside the camp, they had been constantly bombarded; a sickening stench of rotting corpses, both animal and man, had pervaded the air; and the only available water had been polluted by the decaying carcasses which floated in it. Many of the Boers had their families with them and they had urged their unwilling general to concede defeat.

Cameras clicked as Cronje, wearing a slouch hat, an old green overcoat and frieze trousers, was escorted into the British lines. Roberts, snappily dressed, strode forward and shook his hand. 'I am glad to see you,' he said. 'You have made a gallant defence, sir.' Together the two commanders, both well respected among their men, breakfasted under the trees. While they completed the details of the surrender, 4,000 oddly assorted burghers silently handed in their arms. They were sent to a prisoner of war camp on St. Helena, together with Cronje and, with special permission from Roberts, Mrs Cronje.

It was a sad day for the Boers. Cronje was one of their best generals. Strict, but nevertheless popular, he had studied modern warfare and repeatedly proved his bravery by taking the most exposed positions in battle.

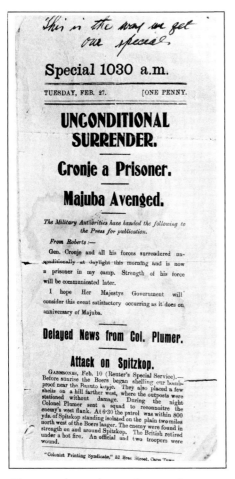

This is the way we get our special.

Special 1030 a.m.

TUESDAY, FEB. 27.   [ONE PENNY.

UNCONDITIONAL SURRENDER.
Cronje a Prisoner.
Majuba Avenged.

The Military Authorities have handed the following to the Press for publication.

From Roberts :—

Gen. Cronje and all his forces surrendered unconditionally at daylight this morning and is now a prisoner in my camp. Strength of his force will be communicated later.

I hope Her Majestys Government will consider this event satisfactory occurring as it does on anniversary of Majuba.

Delayed News from Col. Plumer.

Attack on Spitzkop.

GABBROONS, Feb. 10 (Reuter's Special Service).—Before sunrise the Boers began shelling our bombproof near the Basuto kopje. They also placed a few shells on a hill farther west, where the outposts were stationed without damage. During the night Colonel Plumer sent a squad to reconnoitre the enemy's west flank. At 6·30 the patrol was within 800 yds. of Spitskop standing isolated on the plain two miles north west of the Boers laager. The enemy were found in strength on and around Spitzkop. The British retired under a hot fire. An official and two troopers were wound.

"Colonist Printing Syndicate," 52 Bree Street, Cape Town.

This special newssheet, informing the men in Natal of Cronje's surrender at Paardeburg, fired them with even more enthusiasm. (A)

While Tucker was waiting in the wings, snatching a meal, so Deneys Reitz, on the Boer side, was snatching cover. 'At sunrise next morning,' he wrote, 'the English started in real earnest to bombard the spruit. All day long they shelled us with light and heavy guns, while we hugged the sheltering bank. Shrapnel and lyddite crashed upon us, causing a great many casualties and we suffered a terrible ordeal.'

The Battle of Pieter's Hill   *Map by Mr A. Spark*

the 'nob'. Fighting shot for shot is much more sportsmanlike, I prefer it to waiting and I think everyone else does.

About 3.00 p.m. we moved up to our advanced post near the railway, and there, once more, we came in for a heavy fire. We lined up around a low kopje, opposite Pieter's Hill, and opened fire on the Boer trenches in conjunction with our Marines. What with the Maxims, the big guns, pom-poms, rifle fire and the bursting of shells, the noise was deafening. We caught sight of the East Surreys just up a hill, on our flank; we all gave a good, hearty cheer and a yell of 'Remember Majuba!' and we started off on the race for the top of the hill. Hardly had we left the cover of the kopje before our men began to fall fast. The air seemed to fairly crackle with Mauser rifle bullets and how any of us survived all the bullets, pom-poms and pieces of shell with which we were greeted as we ran the gauntlet to Pieter's Hill, is a marvel to me. It was simply terrific. Men were falling everywhere but we had no time to see to them, they were left behind for the stretcher bearers. We kept rushing forward, stopping every now and then, to fire as we saw a chance. We quickly reached the side of Pieter's Hill, where we lay down and pelted them in such a heavy manner that some Boers, who were able, thought it best to move. As they retired we rushed with the bayonet. We let the Boers know that we were revenging Majuba. White flags meant nothing to us and no notice was taken of them. We got a little of our own back. I shall never forget the way our men took the position. The Colonel of the East Surreys shouted to his men, 'Come on men or these Rifle monkeys will go right through you.' And he had good cause to hurry his men along for we certainly did not intend to be last. When we reached the trenches, Riflemen and East Surreys were all mixed up, so neither regiment could claim the honour of being the first in the trenches. My company had, however, led the attack and really were the first up Pieter's Hill.

It was at this point in the attack that most men were lost, but

Tucker's (Norcott's) brigade was on the left of the infantry advance with Kitchener's brigade in the centre and Barton's on the right. All three sides pressed forward with a common determination. Then, with dramatic suddenness, the British artillery fell silent. The infantry had neared the crest of the hill and had come into their own firing line. Shouts of 'Remember Majuba!' rippled over the men as they fixed bayonets.

Although it was obvious that they were losing their grasp of the battle, the Boers gamely established a false left on a height north of Monte Christo, but it failed to deceive the British and the attack swept on.

The infantry positions, prior to the Battle of Pieter's Hill, can be seen marked out on this photograph. The Boer trenches and breastworks are in the distance. (A)

*A double stone sangar on top of Hart's Hill.
A helmet and a bare head can just be
glimpsed above the rough mound of stones.
(L)*

*At about 5.00 p.m., after three bayonet
charges, men could be seen on the summit of
the hill and airborne helmets announced the
victory! Majuba had been remembered!*

*The Boers fell back to a third kopje on
Pieter's Hill and there, reinforced by men
who had come down from their positions
around Ladysmith, they held the British off
until nightfall.*

*Taking advantage of a more immediate form
of stone defence, a Maxim gun in action,
protected by the wall of a Kaffir enclosure.
(S)*

the dash of the Rifle Brigade could not be stopped, no one even
faltered, though he might see his best chum drop. No time for
anything but revenge for Majuba. And no one can deny that we
took it fully and amply. Their trenches were full of dead, some
with the ghastly wounds which show the horrible work of lyddite
shells, others with the neat, hardly discernible, .303 bullet hole.

The firing continued until dark and then only an occasional
sniper disturbed us. We could not follow the Boers owing to the
darkness, and, as they had the advantage of being mounted and
knew the country very well, they easily got away.

Our much belated cavalry were safe on the other side of the
river, out of harm's way, instead of backing us up during the

After such a dramatic and exhilarating day for the British, one pompous patriot, who had witnessed the battle, was moved to write: 'All the money, all the lives, all the misery caused by the war, are well repaid by this glorious battle. In Great Britain the new century has been baptised in the blood of her soldiers and has opened in the flame of battle, but from the holocaust the courage of the British infantry comes pure and unsullied—a sure presage that the safety of the greatest country in the world is secure forever in the arms of her soldiers.'

The tiny commando force had been finally pushed back from the summit of Pieter's Hill but Buller, instead of despatching his cavalry in pursuit, halted his men. He was then totally unaware of his complete success and cautiously anticipated a further attack. But the Boers had had enough. Joubert, much against Kruger's wishes, had given the order for a general retreat and quickly skipped off to Elandslaagte himself. His flight only caused more panic among the Boers and they hurried away, a disorderly, ragged mob.

Boer women occasionally joined their husbands at the front line—many of them had been trained with their brothers to shoot and were excellent shots—but after Joubert's death, Botha, who succeeded him as Commandant-General, forbade women to visit the Boer laagers. (F)

night and early next morning. They should have been giving chase to the retreating Boers. The victory we had gained would then have been an utter rout to the Boers instead of simply the good retreat it was. Mules of luggage which the Boers had accumulated near Ladysmith, their Long Toms which they had had to take down from their positions on Umbulwana, and all their stores with oxen transport which can only travel two miles an hour; all this was allowed to slip away unmolested while 4,000 cavalry who boast they are the finest in the world were swinging their heels out of rifle range on the other side of the Tugela.

We bivouacked for the night on the hill which we had taken and next morning woke up to perform the sorrowful part of warfare—the burying of the dead, searching for stray wounded and enquiring after absent faces. All this, combined with the sight of the dead in the trenches, makes me truly realize the horrors of war. Two women were found in one trench, they had been fighting alongside their husbands. One was dead, struck by a shell, and the other had a nasty wound. She said her husband had made her stop to fight as she was a good shot. This heartless brute had left her wounded to look after herself while he rode away to save his own skin!

To be fair to the cavalry—much maligned by Tucker—they had strict orders not to pursue. Remembering, from his previous South African experience, the Boers' deadly rear-guard action, Buller preferred to rest his men, allowing a tidy haul in prisoners and supplies to escape before pushing on with the pressing business of feeding the starving town.

For the cavalry this was to be their last major war. Mounted infantry were coming into prominence and, during the whole war, the British Army Remount Department provided approximately 520,000 horses and 150,000 mules, of which 350,000 horses and 50,000 mules were killed or died. The horses came chiefly from Britain (including London bus horses), America, Hungary, Canada, Australia and South Africa itself. The mules were recruited as far afield as Spain and Italy, as well as America and South Africa.

When the news of Cronje's surrender reached London, the public went wild. Stockbrokers tossed their hats into the air, gave ten rousing cheers and sang God Save the Queen. (D)

Under cover of night, and unhurried the following morning, the Boers evacuated their positions, retired their guns and wagons, and fell back with all possible haste to the Biggarsberg.

The only communication the besieged town had received from Buller during a day filled with frenzied battle sounds had been, simply, 'Doing well'. They hardly dared hope.

The British searching for wounded and burying their dead by the light of paraffin lamps. (P)

The work of burying the dead was completed, we buried the Boers in their own trenches—what better graves could they have had than the place in which they fought? Our own poor fellows, seven of them, were laid at the foot of the hill and their grave was dug just under a small tree which grew nearby. We all took a last look at the faces we knew so well. As we stood looking at our dead, General Lyttelton and his Aide rode up, and, catching sight of our row of dead, he saluted and took off his helmet. He

spoke to our Sergeant-Major, whom he knew well, about the fighting of the previous day. He had been on the right at some distance from us: 'So it was the old regiment I saw, I thought I recognized them but wasn't sure, it was a beautiful sight and done me good to see it, glorious, grand!' he exclaimed as he saluted our dead again and rode away, with, I firmly believe, a tear in his eye. Such praise from our old general was quite unexpected. After we had laid the dead in their grave and covered them in, we made a fence of stone around it, and one handy fellow made a cross from a piece of box and placed it on the grave with the names of the dead written upon it. Perhaps, some day the Government of Natal will erect a memorial stone to show passers-by who these brave men were and how they met their death in relieving their comrades in Ladysmith, but I am afraid they will be forgotten by all but their relatives.

The victory had taken six hours to accomplish and had cost 500 casualties. Buller had been attacking the Boers for thirteen continuous days and, although fiercely patriotic, the commandos were undisciplined, so it was only a matter of time before their resistance crumbled. The relief of Ladysmith had cost, altogether, one sixth of Buller's army: 5,000 men killed, wounded or missing.

Feb. 24th 1900.

Cronjé surrendered at day break this morning with 6000 men. There is also a rumour that Ladysmith is relieved.

A patriotic postcard commenting on Cronje's surrender and anticipating Ladysmith's relief. (N)

On 28 February, still unaware of the total success, White signalled reproachfully: 'I am now issuing only half-pound of breadstuffs daily; it is a very inferior meal.'

Buller replied at once: 'I have seventy-four wagons of supplies for you, the arrival of which I can promise very shortly.' And he followed up this mouth-watering promise with news of the battle: 'I beat the enemy thoroughly yesterday, and am sending my cavalry as fast as my bad road will admit of, to ascertain where they have gone to. I believe the enemy to be in full retreat.'

We had buried our dead so we made ready for the advance which we expected to make, but after waiting for some hours we found to our disappointment that this was not to be. We were reinforced by a strange regiment we had not seen before. In fact, we did not even know that they belonged to the Natal Field Force. I suppose that, while we had been busy fighting every day and having a rough time, they had been living in comfort at the Base or Line of Communication, on soft bread and fresh meat. Even the cavalry came across the Tugela and condescended to approve of the way we had twisted the Boers out from Pieter's Hill, but our men didn't want their approval and some of our fellows gave them to understand as much. 'There was plenty of work for you fellows.' I heard one of our men remark to one of the colonial mounted men. 'Yes,' he replied, 'but our horses wanted rest.' I don't know how they got done up for we had not seen them do anything to warrant tiring them. After the guns had crossed the river, the cavalry rode forward to find out if the enemy had gone. They had scarcely gone any distance before they came scampering back as if the devil had them. A few Boers from their rear guard had fired on them and sent them all back to us for protection. However, after being reinforced, they went out

Badges, most commonly depicting war heroes and leading generals, were popular among the men. This one shows Kruger: battered and piratical. (A)

As February gave way to March, so the Boers likewise gave way to the British force, who found themselves no longer on the defensive in their own country, but pursuing a vigorous offensive in the country of the Boers.

again and this time they found nothing. That night, they galloped into Ladysmith, and must have snatched all the honours from the papers at home, while we remained on Pieter's Hill for another night, in the rain, enjoying the horrid stench of dead horses.

1st March 1900

Marched off along the road to Nelthorpe. Nothing of note took place during the march. We bivouacked near Bulwana, near where the Boer's laager had been and we captured the flour and lard they had left behind. We soon had a good dinner cooking, for we made dumplings with the flour and lard and boiled them

In London, vast, traffic-stopping, crowds assembled from Mansion House to Pall Mall to cheer and wave banners. In Cambridge, the undergraduates built an enormous bonfire in the market square, burning everything and anything they could lay hands on in a costly celebration of Ladysmith's relief.

On the road to Ladysmith at last! The relieving force marching the last four miles into town. They had with them much needed supplies and medical equipment. (D)

with our bully beef and preserved vegetables. Me and the other three I mucked in with made a very good stew although the dumplings were a bit weighty. We were very grateful to the Boers for leaving their flour behind.

During the night the rain poured down again and we woke up saturated. We stopped at Bulwana all next day, wondering if we were ever going to get a look at our chums and the much desired town of Ladysmith.

Wading across a spruit. One of the men, recognising the camera, has raised his hat in a gay salute. (E)

The Siege of Ladysmith

On 1 March, 1900, the hills surrounding Ladysmith were unusually empty. The cavalry, headed by Dundonald, who was unaware that the Boers had retreated completely, advanced cautiously across the open plain. Encountering no obstacle they rode on to Ladysmith, arriving at dusk. Many of the towns-people, gaunt and emaciated, broke down and cried as they recognized these unfamiliar soldiers on their well-fed horses as the vanguard of Buller's relief column. 'I thank God we have kept the flag flying,' said Sir George White as he rode forward.

What had the 120 day siege been like for the 21,000 civilians and troops? Encircled by well-fortified hills, which effectively kept the town trapped and the relieving force at bay, they had been bombarded monotonously and regularly. At the end of the siege it was estimated that 16,000 shells had fallen within the town. The Boers religiously ceased fire on Sundays, wet days and mealtimes. Each time Buller tried to break through, the town came in for a more than usually punitive shelling in the hope that the garrison would surrender before help could reach them. Not only did White have to rally his men after the crushing disappointments of Colenso, Spion Kop and Vaal Krantz, he had also to lend his support and iron will to a vacillating Buller whose regular heliographs called helplessly for advice.

Buller wrote to his wife, praising the pluck of his men; 'I am filled with admiration for the British soldier: really the manner in which these man have worked, fought and endured during this last fortnight has been something more than human. Broiled in the burning sun by day, drenched in rain at night, lying not 300 yards off an enemy who shoots if you show so much as a finger, they got but little sleep, and through it all they were as cheery and willing as could be.'

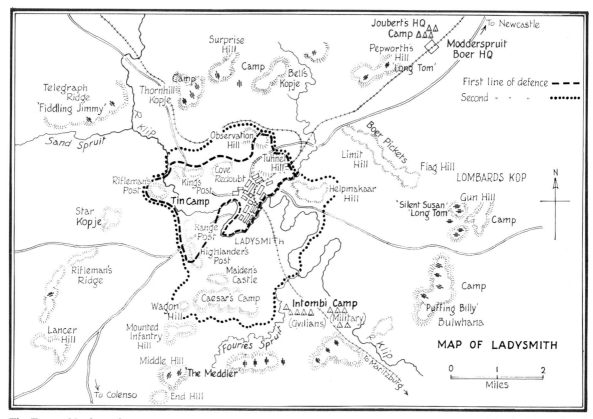

The Town of Ladysmith

Map by Mr A. Spark

The Boers bringing a Long Tom up to their siege positions around Ladysmith. The Boers had four Long Toms; each had a range of 10,000 yards. (A)

Among the many civilians detained in Ladysmith by the siege was G. W. Steevens, special correspondent for the Daily Mail, *who wrote, hopelessly: 'Weary, stale, flat, unprofitable, the whole thing. At first, to be besieged and bombarded was a thrill: then it was a joke; now it is nothing but a weary, weary, weary bore. We do nothing but eat and drink and sleep—just exist dismally. We have forgotten when the siege began; and now we are beginning not to care when it ends.*

'For my part, I feel it will never end.

'It will go on just as now, languid fighting, languid cessation, for ever and ever. We shall drop off one by one, and listlessly die of old age.

'And in the year 2099 the New Zealander antiquarian, digging among the buried cities of Natal, will come upon the forgotten town of Ladysmith. And he will find a handful of Rip Van Winkle Boers with white beards down to their knees, behind quaint, antique guns shelling a cactus-grown ruin. Inside, sheltering in holes, he will find a few decrepit creatures, very, very old, the children born during the bombardment. He will take these links with the past home to New Zealand. But they will be afraid at the silence and security of peace. Having never known anything but bombardment, they will die of terror without it!'

G. W. Steevens died on 15 January of enteric fever before the siege was lifted.

Issuing milk rations for the invalids inside Ladysmith. (D)

The Boers around Ladysmith numbered between 10 and 25,000, depending on where they were most needed. They had an impressive array of field guns, with which the garrison grew so familiar that they named them 'Puffing Billy', 'Silent Susan', 'Fiddling Jimmy', and 'Long Tom'. In his book, *Commando*, Deneys Reitz, a young burgher, described the Boers' stoical patience as they waited for exhaustion and starvation to bring the town to its knees:

'So quiet were things around Ladysmith, that, as time went on, many burghers got ox-wagons brought down from their farms, and some even had their wives and families with them, which tended further to increase the spirit of inactivity that was gaining on the commandos. However, reports from all fronts were good, and we deluded ourselves into believing that everything was as it should be and, so far as my brother and I were concerned, we thoroughly enjoyed the business of besieging Ladysmith, and making regular excursions to see the guns fired into the town.'

Life inside the tortured town was not quite so domestic. The vast stores, which had been husbanded at Ladysmith at the outbreak of the war, were fast dwindling. By the end of January there was no more bread, beef had been replaced by horse meat, and luxuries were available only at exorbitant prices on the black market. The garrison was, however, determined to hold out and the spirit of ingenious enterprise was much in evidence: two mills were set up to convert the mealie stock to flour, several factories produced Chevril paste, soup, oil and sausages from horsemeat. The remaining cavalry horses were fast becoming a burden on the town's resources and they were let loose on the dry veldt to forage for themselves but, distressingly, they kept returning, banded together and whinnying for their accustomed food. The Boers tried to further demoralize the town by polluting the Klip River with the carcasses of dead animals and soon the water supply, which had never been good, gave grave cause for anxiety. The alum supply necessary for filtering the water had been exhausted, as had the coal which ran the improvised condensers—enteric fever and dysentry swiftly followed.

At the start of the siege, Joubert had given permission for a small camp to be set up at Intombi Spruit, just outside the town, for the wounded and for those civilians who chose not to remain inside the town. The camp was made up of portions of two field hospitals and a stationary hospital with a capacity of only 300 beds and with a proportionate staff and supply of drugs. By the end of January, no less than 1,900 sick and wounded, of which 842 were cases of enteric fever and 472 of dysentry, lay crowded within its tents, unable to step over the 'dead-line' which surrounded the camp and lived up to its name. The Boers made frequent visits to the camp and tapped the medical supplies ceaselessly.

The garrison troops erected false fortifications to draw the Boer shells, the townspeople huddled in dug outs along the banks of the Klip and the men who made up the line of defence, fourteen miles around the town, hugged the hills which provided little or no shelter and thriftily returned the Boer fire. There were only two 4.7 guns capable of reaching the Boers' formidable artillery array, and ammunition, like everything else, was scarce.

Two daring night attacks were made by small parties of a few hundred men during the early months of the siege, and they succeeded in dismantling three of the Boer field guns before the Boers reinforced their night pickets and surrounded the guns with wire emplacements.

In addition to the private food supplies, requisitioned by the Army Service Corps, there was 979,000 lb of flour, 173 lb of tinned, meat, 142,000 lb of biscuit, 267,000 lb of sugar, 23,000 lb of tea, 9,500 lb of coffee, 3,965 lb of maize, 1,270,000 lb of oats, 923 lb of bran, and 1,864,000 lb of hay, with spirits, wine and medical comforts in Ladysmith at the beginning of the siege. There were 9,800 mules and horses, 2,500 oxen and some hundreds of sheep, which could all be eaten in an emergency.

The label on a packet of Chevril paste. The hand-printed slogan 'The Iron Horse, None genuine without our signature' implies that several manufacturers had set up in competition with one another. (A)

One of two 4.7 inch guns, known as 'Lady Anne' and 'Bloody Mary', which were capable of reaching the Boer lines but, owing to the scant supply of shells, they were rarely fired. (A)

Heliographic communication—a signalling method which uses the sun's rays, caught on a revolving mirror, to transmit messages in the familiar dot and dash system of the Morse Code—was set up between Buller and White on 7 December and continued until the siege was lifted. In the clear atmosphere of South Africa messages could be flashed up to seventy miles, although bogus ones were so often substituted by Boer signallers that British recipients could never be wholly sure of their validity. White also had a number of pigeons, trained to carry news to Durban and a reconnaissance balloon. (S)

Winston Churchill was in Ladysmith on 3 March and described the scene: 'All through the morning and on into the afternoon the long stream of men and guns flowed through the streets of Ladysmith, and all marvelled to see what manner of men these were— dirty, war-torn, travel-stained, tanned, their uniforms in tatters, their boots falling to pieces, their helmets dented and broken, but nevertheless magnificent soldiers, striding along, deep-chested and broad-shouldered, with the light of triumph in their eyes and the blood of fighting ancestors in their veins. It was a procession of lions.'

On 6 January, the Boers, made uneasy by Buller's movements, attacked Caesar's Camp, one of the town's outposts, hoping to precipitate a surrender. They were finally beaten back with severe casualties on both sides but it was a close shave for the British, who, weakened by continual deprivation and surely unable to withstand a further onslaught, prayed desperately for relief.

By the end of February, when Buller finally broke through the Boer lines and crossed the twelve miles dividing him from the beleaguered town, most of those within had had their hopes baffled, their rations halved and the price of eggs tripled so many times that is was small wonder Tucker and the rest of the force received such a subdued welcome. On entering the town on 3 March. J. B. Atkins was moved to write, 'I have been greeted with as much ardour in the afternoon in London by a man with whom I had lunched two hours before.'

Nevertheless, Britain, and Buller's, fortunes were looking up. In the space of two weeks both Kimberley and Ladysmith had been relieved, the Boers had been put to flight and the traffic in London had been brought to a standstill.

3rd March 1900

Paraded at 8.00 a.m. As we marched to Ladysmith we saw where the Boers had tried to dam the Klip river with sand bags; their intention had been to flood Ladysmith.

At the sack of Badajoz, Harry Smith, a Rifle Brigade officer, rescued a beautiful, young Spanish woman and subsequently married her. The town of Ladysmith is named after her.

Harry Smith was born in Whittlesea in Cambridgeshire in 1788, his distinguished military career included services at Waterloo. In 1847 he was appointed as Governor of the Cape, where he won universal admiration for his work. Another town, Harrismith, linked by rail to Ladysmith, is named after him.

The Doorbraakder dam on the Klip River. Five hundred natives were employed piling sandbags up and a tramway had been built to carry the sandbags to the extreme end of the dam. The plan, designed to precipitate the surrender of Ladysmith, failed when the river swept the dam away. (T)

The troops of the garrison lined the streets and although they looked a bit pale compared to us who had not had a good wash or change of clothing for such a long time, I don't think they had done so bad as some imagine; they certainly looked much better than us with their clean faces and clean clothes. General White and his staff were in front of the Town Hall and watched the troops march by, some slight attempt was made to cheer us, but it was quite a different reception from what we had expected.

These barricades were no defence against shells from the Boer Long Toms. On Christmas day only one shot was fired by the Boers. The shell did not explode and, on closer inspection, was found to be full of plum pudding. (A)

Sir George White was an Irishman born in 1835. He was given an extravagant welcome when he returned to England. The fact that he had chosen the indefensible town of Ladysmith as his military centre and monopolised the cavalry profitlessly and expensively was generously overlooked. (A)

AT LAST!

AT LAST!
Sir George White. 'I hoped to have met you before, Sir Redvers.'
Sir Redvers Buller, V.C. 'Couldn't help it, General. Had so many engagements.' (B)

The only apparent damage to the low storeyed buildings was the missing corner of the Town Hall. (A)

Instead of being cheered by all as we had imagined, most of them seemed to say with their looks, 'Well, you have come at last, but you have taken your time over it.'

The town did not appear to any of us to have suffered much damage from the Boer shells. The tower of the Town Hall had had one corner knocked off; this was most noticeable but only a few houses had holes in the walls. Most of the shops were closed up, having sold out, I suppose.

We bivouacked near Surprise Hill, about three miles from the town. The next day, Sunday, our tents arrived and we were soon busy pitching camp and enjoying a clean change of underclothing which was greatly needed by us all! During the day we were visited by some men of the 2nd Battalion who had assisted in the defence. All the conversation was taken up by them telling us of the bad times they had been through and all they had suffered: how they were kept on short rations, without potatoes or bread for some time. Reduced to eating biscuits and horse flesh they had been forced to drink river water. We let them talk on in this strain. They thought nothing of what we had gone through for months in the field. Had we never gone without food or water? Had we never experienced sleepless nights nor marched almost

Weighing and distributing rations to the troops inside Ladysmith. Six hundred men died during the siege, of sickness, fever or shellfire. (C)

The three sieges differed vastly from each other. Each had its own dominant personalities, its own methods of defence (Ladysmith was the only besieged town with a strong army force present to maintain the defence) and improvisation, the only common factor appeared to be hunger.

In Mafeking, Baden-Powell—the most inventive general—had several ingenious ways of carrying messages beyond the town. He used natives, who hid them, written in cypher on the thinnest paper, in their curly hair, or the stems of their pipes, or even stowed in their nostrils.

barefoot and in rags over the rocks, waded through rivers, fought, marched and suffered three reverses? Had we not lost more men than their garrison contained, in our efforts to relieve them? No, the relieving force had done nothing and they were only to be pitied. We were keenly disappointed with the whole lot and longed for the time for us to move again.

A naval gunner on the *Powerful* also came to see a relative, a friend of mine. He said the civilians of Ladysmith had prepared for a siege. They had laid by a store of spirits, tea, sugar, coffee and tobacco for their own use, and they had taken care to keep it

A primitive X-ray machine in Ladysmith. X-rays had been discovered in 1896 by Röntgen and every available machine was despatched to South Africa during the war. (A)

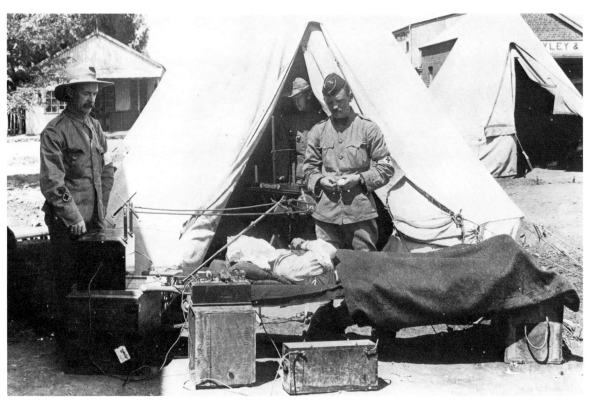

There were two siege newspapers. The Ladysmith Bombshell *was written, often in long hand, on everything from ledger sheets to brown paper.* The Ladysmith Lyre, *which was composed largely of sarcastic swipes at Buller's impotent force and the War Office, produced a number of issues. This extract, 'From our own Despondent', is a clear example of the style:*
'A shell from Long Tom burst in the War Office this afternoon. General Brackenbury, Director General of Ordnance, accepted its arrival with resignation. Several reputations were seriously damaged. Unfortunately the Ordnance Committee was not sitting. A splinter broke into the Foreign Office and disturbed the siesta of the Prime Minister.'
(C)

Around all three towns the besiegers played constant hosts to streams of visitors—many of them ladies—who arrived, complete with picnics, to watch the guns bombard the towns.

Business as un*usual. The town barber sets up his shop on the riverbank, protected from the Boer shells. (A)*

to themselves, but they also drew their usual rations of biscuits, etc. He took an oath and claimed they had given their surplus siege rations to their dogs, as they had enough without! A lot has happened during this war that would not stand much looking into.

There is only one thing worth taking note of during our stay at Surprise Hill: a special order from Sir Redvers Buller.

Special Army Order
3 March, 1900
Ladysmith

Soldiers of Natal, the Relief of Ladysmith unites two forces both of which during the last few months have striven with conspicuous gallantry and splendid determination to maintain the honour of the Queen's Country.

The Garrison of Ladysmith have, during four months, held their position against every attack with complete success and endured many privations with admirable fortitude. The relieving force had had to force its way through an unknown country across an unfordable river and over almost inaccessible heights in the face of a fully prepared and tenacious enemy. By the exhibition of the truist courage, the courage that burns steadily as well as flashes brilliantly, it has accomplished its object and added a glorious page to the history of the British Empire.

Ladysmith has been relieved. Soldiers and sailors, colonial and home-bred have done this united by one desire, inspired by one Patriotism. The General Commanding congratulates both forces upon the metal qualities they have shown. He thanks them for their determined efforts and he desires to offer his sincere sympathy to the relatives and friends of those good soldiers and friends who have fallen in the fight.

Redvers Buller (General) 4th Brigade

"French is scouring the Country"
Lord Roberts' Dispatch

To scour the land
Use Monkey Brand.

Chapter Four:
Buller's Leisurely Advance

Roberts predicted a speedy end to the war and, indeed, his prophecy seemed close to being realized for the Presidents of the Transvaal and the Orange Free State, Kruger and Steyn, had opened peace negotiations. On 5 March, 1900, they sent a telegram from Bloemfontein to the Marquess of Salisbury, stating that they were 'desirous of seeing peace re-established in South Africa, and of putting an end to the evils now reigning over South Africa'. However, there were conditions. They insisted on independence for the two Republics and referred to 'the unextinguishable fire of the love of freedom' which God had lighted in their hearts.

Salisbury remained unmoved. His stiffly polite reply went to great pains to remind the two Presidents that the 'insulting ultimatum' had come from them. They had planned the war, prepared for the war, and now must suffer the consequences of war. 'The British Empire,' he wrote, 'has been compelled to confront an invasion which has entailed upon the Empire a costly war and the loss of thousands of precious lives. This great calamity has been the penalty which Great Britain has suffered for having in recent years acquiesced in the existence of the two Republics.'

Clearly independence was not on the cards. Kruger threw in his hand and the war chugged on.

7th March 1900

We paraded at 9.00 a.m. and marched to Modder Spruit. It was a very hot day and during the long march the men suffered severely from thirst. As soon as we got there it commenced raining. It poured down, we were soon wet through, and, as usual, we had no tents, coats or blankets, so we spent another pleasant night on the veldt in our wet clothing, lying in water and mud. The next morning our wagons came in and, as we were not moving again that day, camp was pitched and so we got one good night's rest.

9th March 1900

Struck camp and marched to Sunday's River, past the Elandslaagte coal mines where we saw some of the handiwork left by the Boers as they retired. Every bridge and culvert along the railway line had been blown up; sheds and houses had been torn to pieces, some burnt; and a lot of damage had been done to the

The Boers at Elandslaagte were eventually captured by the British and sent to the prisoner of war camp on St. Helena. (L)

coal mine shafts. Along the road we passed many of the enemy's broken down wagons and dead horses.

On our arrival at Sunday's River, we pitched camp and were soon busy digging trenches and building sangars. Our brigade were the most advanced, we were within a few thousand yards of the enemy who were reported to be strongly entrenched on the Biggarsberg. We fully expected to be attacked so we prepared ourselves, but they did not trouble us for some time.

12th March 1900

We were treated to soft bread again in lieu of biscuits; this was the first bread we had tasted since 12 February. We were not sorry for the change, for a month on biscuits of the army type is enough for any man—even if his teeth are like steel.

After we had made ourselves secure by building stone walls, we were turned into novices and set to work repairing the railway line. I must say, we made a good job of it. At one place we made a

Roberts wanted all the columns in South Africa to converge on Pretoria concurrently with his own and so bring the war to a decisive finish. On 24 February, he telegraphed Buller outlining his plan. But Buller, having successfully relieved Ladysmith, seemed content to sit back and contemplate his victory. His force now numbered 55,000 men, but if he had any intention of pre-empting Roberts by sweeping through the Transvaal, he certainly gave no indication of it.

For two months Tucker was employed repairing the railway lines, building walls and playing football. The stores were replenished and the Natal Army, which from the very outset of the war had been the most well-cared-for force, took things easy.

Almost fifty telegrams passed between Buller and Roberts during these two months. Roberts implored Buller to begin his advance, or, at the very least, send him a portion of his healthy force. Buller appalled at the thought of forfeiting some of his men, sent evasive replies, occasionally advocating a line of attack Roberts might take, but always cancelling the plan out by a new one in his next telegram. Finally, Roberts' patience came to an end and he left Buller to his own fanatical preparations.

Tucker's worst enemy: a British army ration biscuit. (A)

Following the failure of the peace negotiations, Kruger called a council of war on 17 March, 1900, at Kroonstad. Many of the younger generals raised objections to the wagon camps, containing wives, children and household goods, which trailed behind the Boer columns, weakening them as had been proved by Cronje's surrender at Paardeberg. The council agreed to forbid them, although after Roberts' policies of farm burning and concentration camps, the decision was, by necessity, disregarded as homeless, frightened families joined the Boers in the field. (A)

Having relieved Ladysmith, Buller's troops turned their attentions to restoring lines of communications. (A)

loop line around a bridge which the Boers had blown up, and even though we had to take it across a spruit, we turned it out in first class style.

24th March 1900

General Lyttelton had the Battalion formed up and made us a farewell speech. He introduced our future Brigadier to us: Colonel Cooper of the Dublin Fusiliers. General Lyttelton told us he had been given the command of the Ladysmith Garrison.

We were all extremely sorry to lose him and he to lose us for we had been together through all the rough, hard times of Colenso, Spion Kop, Vaal Krantz, again in our long but successful fight for Hussar Hill, Cingolo, Monte Christo Valley and the last big fight, Pieter's Hill. We knew each other well and speaking for my own regiment (1st Rifle Brigade) we would go anywhere with him and do anything for him. He is the only general in our forces who has not made a mistake. He also spoke well of us, praising our part in the relief of Ladysmith and gave the regiment many compliments. he did not care much about being left with the invalid garrison of Ladysmith where, formerly, he had always been with us, the advance guard of General Buller's forces.

Towards the end of March, General Clery, who had been in hospital since Vaal Krantz, returned to duty and took over the 2nd Division from General Lyttelton, who was given command of the 4th Division, consisting of the 7th and 8th Brigades, formed of the Ladysmith Garrison. General Hunter was given command of the 10th Division, consisting of Hart's (5th) and Barton's (6th) Brigades.

Nothing of importance occurred for a few weeks except that the Battalion received a free issue of stout, sent from home. This was the first chance we had had of drinking since January and each man received one pint. Our exposure to hard work prior to the relief of Ladysmith began to tell on us. Fever and dysentry were very common, big strong men were reduced to mere walking skeletons, and every night we heard the orders read out: The Officer Commanding announces with regret the death of No . . . Private . . .

The combined effects of the recent hard struggle and the bad water caused an outbreak of enteric fever. At Elandslaagte, seventy-five out of every 1,000 men fell prey to the illness and, together with the wounded and the Ladysmith sick, they filled the Natal hospitals to bursting point.

Piet Joubert (above), the old and cautious Commandant-General, was taken ill immediately after the council of war and forced to retire to his farm. There, on 27 March, 1900, he died. A stern republican, he had a broad and powerful face, and a nepotic system of appointments. An oft-repeated story was that of a young man, who asked if he was an officer, replied, 'Of course I'm an officer. I am the Commandant-General's nephew.' In 1893 he had failed to beat Kruger (left) in the presidential election and his influence as a politician had waned somewhat although he was still held in affectionate esteem by the Boers. (C)

10th April 1900

Just as we were having breakfast, the Boers surprised us by shelling the camp. At once we struck camp, packed up and prepared to receive them, but with the exception of shelling, they left us alone. Our naval guns returned the fire and soon everything was quiet again. During the night we moved our camp further away, under cover of the hills, out of sight.

Every night the Boers gave us a treat in the form of illuminations by setting fire to the grass and shrubs along their

At Joubert's State Funeral, Kruger said, 'he died as he has lived, on the path of duty and honour. . . humbly and modestly taking his share of privations and the rough work of the campaign like the poorest burgher, a true general, a true Christian, an example to his people.'

In Britain the Queen had added the Irish Guards to the Household Brigade in recognition of their valour. The Government, less generously, had added fivepence to the income-tax, raising it to one shilling, in their April Budget. However, the majority of the population accepted it as an inevitable war tax and remained in high spirits.

With many men away at war, cigarette sales took a dive. They were also heavily taxed in the latest budget so advertisers stepped up their campaigns, featuring famous faces in their endeavours to boost profits. (D)

In London a khaki uniform entitled its wearer to free seats in the music halls and in fashion circles khaki cloth was in great demand for ladies dresses. Punch *picked up on the trend publishing the above fashion sketch and insisting that, in future, the town was not to be painted bright red, but khaki instead! (B)*

The 'thin red line' is now quite out-of-date,
 The tar's blue jacket shares its fate,
  Our garb is in a state
   Of transformation!
Needless to say khaki is all the rage,
  For Camp and Court, for Church and
   Stage,
    For folks of ev'ry age
     And occupation.

position on the Drakensberg Mountains and it really looked good. The idea behind this was to make the ground we had to pass over black and to show our khaki up plainer and thus make us better targets. Our inactivity seemed to make them very restless and we expected them to attack us any night. We knew they would not come in the daytime, they didn't have enough courage.

I think the Boers were greatly disappointed by us not attacking them for they had been preparing their fortifications and were ready to give us a good reception.

13th April 1900

We prayed for the Boers to attack and so give us the opportunity of surprising them, for we were thoroughly prepared and meant business. Although we kept ourselves in readiness from 2.00 a.m. onwards, we were disappointed again.

15th April 1900

Easter
'A' Company paraded at 4.50 a.m. for outpost duty.

17th April 1900

Two Battalions of the brigade moved closer to Elandslaagte Station. We joined the 10th Brigade with the Scottish Brigade, while the other two battalions marched to Modder Spruit.

21st April 1900

The Boers shelled the coal mines but did no damage. Every day we are employed fortifying the station and our work should last for a good many years if it isn't destroyed for other purposes. We utilised thousands of iron sleepers and formed them into a palisade, four feet six inches high. This meant we could stand up to fire over them. They wouldn't stop a shell but they were proof against rifle bullets.

2nd May 1900

General Lyttelton gave each man in the 4th Brigade one pint of stout per man.

7th May 1900

'A' and 'I' Companies were on outpost duty at the station. The officers were told to expect an attack. We didn't take much notice, the same warning had been given every day and nothing had come of it. However, sure enough, the next morning about 4.45 a.m. we were alarmed by a rattle of musketry on our left, by the coal mines where 'I' Company were on duty. We thought the long expected attack had commenced at last, but after a few minutes it gradually died away and we found it was only a Boer patrol of twenty men. They had got through our cavalry patrol

Buller's inactivity did not reflect that of other British commanders. In the Orange Free State, Roberts had already left Bloemfontein and, with his vast army, was marching on Pretoria. While in Kimberley, a small column of only 1,200 men, led by Colonel Mahon, struck north with the intention of reaching Mafeking, 250 arid miles away, as quickly and as unobtrusively as possible. Although every attempt had been made to keep the advance secret, the Boers were, as usual, perfectly informed of the plan and the younger Cronje, with a force of 1,500 Boers, was directed to arrest the advance. The following ten days resembled a race more than a march, as Mahon strived to reach and assist in the relief of Mafeking, and Cronje contrived to stop him.

DESIGN OF THE WATCH PRESENTED TO OFFICERS AND MEN OF H.M.S. "POWERFUL."

On their return, the Mayor of Portsmouth presented each of the officers and the men of the H.M.S. Powerful *with a watch as a memento of the siege of Ladysmith. (D)*

A QUESTION OF THE DAY.

A QUESTION OF THE DAY
Enterprising British Election Agent. 'Beg pardon, Mr. Kroojer—but can't you give us any idea of when the war will be over? So that we can arrange for our General Election.'
    The war in South Africa was one of the biggest electoral issues fought during the campaign. (B)

"SEATS OF THE MIGHTY."

'SEATS OF THE MIGHTY'
According to the newspapers, a large number of armchairs have been sent to the Cape for the use of officers in the field. The above 'Seats of War' are all 'Front Seats'; they are 'Strictly Reserved'; and are not to be sat upon by the enemy.

Left to right, Methuen, Buller, Roberts, Kitchener, French and White. Mafeking had still to be relieved and Baden-Powell had not yet reached 'hero' status. (B)

As far as Buller was concerned, the most urgent business outstanding was the repair of the railways and the telegraph lines. Without these essential communications, his vast force was stranded, unable to eat, move, fight or sleep.

The Boer commandos in the vicinity, led by Ben Viljoen, were equally as intent on preventing this work. Swift moving and self-sufficient, they swooped down in small bands and harassed the British repair teams.

RINGING THE CHANGES
Tompkins. *I see they're forging British florins at Pretoria.*
Jobson. *Very likely, but I'll be hanged if they'll counterfeit British 'Bobs'.*
Punch

and were making for the main shaft of the mine with the intention of blowing it up, when they ran into a picquet of a Sergeant with a few men from 'I' Company who gave it to them in such a hearty manner that they soon retired leaving one man dead and several wounded. They escaped, with their wounded strapped on to their horses. Even then our cavalry let them get away, without capturing even a horse! There were three patrols of mounted infantry in front of our line of outpost. They had allowed this party to get through their ranks in the first place, and, after being alerted by our rifle fire, they allowed them, handicapped as they were with several wounded men to look after, to get away again! A fine body of men are our cavalry! They relieved Ladysmith in just about the same way. I suppose when they get home to England again, they will strut about with all the assurance in the world and talk of the war in South Africa; bragging of how they made the Boers run. But to my knowledge it has generally been the other way about—the Boers have chased them, instead of them chasing the Boers!

8th May 1900

Received orders to prepare for marching at 7.00 p.m. Although we were ready on time, we had to wait until 9.00 p.m. before starting. We marched until 1.30 a.m. finding ourselves at Modder Spruit again and heard we were to go around Zululand to out-flank the Boers. We bivouacked for five hours and started again in the morning.

After doing about twelve miles we halted at Pieter's Farm. On

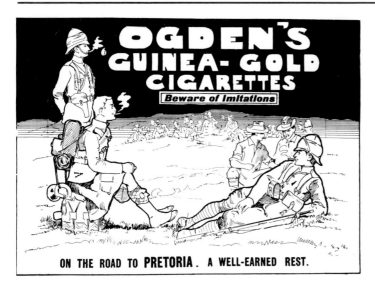

ON THE ROAD TO **PRETORIA**. A WELL-EARNED REST.

While Roberts continued his march on Johannesburg and Pretoria, Tucker was marching in circles, constantly stopping and starting. (D)

the following day, we started at 4.00 p.m. and marched till 10.00 p.m. until we arrived at the bivouacks of the remainder of the brigade.

We were told that we were detailed for convoy duty on the following day. This duty is, I should say, one of the most tiring and trying that one can possibly have on the march, for you have so much stopping and starting off, having to assist every breakdown on the road, and, with ox transport, which only travels two miles an hour, it is very tiring.

Unharnessed, the Rifle Brigade baggage mules pose for a photograph. Forage had to be carried for the mules, while the Boers, who travelled with fewer mounts, relied on the veldt to provide for their ponies. (A)

Although Tucker hated convoy duty and was vociferous in his complaints, the new system Kitchener had instituted was proving more effective than the old. The troops now carried two days rations with them as they advanced and the great bulk of supplies was carried by ox wagons following in convoy.

Kitchener was aware of the disruptions he caused. In a letter to a friend, he confessed: 'I am afraid I rather disgust the old red-tape heads of departments. They are very polite, and after a bit present me with a volume of their printed regulations generally dated about 1870 and intended for Aldershot manoeuvres, and are quite hurt when I do not agree to follow their printed rot.'

Overcome by the heat and utterly exhausted, many men collapsed during the march. They were collected by members of the Red Cross and carried in ox wagons at the rear. The worn out horses were left where they had fallen, without shade or water. (F)

By May, Buller had, at last, decided to advance and attack a range of mountains known as the Biggarsberg, upon which the Boers, commanded by the young general, Ben Viljoen, were gathered. Buller's numerical strength and the intelligent way he deployed his forces succeeded in ousting the Boers, who fled back into the Transvaal on the 13 and 14 May. With less than twenty-five casualties, Buller had cleared Natal of Boers. three days later the final siege was lifted.

We crossed the Sunday River Drift and found the road very rough and hilly; the poor bullocks were almost dropping with fatigue. At 3.00 a.m., after nine hours on the road, we arrived at our place of bivouack: Waschbank. After two hours sleep I was woken by shots at the head of the column. I slept intermittently and at 9.00 a.m. we started again, still on convoy guard. The Boers kept up a vicious sniping fire all day, their object being to stop the progress of the convoy, but they were too afraid to come close enough to do us any harm. We got to our bivouack at 8.00 p.m. and found ourselves close to a fine farmhouse with a good orange orchard and we were soon enjoying some of the ripe fruit. Afterwards, I slept soundly, I had been marching almost all day and night and desperately needed the rest.

13th May 1900

We found next morning, that during the night the Boers had been busy on our left, getting guns up on the Helpmakaar Road, ready to shell us as soon as the daylight came. The garrison artillery gunners, who had taken over the 4.7 guns from the Navy, were

A Boer Long Tom (Creusot 5.9) about to be loaded. The men of the commando are grouped proudly around their prize possession. (A)

watching them through their powerful glasses as they built two sangars for their Long Toms. The gunners could see two Long Toms and so they brought the two 4.7s forward to reply as soon as the Boers opened fire. We did not have long to wait. We had just fallen in on parade when the first shot rang out close by my regiment. The next came in right amongst the Durham Light Infantry, wounding several. We, at once, opened out in loose order and retired clear of the naval guns giving them room to fire. They soon silenced the Boers! It was said that the second shot we fired landed right in the sangar and completely smashed the Boer Long Tom. General Buller complimented the garrison gunners on their excellent shooting. It really was good shooting too, for our guns were on the level plain, while the Boer guns were on a high hill, well protected by rocks several feet thick. The Boers retired and our cavalry, with a battery of artillery, went in pursuit, and for once our cavalry worked smartly, keeping them on the move up through the Helpmakaar Pass.

Medical men purchasing shells from a Kaffir woman. As curios, shells, and even fragments of shells, were popular. In the siege towns they were put up for sale in shop windows. (L)

Flushed with victory, the cavalry gleefully pursued the disorderly Boers as they fled from their positions on the Helpmakaar Heights. (K)

What was, for Private Tucker, a perfect picnic spot, had been, in 1879, a site for carnage and the complete annihilation of a British column by the main Zulu army.

At Rorke's Drift a small British force had held the Zulus at bay throughout the night until reinforcements could reach them.

When Cetewayo and his Zulu army was finally defeated by Lord Chelmsford at the capital, Ulundi, Zululand was divided up among several chiefs and the power of the tribe was broken. Cetewayo was hunted down and captured. He was restored a few years later, but he had lost his authority and died soon afterwards.

We—the 1st Rifle Brigade—were the advance guard of the convoy and came in for a little sniping but that was all. We passed the house in which the Zulus had massacred our wounded during the Zulu War. It was at the foot of the pass in a beautiful shady spot surrounded by trees, near a spruit of cool, clear water. We halted there for about ten minutes and filled our water bottles. Our cavalry captured a lot of horses and cattle from the Boers' laager, which our artillery had been shelling.

British troops taking the opportunity to fill their water bottles from a cool, running spruit. (A)

We bivouacked in the pass, about six miles from Rorke's Drift—another place where the Zulus had cut our fellows up so badly—with Isandhlwana on our right. The Boers were reported to be strongly entrenched on the top of the pass so we expected to be hard at it the next morning, but we were disappointed. During the night they had done another of their mid-night flits and we found the pass, and their trenches, empty. Our cavalry and the Royal Horse Artillery went in pursuit and shelled them from their main laager on the Dundee Road. Their position was first class, commanding every inch of the road. What could have made the Boers leave so easily was a marvel to us all, we had never seen such long walls and trenches before. They had built some

'WHO SAID BOBS?'
One of F.C.G.'s famous series of tortoise cartoons which appeared in the Westminster Gazette. *(R)*

Men of the Transvaal artillery at work building stone wall defences around their laager. (D)

beautiful emplacements for their guns, especially their pom-poms. They were so well built, with neat trenches either side for the gunners to dodge into, that I firmly believe a few hundred men could have held it against a couple of brigades quite easily. The walls were sometimes a mile in length and strongly built, every gun position was placed well and in commanding positions, well protected by walls. They could have given us a warm time of it if they had only made a stand but as they had retired, we went forward towards Dundee.

We bivouacked on the same camping ground the Boers had used—their laager. In their haste they had left a lot of flour and lard behind and our men made good use of it. We found this laager had been occupied by the Johannesburg commando.

At 7.30 a.m. the next morning we marched off again unopposed through Dundee. We passed by coal mines which the Boers had completely wrecked, also several houses in the town had been smashed up. Plenty of British flags were flying, I suppose the European residents (there were several) took the Boer flags down just before we marched into the town. We were bivouacked about a mile outside the town on the very ground on which the Battle of Dundee had taken place, close by Talana Hill where General Symons had been mortally wounded and Colonel Sherston had been killed. General Cooper, who had then been Colonel of the Dublin Fusiliers, found the big drum that the regiment had lost in that battle.

The next day, as our transport oxen were done up, we were given a day's rest. We were glad of the rest, having marched for eight days solid.

Dundee was a small coal-mining town, boasting a station, an English church and a line of tin-roofed houses. It had, however, been the site of one of the first battles of the war in October 1899.

At the Battle of Talana Hill the British succeeded in defeating the Boers but they were still surrounded and threatened by another attack. Their commander, General Penn-Symons, lay dying, mortally wounded in the stomach. General Yule, the second in command, decided to withdraw. Under cover of darkness, he marched his men sixty-four miles on a circuitous route to Ladysmith where he joined forces with White. The supplies, equipment and tents—still standing—were left behind and everything fell into the hands of the delighted Boers.

Camp cooks at work. Catering for such large numbers involved continual effort, gathering and chopping wood and collecting water. The covered pans were built up in a pyramid shape over the fire. (M)

Cooking dinner in the Dorset Camp

*A small group of armed Boers below a
partially destroyed railway bridge. (A)*

*The first hint that Mafeking had been
relieved presented itself to London in the
form of an unconfirmed Reuters report,
written in huge letters and displayed outside
their office in Fleet Street. The news spread
rapidly throughout the capital and beyond,
as crowds beat a jubilant path to the centre
where they 'mafficked' (Chambers
Twentieth Century Dictionary defines this
new addition to the English language as 'to
rejoice with hysterical boisterousness') for
two nights and a day.*

*Baden-Powell's spirited and audacious
defence of the beleaguered town had
captured the imagination of the Empire, and,
throughout the world, news headlines united
in common praise.*

*During the 217 day siege Baden-Powell
had done more than simply defend the town.
He had succeeded in keeping nearly 10,000
Boers idle during the first critical month of
the war, and never less than 2,000 for the
remaining months. Within the town, his
enthusiasm had been indefatigable. He had
organized cycle races, concerts, fêtes and
parties. The Sunday shindigs so incensed the
devout Boers that they threatened to shell
the town if they did not cease.*

*Each battered building testified to the
heavy bombardment which the town had had
to endure, but the casualties had been
surprisingly slight: thirty-five killed, 101
wounded and twenty-seven taken prisoner.*

17th May 1900

We left Dundee at 6.30 a.m. and marched to Dannhauser
arriving there at 1.00 p.m. The Boers had blown up the bridges
along the railway line.

18th May 1900

We paraded at 4.30 a.m. to march into Newcastle, a distance of
twenty-five miles. We were given two hours halt on the road for
dinner and, as we were close by a river, we were able to have a good
wash and start again on the march quite refreshed. We arrived at
Newcastle at six in the evening feeling rather tired. The
inhabitants of the pretty town lined the streets and gave us a
welcome; a great many flags were flying and all the women were
wearing red, white and blue ribbons. I think we saw about forty
women who were wearing deep black, signifying someone dear to
them had fallen in this strife while fighting against us.

*Before the arrival of the British, a group
photograph of the Boer commando at
Newcastle, on the steps of the town hall. (A)*

Surrounded by approving townspeople, General Buller listens to a welcoming speech read by the landdrost at Newcastle. (A)

We expected to be stationed here for a time but the 4th Brigade were ordered to the front again as an advance guard as usual. So, early the next morning, we marched to Ingogo and bivouacked for nine days, leaving the other brigade at Newcastle. Our camping ground was just opposite Majuba Hill, where in 1881 the Boers had cut our troops to pieces during the last Boer war. The 3rd King's Royal Rifles were bivouacked close by a monument which had been erected in memory of the men of the 81st Regiment and the 3rd King's Royal Rifles who had fallen in that ever memorable disaster.

Kruger had been negotiating for peace on the very day that the fateful Battle of Majuba had taken place. However, by some misunderstanding, Sir George Colley, the general in Natal, had not been informed of Kruger's move and so he had continued with the war. On 26 February, 1881, he had made a night march with 600 men and had seized Majuba Hill, a height commanding Laing's Nek. The next day, a considerable force of Boers had stormed the hill and Colley had been among those killed.
· Lord Roberts, who had been sent out to South Africa with reinforcements, had landed at Cape Town only to find that peace had been signed, so he had promptly returned to England.

Newcastle town hall filled, not with people but with looted furniture. The Boers had cleared the houses of British sympathizers and made a huge bonfire of their contents, intending to burn the whole building down. (W)

A sixpenny badge issued by the War Employment Bureau to commemorate Queen Victoria's birthday. The proceeds went to a charity which aided war sufferers. (D)

Roberts marked the Queen's birthday by flamboyantly annexing the Orange Free State and adding it to her dominions under the name of the Orange River Colony. It was placed under martial law on 31 May, and the following day it was announced that any burghers who refused to hand in their arms within fourteen days would be dealt with as rebels. The burghers duly sorted out their decrepit, useless weapons and traded them for Roberts' promise of immunity, and returned to their farms until they and their lethal, modern weapons were called to action once more.

Before leaving Bloemfontein, Roberts had taken over the offices of the 'Friend', and installed Kipling on the editorial staff of the new army newspaper. Kipling stayed for some months and wrote verses and short pieces under the title, 'A Kopje Notebook'.

We find the weather bitter cold. The troops are employed nearly all day digging trenches and building walls so as to be well prepared in case of an attack. The Boers are reported to be strongly entrenched, and in great numbers, on Majuba Hill and at Laing's Nek. For the last two days we have been very short of rations. We are eating trek oxen—their flesh is more fit for repairing boots than for human consumption. Hardly surprising when you think they have been dragging wagons about for the past twenty years.

24th May 1900

Queen's birthday

All troops paraded and gave three hearty cheers for Her Majesty, but no guns were fired. We were given an extra ration of rum in honour of the event. General Buller complimented the Battalion on our eleven days marching.

28th May 1900

The 4th Brigade advanced again to Inkwelo Mountains, six miles from Ingogo. My regiment (the 1st Rifle Brigade) was stationed on the top of a 6,600 feet high mountain. It was a very steep climb and everything—rations, wood, etc—had to be carried from the very bottom to the top by us each day. On our arrival, the Boers let us get safely to the top. Half the Battalion—my company among them—was sent to the bottom again to collect our blankets and coats. The Boers took this opportunity to send several shells amongst us, but luckily only one man—of the King's Royal Rifles—was wounded. Our naval 4.7 guns were hauled up the steep hill; it took sixty oxen and 200 men to drag each gun up. They opened fire as soon as the guns were in position. It took them a little time to find the exact range, but they soon silenced the Boer guns.

Oxen and men combining forces to haul a gun up to the top of a hill. This close up of the rocky terrain makes it easier to understand why the British columns moved at a snail's pace. (S)

Out in the open. A British soldier cocoons himself in blankets against the morning cold of the South African winter. (E)

As Roberts closed in on Johannesburg, French and German mine-owners grew extremely anxious, for the Boers had threatened to blow up the mines and thus deprive the advancing British of this lucrative source of income. Finally, fearing the loss of both public and foreign support, which was noticeably flagging, they changed their minds and 30 May found Roberts and his force on the periphery of the city.

Displaying a line of courtesy now long since out of supply, Roberts agreed to wait for twenty-four hours while the Boers made good their escape! This, he rationalized, would avoid any street-fighting and possible danger to innocent townspeople. Kruger, forced to forsake his capital, gathered together what gold was left in the mint, and moved his government sixty miles to Middelburg.

Most of the Uitlanders, for whom the war was being fought, had pulled out long ago and the weary troops were met with a lukewarm welcome as they marched along the dust—rather than gold—paved streets. Roberts stayed to hoist the Union Jack (a silk one made for him by his wife) before moving on to Pretoria.

We made ourselves comfortable for the night. It was too cold to sleep and in the morning I found my top blanket was quite wet and stiff, and I was rather surprised to find a sharp white frost over everything. This was a change that required some getting used to. I tried to make some coffee but found my water bottle full of ice, so I had to thaw this over the fire before I could make the coffee.

In addition to the 4.7 guns we had two 12-pound guns with us, and these opened a heavy fire on Majuba Hill. The Boers replied for a few hours but did no damage. It didn't freeze the second night but there was a very strong, keen wind which seemed to cut through me. It was impossible to keep warm and I think every one spent a very miserable night.

2nd June 1900

General Buller and General Clery went out under a flag of truce to interview the Boer Commanders. They told them they were surrounded and, I suppose, tried to close this fight without further bloodshed. An armistice was agreed on until Thursday, 6 June, so we spent a few quiet days.

Buller's procrastinations in Natal contrasted sharply with Roberts' undeviating advance on Pretoria. On 29 May 1900, before going to Roberts' aid, he sent General Hildyard into the town of Utrecht with instructions to secure its surrender. Hildyard and the landdrost of the town conferred for a considerable time before the landdrost handed over the Transvaal flag and six rifles as a token of the town's submission. The commandos had agreed to move out of the town and not return, but they waited in the surrounding hills until Hildyard—mission accomplished—marched on to Coetzee's Drift. Immediately he had left, the commandos reoccupied the town, tore down Buller's proclamation and arrested the landdrost.

A Boer camp for British prisoners. Several of the men have hidden their faces in this photograph although one, bolder than the others, gestures rudely. While in the prison camps, British soldiers had their pay stopped. On release, enquiries were set up and the arrears were handed over. (J)

SHIFTING HIS CAPITAL
('It is not true,' Mr. Kruger is reported in the Daily Express *to have said, 'That I have brought with me gold to the value of two millions. Whatever monetary resources I may have with me are simply those we require for State purposes.') (B)*

Buller wrote to Christian Botha at the end of May. His situation on Laing's Nek, he cautioned, was hopeless and he would do best to come to terms. As a result of this letter, Botha sent in a flag of truce and the two men, accompanied by their respective staffs, held a conference between their front lines on 2 June.

While waiting for Roberts' terms to come through (Buller was not authorized to make any himself) there was a three day armistice, during which both sides edged themselves into more favourable fighting positions in the event of a deadlock. Roberts demanded an unconditional surrender. The Boers answered with a defiant burst of gunfire.

On 5 June, 1900, Roberts entered Pretoria. The effect on the British morale was one of elation, for the Boers it spelled devastation.

Even as Roberts was watching his wife's flag hoisted once more, Botha, De la Rey and the other Boer generals were making plans for surrender. Pride or indecision made them delay and in the interval Christian de Wet stepped up on the stage and infused new hope in the flagging Boers. At dawn on 7 June, he made three simultaneous, successful attacks in the Orange Free State and captured stores, took 700 prisoners, wrecked a bridge and severed Roberts' vital communications with Bloemfontein completely.

Taking their lead from the daring De Wet, the Boers were now getting their second wind. The three sieges had been lifted, Roberts was in Pretoria, their Presidents were fugitives in their own countries, but the Boers were determined to fight on. To do this, they had to adopt a more irregular style of fighting, shedding much of their heavy artillery, and relying on sharp, swift, surprise attacks: guerilla war had been declared.

As the British bounded into Pretoria, the Boers slipped away. Both Botha and Kruger had to leave their wives behind in the town. (D)

SHIFTING HIS CAPITAL.

5th June 1900

We received our serge khaki clothing. This clothing should have been issued to us quite a month earlier but our Colonel liked us to wear our thin khaki as we could wash it and so appear clean—he has no regard for our health and comfort!

6th June 1900

The armistice ended and our guns opened fire again at daybreak. The Boers will not give in, they prefer to fight.

During the morning we were told that the flag was flying at Pretoria at last and all the regiment gave three cheers. Our Colonel has issued an order forbidding any man to wash himself

Interior of "Bird Cage" where 168 British officers were imprisoned in Pretoria for over 4 months

before 11.00 a.m. He does not like cold water himself! Thinking it 11.00 a.m. (it only wanted two minutes) a man of my company and eight others had a wash in front of a sentry, who had been posted there to see that the order was observed. He watched them strip and wash (most of them, at least), and then said, 'You are not allowed to wash before eleven,' and called the Sergeant of the Guard. The Sergeant took their names and company and they were told they were *prisoners*!! The following morning they were brought before their respective Company Officers, who sent them before the Colonel, their *crime* being not complying with an order. The sentry and the Sergeant gave evidence against them, saying they refused to go away when ordered. This was a deliberate lie and, as a private soldier's word (especially a reserve man) is never taken against a man with a stripe, or stripes, on his arm, the Colonel gave them each eight days defaulters. Another typical indication of the sort of man we have in charge of us.

A heavy firing was kept up all day from our guns and severe fighting took place close by us—General Hildyard's brigade and the 10th Brigade.

Rain came on in the afternoon and in the evening, very heavy fog. It was intensely cold.

The night before Roberts' entry into Pretoria, the 168 British officers, imprisoned in the 'Bird Cage', were instructed to make ready for a move. The officers promptly arrested their wardens and overpowered their guards. (D)

The moment Roberts entered Pretoria he increased his force by 5,000 men—prisoners of war whom the Boers had been unable, in their haste, to take with them.

In England, the Illustrated London News *published a letter from the Secretary of the American Hospital-Ship Fund for South Africa, praising the 'Cloudy Fluid Ammonia' sent by Messr's Scrub and Co. and thanking them also of the antiseptic soap which was a great success.*

Chapter Five:
Guerilla Warfare

9th June 1900

Still surrounded by a very thick mist. All operations have been suspended. Five companies from my Battalion were stationed on outpost in case the Boers tried to take advantage of the fog and rush us. If they had made such a movement, it would have given us great satisfaction. About 11.00 a.m. the fog lifted and our guns opened fire : a duel of artillery was kept up all day.

10th June 1900

Sunday was a very quiet day, without any firing. At 8.00 a.m. on the next morning the Boers opened fire, they had calculated the exact range of our bivouacks and common shell and shrapnel fell among us. One shell fell within a few yards of a man's bivouack

A rest and a smoke. Two men remain on look out while the others talk and relax over their cigarettes. (L)

A military butcher cutting up meat with a saw. In the foreground are crates of corned beef. (J)

and several men had narrow shaves, especially the cooks who were busy cutting meat up for our dinner. We all had to seek shelter in a donga close by and remained there for the rest of the day. The Boers sent about thirty shells into our position but I think they were only using up their spare shells because during the night they left their positions on Majuba, Pugwana and Laing's Nek. They left behind their Long Toms, taking only the breaches away. The next day, Tuesday, 12 June, our troops advanced through Laing's Nek leaving us (1st Rifle Brigade)

On 11 June, in a daring bid to force Botha's hand, Buller launched an attack on the seemingly impregnable Alleman's Nek. (Tucker's brigade were not involved in the attack.) As before at Pieter's Hill, he utilized his force well, making excellent use of his artillery and keeping his nerve until the very end when the Boers galloped off in retreat under cover of their customary grass fires.

The victory of Alleman's Nek was decisive. Buller had gained an excellent position, but his tardy progress and his failure to grasp the strategical importance of his victory gave the Boers ample time to make good their escape. By 12 June they had evacuated Laing's Nek and retired back into the Transvaal, bent now on protecting their own borders and lines of communication.

A panoramic view of Ingogo, Majuba and Laing's Nek, the scene of hostilities in 1881 and in May 1900. (D)

PROCLAMATION.

Whereas small parties of raiders have recently been doing wanton damage to public property in the Orange River Colony and South African Republic by destroying railway bridges and culverts and cutting the telegraph wires, and whereas such damage cannot be done without the knowledge and connivance of the neighbouring inhabitants, and the principal civil residents in the districts concerned.

Now therefore I, Frederick Sleigh, Baron Roberts of Kandahar and Waterford, K.P., G.C.B., G.C.S.I., G.C.I.E., V.C., Field Marshal, Commanding in Chief Her Majesty's Troops in South Africa, warn the said inhabitants and principal civil residents that, whenever public property is destroyed or injured in the manner specified above, they will be held responsible for aiding and abetting the offenders. The houses in the vicinity of the place where the damage is done will be burnt, and the principal civil residents will be made prisoners of war.

ROBERTS,
F. M.,
Commanding in Chief, South Africa.

Army Head Quarters, South Africa,
Pretoria, 16th June, 1900.

PROCLAMATIE.

Aangezien in de laatste tijden kleine getallen van vrijbuiters in de Oranje Rivier Kolonie en de Zuid-Afrikaansche Republiek onnoodige schade hebben aangericht aan publiek eigendom door het vernielen van spoorwegbruggen, duikers en het afsnijden van de telegraafdraden, en aangezien zulke schade niet veroorzaakt kan worden zonder medeweten van de omliggende bewoners en de voornaamste inwoners van de betrokken districten,

Zoo is het, dat ik, Frederick Sleigh, Baron Roberts of Kandahar and Waterford, K.P., G.C.B., G.C.S.I., G.C.I.E., V.C., Veldmaarschalk, Opperbevelhebber van Harer Majesteits troepen in Zuid-Afrika, gezegde inwoners waarschuw, dat, waar publiek eigendom vernield of beschadigd wordt op de wijze zooals hierboven aangehaald, zij verantwoordelijk zullen gehouden worden voor het helpen en samenspannen met dusdanige vernielers.

De huizen in de nabijheid waar de schade aangericht is, zullen afgebrand worden, terwijl de voornaamste inwoners krijgsgevangen zullen gemaakt worden.

ROBERTS,
V. M.,
Opperbevelhebber in Zuid-Afrika.

Hoofdkwartieren, Zuid-Afrika,
Pretoria, 16 Juni 1900.

One of Roberts' many proclamations, dated 16 June, 1900, and posted in every town. (A)

British troops guarding a tunnel at Laing's Nek, which had been partially destroyed when two trains entering the tunnel from opposite ends had collided with a truck load of dynamite, strategically placed in the centre by the Boers. (W)

Overlooking, for the moment, the delay, Buller was riding high on a crest of success. His recent operations had been well-planned and skilfully executed and he was finally advancing. On 19 June he occupied Volksrust, his first town in the Transvaal.

behind to escort the guns and help move them off the hill. This we accomplished on Wednesday, 13 June. We moved off at about 1.00 p.m., escorting six guns (two 5-inch, two 4.7 guns and two 12-pounders). We marched by Majuba, pitched camp about four miles from Charlestown and spent a very comfortable night under canvas. This was our first time under the shelter of a tent since 7 May.

On Tuesday, the casualties from Hildyard's brigade were thirty killed, 120 wounded. The Boers lost heavily: 150 were buried by the 10th Brigade. Most had been killed by the shrapnel from the howitzer battery. The exact number of Boer wounded is not known.

We remained at Laing's Nek until Tuesday, 19 June. During our short stay, the men were employed repairing the damaged tunnel and railway. The first train came through the tunnel on Monday afternoon, 18 June. Some of the men paid a visit to the top of Majuba Hill to view the monument and graves of those who fell in the last Boer War, fought on this spot. The trenches and breastworks used by the Boers were a marvel of engineering.

19th June 1900

The 2nd Division moved forward. We passed through Charlestown and found it very much damaged, nearly very house was broken up. Then we passed by on the outskirts of Volksrust, a

rather large town on the Transvaal border. We didn't see much of the town but were told that little damage had been done. As it was a Boer town, there were several inhabitants still there; the women, we noticed, were mostly dressed in black showing respect for their dead relatives who no doubt had fallen by our army.

We camped at Joubert's Farm.

Checking and serving out ammunition at Volksrust. All supplies and ammunition were brought up by trains, without which the British army was paralysed.

Majuba Hill can be seen in the background. (L)

20th June 1900

We continued our march and, after six hours, we bivouacked at Sandspruit. The weather was very bad for bivouacking; in the morning our blankets were wet through, stiff and covered with white frost. The mist and rain hung about the whole morning and we continued our march very cautiously with the Rifle Brigade leading. We arrived at Paarde Kop after a seven hour march and bivouacked.

De Wet, who had become the thorn in Roberts' side, was causing ructions up and down the country. Burghers, emboldened by his spirited raids, were returning to their commandos in their hundreds. On 12 June, Kitchener himself narrowly escaped De Wet, who was approaching his camp near Heilbron with a raiding party, by galloping to safety in his pyjamas.

22nd June 1900

We set out on a twenty-three mile stretch, halting half way at Platrand Station to eat dinner and to rest. We finally finished our march at 6.00 p.m. when we arrived at Katbosch Spruit. We pitched our canvas in the dark and after making some tea we had a good night's rest.

The shortage of horses in South Africa was becoming so acute that the government began requisitioning bus-horses. A wit at Punch *cantered into print with this poem:*

THE NEW CHARGER
Ride a bus-horse
To the far Southern Cross,
Says the War Office,
For mounts at a loss;
With wrings on his withers
And balls from his foes,
He'll face the music wherever he goes!

Midday halt near Standerton. After tea one man settles down to read under the shade of the wagon. (A)

On 23 June Tucker brags importantly of the mileage he has covered. The strategic importance of the position should not be overlooked. The advance had succeeded in isolating the Free State forces, who used Standerton as their chief centre of communication with the Transvaal headquarters. The net was tightening around the Boers.

23rd June 1900

We finished our march, arriving at Standerton about 2.00 p.m. and pitched camp. We are to rest here for a few days. After all, we have marched eighty miles in five days!

Standerton is rather a large town with tin-roofed houses scattered about. There is a very pretty, well-built church standing almost in the centre but we are not allowed to visit this place. Instead, we are encamped about one mile to the left of the town, where we found nineteen engines and a lot of trucks. The Boers blew up the centre span of the three-span railway bridge that crosses the Vaal River just outside the town. This caused us great delay in getting provisions up by rail. We were all glad of the few days rest at Standerton and being near the river we were able to bath, and wash our dirty underclothing. However, we did not get the chance to remain there long, for on Saturday, 30 June, the 4th Brigade Cavalry and Artillery moved forward again leaving their 2nd Brigade behind at Standerton.

The demolished centre span of the Vaal River bridge. The men have stripped off for a welcome bath. Many were infested with lice, which had to be prised out from the seams of their uniforms. (A)

We marched, without opposition, to Waterval and pitched camp, a distance of twelve miles. Some sniping took place between our outpost just as it was getting dark. This small affair caused us to keep our boots and straps on all night.

'What are your looking for, Sylvie?'
'Why, Papa said that when the Boers fired on the white flag, ''Lord Methuen took Umbrage,'' and I can't find it anywhere!'
(B)

1st July 1900

The next morning, Sunday, was very cold and wet. We struck camp at daybreak and soon moved forward again. The Rifle Brigade formed the advance guard of the column followed by the cavalry. We had got about six miles along the road when the Boers began sniping again. The cavalry chased them and our artillery fired a few shells. Here our Canadian Cavalry experienced the Boer treachery of the white flag. Some of these men advanced to a farmhouse, which was flying the white flag, and when within fifty yards, two Boers came out and gave themselves up (or gave signs that they would) so our Canadian

Along with Tucker and the other men from the 4th (Cooper's) Brigade, Thorneycroft's Mounted Infantry, Strathcona's Horse and sixteen guns set out for Heidelberg. (Strathcona's Horse came from Canada. Lord Strathcona had raised, at his own expense, a 400 strong force of 'rough riders'. They were all single men, good horsemen and excellent shots.)

A Boer woman raises her fist to the British soldiers who are burning her farm despite the fact that it is flying a white flag. Farm burning began in February, although Roberts issued no formal proclamations until August. (C)

'White flag incidents' were widely reported in Britain and caused much outrage among the patriotic public. Some justification can be found during the denser battles, for fighting burghers were very much their own commanders and although one group might elect to surrender, it was quite usual for the rest to go on with the fight. However, the more dubious cases of chicanery—attempts to mislead the British troops by calling out in English; flying white flags to gain a brief ceasefire but not a surrender; commandants requesting armistices simply to regroup and replenish their forces—were legion.

friends advanced and soon got a volley from some more Boers, killing one and wounding two others, but soon everything was quiet and we continued our march.

We camped at Vaal Spruit.

2nd July 1900

We continued our march amid more sniping. One Hussar had his horse shot from under him.

We arrived safely at Greylingstad and pitched camp.

3rd July 1900

A day in camp.
My company on outpost at night.

4th July 1900

Several Boers came into our camp and gave themselves up, also fetching in their rifles and ammunition. We were rather amused by two Boers who came in: they drove up in two, two-horse gigs and brought their wives and children, but their families were sent safely back to their homes. The husbands were detained to sign a declaration.

General Christian de Wet was born in 1852 in Harrismith. He came from a well educated farming family but lost his fortune on the Johannesburg stock exchange.

One of the most flamboyant and obstinate Boer generals, he had had no military education whatsoever but proved himself repeatedly to be a brave and intelligent strategist. (A)

A Boer is led blindfolded into the Rifle Brigade camp. The British took this precaution just in case the Boer was a spy who had not come to give himself up but to gain information on the British defences. (H)

During the day the Durhams and Scottish Rifles and half the Battalion of the 60th Rifles', marched forward to Vlakfontein leaving us to garrison in Greylingstad.

Another old Boer of about seventy came in but was soon released.

5th July 1900

The half Battalion of the 60th Rifles' that was left behind with us moved back to Waterval.

During the day our men got a convoy ready. In the evening four companies were covering party for another convoy of stores from the station to our camp.

The persistence of the roving guerilla bands was equal to that of the mosquito, and their effect was just as swift and painful. Surveying the scars of wrecked railways, ambushed convoys and broken lines of communication, which covered the body of the British Army, Roberts decided to intimidate the burghers into surrender by notices, like this one below. They were put up in every town and, as we can see from Private Tucker's accounts, they were having some success.

Public Notice
It is hereby notified for information, that unless the men at present on commando belonging to families in the town and district of Krugersdorp surrender themselves and hand in their arms to the Imperial Authorities by 20 July, the whole of their property will be confiscated and their families turned out destitute and homeless.

By order G. H. Ritchie,
Capt. K. Horse, Dist. Supt. Police
Krugersdorp, 9 July, 1900.

Later, on 14 August, a further proclamation was issued, urging those burghers who had returned home and taken an oath of neutrality to 'acquaint Her Majesty's Forces with the presence of the Enemy'. In other words, to act as British spies and renounce their neutrality.

A burgher with his son and Kaffir cook poses proudly by the side of his wagon. Many Boer farmers, believing the war to be over, returned peacefully to their homes for several months before rejoining their commandos. (L)

Kaffir girls, guilty of having sold beer illegally to the troops, are brought before the provost-marshal. (M)

A convoy of British supply wagons moving off under escort. (A)

6th July 1900

Four companies of the Rifle Brigade—myself included—escorted the convoy for five miles towards the remainder of the 4th Brigade, then met the Scottish Rifles who took the convoy over and escorted it to its destination. We returned to our camp at Greylingstad. Whilst on this convoy escort, I watched our guns shelling a Boer laager—didn't it make them run. Our troops come in contact with the enemy each day but the Boers will not stand up for a good fight. A few give up their arms to us each day.

After our return to camp, three companies went on outpost duty.

7th July 1900

We had a day's rest.

8th July 1900

We struck camp at 7.00 a.m. and loaded wagons ready for a move at 8.00 a.m. Then we were told the move was cancelled, so we pitched camp again. At 1.00 p.m. we were ordered to pack up *again* and this time we marched for four miles to a new camp on some high hills just opposite our old camping ground. Our baggage wagons were a long time getting up to us but, after waiting several hours, shivering with the cold, the wagons arrived and we pitched camp at 10.00 p.m. in the dark. I soon made some coffee for me and my chum and by 11.00 p.m. we were asleep.

A British 5-inch howitzer in camp.
By now the Boers had shed most of their heavy artillery. They buried some on the veldt but the British usually discovered these caches. (A)

9th July 1900

General Buller is here with us.

We escorted one of our 5-inch guns up to our brigade and brought back an empty convoy. The Boers have damaged our telegraph wires and the railway between us and Standerton. This is causing a delay in provisions for no train has been in three days. Small enemy forces are still nearby, our 5-inch gun has been shelling them.

This evening we go on outpost.

10th July 1900

I had a day in camp.

Four companies go on convoy duty again. They escorted General Buller to railhead at Groot Spruit.

11th July 1900

On convoy duty. Returned to camp at 8.00 p.m. Our brigade has concentrated here again.

12th July 1900

Company on duty repairing the railway. Return to camp at 7.00 p.m. and go on outpost at 8.00 p.m. We are left here again. The brigade has moved off to clear enemy forces. From the position we watched them shelling the Boers.

13th July 1900

A day in camp. We watched our brigade shelling the Boers.

A wounded and decorated dummy often used on outpost duty by the British as an amusing decoy, designed to draw the Boer fire. (A)

An Odgen cigarette advertisement, gleefully predicting that Kruger would soon be with General Cronje in the prisoner of war camp on St. Helena. (D)

Diyatalawa prisoner of war camp in Ceylon. 4,000 feet above sea level, the camp was constructed upon a similar terrain to that in South Africa. (F)

14th July 1900

Employed wall building.

15th July 1900

A quiet day in camp.

16th July 1900

Wall building again. No chance to get a wash.

17th July 1900

Wall building again. We are making this hill like Gibraltar.

18th July 1900

Outpost.

19th July 1900

Unloading stores in camp.

20th July 1900

Wall building.

21st July 1900

Draft arrived: 190 men, mostly section D men.

22nd July 1900

Outpost. Wet night.

23rd July 1900

In camp.

24th July 1900

Four companies, 'A'. 'B'. 'C'. and 'D', proceed out for about seven miles acting as escort to a party of Engineers, who are to repair the railway. Before leaving camp we packed up as we were not to return to the top of the hill again. This we were thankful for. We found the railway completely torn up for half a mile and a bridge blown up. The Engineers worked until sundown and we returned to camp in a train sent specially for us. We found our division had arrived at Greylingstad. The Scottish Rifles had relieved us from the top of the hills. We joined our brigade.

Kaffirs, suspected of spying, are led blindfolded into the Rifle Brigade camp. (H)

Kaffirs who sympathized with the British cause were employed as drivers, and later, as guards. This picture shows a Kaffir driving the Rifle Brigade's water cart. (H)

A Boer despatch rider. (A)

A derailed train lies forlornly on its side, surrounded by debris and spilling cargo. (T)

Lord Roberts was heartened by Buller's march up from the Natal line. On 29 July, he asked Buller to send a division of infantry, with cavalry, to clear the country between the Natal and Delagoa Bay Railways, and eventually to cover the right flank of the force already at Middelburg. It took Buller some time to prepare and assemble his force, meanwhile, Christian Botha concentrated his scattered bands of commandos (approximately 3 to 4,000 men with fourteen guns and a few pom-poms) on raiding the railway.

While Private Tucker remained in Heidelberg, Buller despatched a division of 9,000 men. His mounted troops forged forward, followed by the infantry and artillery, and succeeded in dislodging the Boers along the Komati River. Christian Botha, finding himself driven back, decided to divide up his force and scatter his line over fifty miles.

The Transvaal government had retired to a temporary base at Machadodorp and Kruger was housed in a private railway carriage, poised for flight.

'Mobility versus Immobility.'
A satirical sketch showing De Wet galloping away from the encumbered British, which was published in The Owl, *a South African paper, based in Cape Town. (R)*

25th July 1900

In camp at Greylingstad. Very cold and wet.

26th July 1900

At 2.00 p.m. we received sudden orders to pack up and move. This was quickly done. We marched to Vlakfontein: a distance of ten miles. It was quite dark when we reached camp. We pitched camp and got an issue of rum.

27th July 1900

Struck camp at 9.00 a.m. and marched to Zuikerbosch Spruit: arriving at 2.30 p.m.

28th July 1900

The morning was very misty so we stayed waiting for the fog to clear. At about 10.00 a.m. we were able to march for Heidelberg. Arrived there at 3.00 p.m. and camped about a mile and a half west of town. Heidelberg is a fair sized town and I expect we will have a long stay here.

29th July 1900

A day in camp.
   In the evening I heard some bells ringing for church service. This is the nearest approach to civilization I have encountered since the campaign started.

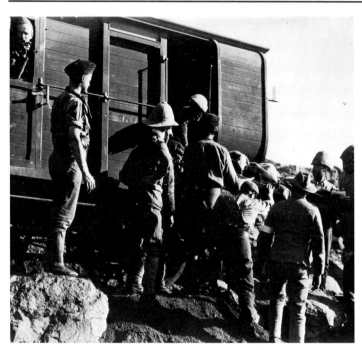

The Boers kept up a constant sniping fire in their efforts to deter the British from repairing the railway. This man, wounded in the stomach and hand, is being sent down to Greylingstad, the nearest hospital. (L)

30th July 1900

We are allowed to visit the town daily from 2.00 p.m. until 6.00 p.m. when not on duty. Today I had a run into town. There is not much to be seen. I indulged in a hot dinner of roast pork and vegetables, the price was 1/6d, and I also bought some beef sausages for 1/3d per pound.

31st July 1900

A day in camp.
    On outpost duty in the evening.

Visitor. 'What! You want to go too? But I'm afraid you're not big enough. You know the Boers are great, big, strong men.'
Bobbie. 'Well, but I s'pose there's Boer children, aren't there?'
    Indefatigable enthusiasm from the mouths of children. (B)

Erecting rough shelters for the men on outpost duty. The guards took turns to sleep for a few hours during the night. (A)

General Buller's camp at Paarde Kop, 3 August, 1900. From here he made his preparations for an advance on Ermelo.
In the background Paarde Kop rises, its peak shrouded in fog. (L)

1st August 1900

The Battalion moved to fresh camping ground; a more sheltered position under the hills. The Battalion has only five companies as three are away on detachment.

2nd August 1900

Every day, when not on duty, we are employed wall building or road making from 2.00 p.m until 5.00 p.m. This arrangement just prevents us from visiting the town or ever having an afternoon to ourselves!

3rd August 1900

Two more companies were sent on detachment, leaving three companies for duty.

4th August 1900

Every morning we parade for Arms Inspection at 10.00 a.m. and are then marched to the water for washing. We all try to attend this parade.
    Another half company sent on detachment.

5th August 1900

Stationed on outpost close by the town. While on sentry duty I could hear the hymns sung in the English church: it was just another reminder of home.

6th August 1900

August Bank Holiday, but the usual parade in the morning and inevitable road making in the afternoon.

Making coffee during a break from outpost duty. Life was rapidly settling down into a steady routine. (E)

7th August 1900

Usual duties.

8th August 1900

Great excitement about the capture of De Wet. Mail arrived today.

De Wet represented more to the Boers than simply his position as a leading general. He had become their driving force and Roberts, hoping to dampen their fighting spirit, made his capture a priority. However, despite the enormous force hunting him, De Wet travelled virtually unimpeded around South Africa. His force was much more mobile that the British columns, who could only hope to slow him down by commandeering every available horse in the vicinity, but somehow he and his men always managed to secure fresh mounts.

Tucker's cheerful entry, 'Great excitement about the capture of De Wet', is merely the result of a rumour. For those in pursuit, the game had become a nightmare. Many of the men were marching in rags and with hardly any boots; they had little sleep, often no food or water and hardly any fighting to whip up enthusiasm. The weary disappointment of the pursuing force was not reflected or understood in London. Music hall songs were peppered with thrilling references to the hunt and the Prince of Wales said of a zealous mother, who was determined to find an eligible husband for her daughter, 'They ought to set her to catch De Wet'.

Some of De Wet's Boers.
Most Boers went to war in their farm clothes, some—like General Cronje—carried parasols or umbrellas. Their only military insignia were Vierkleur ribbons round their slouch hats, adorned with the motto 'For God, Country and Justice,' or even a photograph of Kruger on the upturned brim. (A)

9th August 1900

Usual duties.

10th August 1900

Half company on picquet: half company on outpost. Same next day.

12th August 1900

Church service at 9.30 a.m. This is the first church service we have held for a long time. Sunday evening we were permitted, with a

Kruger and his government were now housed in two private railway carriages at Machadodorp, poised for flight. Except for Kruger, everyone ate at a nearby hotel which was doing amazing business even taking into account the fact that the value of Transvaal paper money had dropped by over half. The proprietor, loyal to his new customers, flew the Transvaal flag, except when there was an alarm, then he ran up the more neutral German flag.

A cloth-bound Boer hymn book. The Boers were a fervently religious people, indeed, Kruger based his policies on biblical texts and would issue circulars to his generals advising them to build their hopes on a particular Psalm. Thirty-three was a favourite.

The British and Foreign Bible Society, anxious in turn for British souls, sent 40,000 copies of the 'Psalter and Gospels' out to the troops in South Africa. (A)

Boers taking the oath of neutrality at Greylingstad. These men were dubbed 'hands-uppers' by the Boers still in the field and were often harassed. In a despatch to Lord Salisbury, Kitchener wrote, 'Numerous complaints were made to me by surrendered burghers, who stated that they had laid down their arms, their families were ill-treated and their stock and property confiscated by order of the Commandant Generals of the Transvaal and Orange Free State.' (K)

pass signed by the Company Officer, to go to church in town. I went and quite enjoyed the service: it was like being at home.

13th August 1900

Usual duties, parades and road making for the next few days.

Men settling down beneath the trees to read their mail: letters and newspapers were their only contact with home. (E)

On 14 August 1900, Roberts officially introduced a policy of farm burning. He had gradually severed the Boers' main supply routes; farms were the only potential depots left to them. Cattle and sheep were captured in their thousands, grain was seized or destroyed, crops were burnt, mills and farm-buildings were destroyed. The Boers, however, were by nature a self-sufficient and enterprising people. They could survive without too many material possessions and what they lacked in food and luxuries was easily obtained by raiding British convoys. Indeed, British weapons became so popular that, by the end of the war, the Boer forces were almost entirely re-equipped with them. It was normal practice for the Boers to trail the British columns, sometimes for a week or more, gleaning quantities of carelessly dropped ammunition.

Transport was a problem for the Boers as well as for the British. But they contrived to conceal their movements as successfully as the British managed to advertise their own.

'Saddle up! Khaki's coming!' was the warning cry, which would alert the Boers to the presence of the British.

17th August 1900

Usual parades. Mail came in.

19th August 1900

Church parade in camp.

20th August 1900

On town picquet. I patrolled the town from 4.30 p.m. to 8.00 p.m. Very dark with thunder-storms.

21st August 1900

Parade as usual.

22nd August 1900

Very wet day. Half company came off outpost wet through. I go on this evening.

23rd August 1900

I came off outpost at 6.00 a.m. with everything wet through. At 10.00 p.m. I was back on sentry duty. First it began to thunder and lighten, then the rain came down all night and it poured. I stayed on sentry for four hours and then lay down in my wet blanket and slept until nearly 6.00 a.m. During the day the sun came out and dried my blankets.

Road making in the afternoon.

24th August 1900

In the afternoon, we get news of the good work done by our 2nd Battalion.

Louis Botha with his decorated Mauser rifle. Throughout August, until he was stricken with quinsy, he was extremely active, rallying his men, determined to give Buller battle. (F)

Schalk Burgher, born in 1852, the Vice-President of the Transvaal, was elected acting President when Kruger crossed the frontier into Lourenço Marques. Originally a firm pacifist, he spent the next two years roaming the veldt with his staff, constantly dodging the British columns. (D)

25th August 1900

Each Saturday is a half day holiday for us. A cricket match generally takes place on the market square in the town between the garrison and civilians.

26th August 1900

Church parade in the morning.

Outpost at night.

We had rather an exciting time on outpost. About 10.00 p.m. a message was brought to our Captain, stating that an attack was expected about 1.00 a.m. (which would be about the time the moon went down). A party of Boers were known to be close to us; they had detained a Captain and some of Thorneycroft's Mounted Infantry who were out under a flag of truce. At 1.00 a.m. a train was due from Greylingstad to Heidelberg. Although they knew it was dangerous, the Boers attacked this train about a mile in front of us. The idea, presumably, was to blow the train up, but the dynamite exploded after the train had passed. They then fired on the stoker and driver, killing the stoker and seriously wounding the driver, who, despite his wounds, managed to fetch the train into the station all right. The Boers were supposed to be short of provisions and that was the reason they attacked the train.

27th August 1900

All quiet again. In the evening the Boers burned fires where the attack took place. We slept with boots and straps on in case they attacked us.

Boers waiting in ambush. There were 1,310 miles of railway to defend against the Boer attacks. Between June 1900 and June 1901, approximately 250 attacks took place. (F)

TO AVOID DETECTION—IF CAUGHT—OOM PAUL HAS SHAVED OFF HIS WHISKERS.—*Vide Daily Press*

"*They'll never think I'm old Kruger giving a hand with the blooming Commissariat!*"

Various rumours circulated on the whereabouts of Kruger at this time, it was even suggested that he had shaved his famous whiskers off to avoid detection. (D)

28th August 1900

Parades as usual.

29th August 1900

We went out at 3.30 a.m. to look for Boers—my company and a few of 'Thorney's' M.I.—but we didn't find any and returned about 2.00 p.m. Mail arrived.

31st August 1900

A day in camp, usual duties.

1st September 1900

Saturday. Usual duties. A very cold day.

2nd September 1900

Outpost again.

Spreading the news in London. (A)

On 1 September, Roberts formally annexed the Transvaal. Kruger issued a counter-proclamation stating that the annexation was null and void. But he was, by now, a fugitive in his own country and rapidly becoming a mill-stone around the neck of the mobile guerilla bands. It was decided, therefore, that he should leave for Europe, nominally for six months. On 11 September he left for Lourenço Marques, where he stayed as a guest of the Portuguese government until 19 October, when he sailed for Europe aboard the Netherlands cruiser, Gelderland, *placed at his disposal by the Queen of Holland. He was never to return to South Africa.*

British troops building roads in South Africa: a typical example of Tucker's 'usual duties.' (A)

Cornered! _ Bobs: "Guess I have time to enjoy an Ogden's 'Guinea-Gold' Cigarette." (Beware of Imitations)

Roberts was now convinced that the Boers would surrender. Without their President or any stable governing body he felt sure their defence would simply melt away, but he had not reckoned with the mercurial qualities of Steyn and Schalk Burger. (D)

3rd September 1900

Flying column arrived from Johannesburg, consisting of several companies from the Lancasters, Cheshires and Stafford Regiments, Brabant's Horse, Cape Mounted Rifles, Border Horse and several guns. This column is commandeering cattle and burning every Boer farm they come across. They expect to move off again shortly. I was on picquet in the evening.

A Boer farmer being arrested by Buller's men. Surrendered Boers were in an uneasy situation. Botha was busily forcing the men to join their commandos again, confiscating their property and leaving their families on the veldt if they refused, and yet, if they remained on their farms they immediately became suspect by the British. (D)

4th September 1900

Usual work road making and stone breaking. Same next day.

6th September 1900

Outpost in the evening.

7th September 1900

Column moved off at 6.00 a.m. Usual work, no fresh news.

9th September 1900

Church parade.

In September some attempt was made to reorganize the Boer forces and for the first time a scale of pay was introduced:

Commandant-General	20s	per day
General	15s	per day
Commandant	10s	per day
Field Cornet	7s 6d	per day
Rank and file	5s	per day

Half the pay was to be given every two months and half at the end of the war, but no pay was ever received.

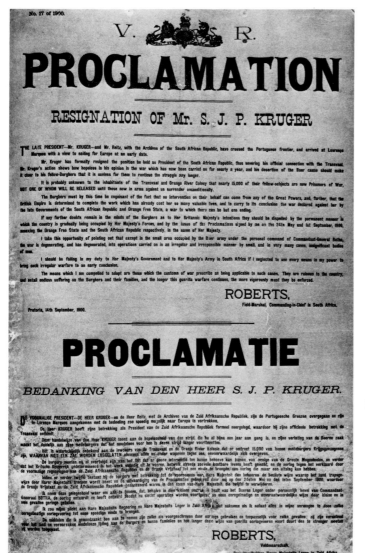

THE PILGRIM'S REST.
Pilgrim Kruger. 'Farewell, a long farewell, to all my greatness! Kruger's "Occupation's" gone!' (B)

A fairly threatening proclamation from Roberts reminding the Boers of Kruger's departure. The men on commando, however, defused these 'paper bombs' with a few derisory comments. (A)

The farm burning was causing hostility and resentment among the Boers, especially when it became evident that Roberts' orders were being exceeded and looting had become prevalent.

After almost a year, Christian De Wet wrote to Roberts: 'Complaints are repeatedly reaching me that private dwellings are plundered, and in some cases totally destroyed, and all provisions taken from women and children, so that they are compelled to wander about without food or covering. To quote several instances: It has just been brought to my notice by way of sworn affidavit that the house of Field-Cornet S. Buys, on the farm, Leeuwspruit district, Middelburg, was set on fire and destroyed on 20 June last. His wife, who was at home, was given five minutes' time to remove her bedding and clothing, and even what she took out was again taken from her. Her food, sugar etc. was all taken, so that for herself and her children she had neither covering nor food for the following night. She was asked for the key of the safe, and after it was given up by her she was threatened with a sword, and money was demanded. All the money that was in the house was taken away, all the papers in the safe were torn up, and everything at the homestead that could not be taken away was destroyed.

'It has also been reported to me that my own buildings on the farm, Varkenspruit district, Standerton, as well as the house of Field-Cornet Badenhorst, on the adjoining farm, have been totally destroyed, and such of the stock as was not removed was shot dead on the farm.'

Even after Roberts had clamped down on his men, imposing stringent punishments for looting, there were still some Boer farms wrongfully destroyed. A nearby commando raid jeopardized any surrounding farms, because they were often accused of harbouring snipers, and so destroyed.

Each regiment of the British Army had its own march past tune. The Rifle Brigade, who marched in short, jaunty steps, strode by to the tune of Ninety-five, *while the King's Royal Rifles filed past more sedately to the strains of the* Huntsman's Chorus.

A military funeral; under a warm South African sun the Chaplain reads the final address. (A)

10th September 1900

Outpost in the evenings for the next few days. Mail arrived on the Wednesday, 12 September.

14th September 1900

Friday, news of General Babington making a big capture of rolling stock and guns.

16th September 1900

Church parade.

18th September 1900

Outpost. Next day the same.

20th September 1900

Band instruments arrive from Pietermaritzburg.

21st September 1900

A slight engagement took place between one hundred Boers and thirty of 'Thorney's' M.I. The Boers ambushed the M.I. and killed one and wounded two or three. Four Boers were killed.

22nd September 1900

The band played the Dead March at the funeral of one of 'Thorney's' Mounted Infantry. General Cooper was present.

THE SINKING SHIP.

THE SINKING SHIP
British newspapers carried reports that Kruger had taken two million pounds out of the country with him. The 'Kruger Millions', if they existed, were never recovered. (B)

By the end of September the Boers in the eastern Transvaal were entirely cut off from their base of supply and from communication with the outside world. They had destroyed nearly all their artillery and a vast quantity of stores for the sake of mobility. Kruger was in Europe, most of the foreign volunteers had returned home, but the Boers appeared to be as determined as before.

23rd September 1900

Church parade. This day we had a proper service, the first for a long time. The band played the Battalion to church.

At 7.00 p.m. the Battalion were ordered to escort a convoy to our detachment at Nigel, eleven miles distance. Thorneycroft's Mounted Infantry and one gun went with the party as an attack was expected. The men that remained in camp were in high fever, for in the evening a party of Boers, numbering 2,400 men with guns, were reported to be near them, but they never saw any. We returned about 10.30 p.m. after marching about twenty miles. The bandsmen and those left in camp went on outpost instead of 'A' company.

Everyone in the Battalion kept their belts and boots on all night but no Boers came near us.

The regimental band was an enormous boost to the morale of the men in the field. Every Sunday morning the sound of Bonny Christchurch Bells *would summon the men to church. And, if a soldier was unlucky enough to be 'drummed-out' of the army— usually for bad conduct—the band would be right there with him, playing, naturally, the* Rogue's March.

'From Different Points of View!'
A cartoon from the Dutch magazine, Amsterdammer, *showing the Boer idea of the Englishman as a piratical burglar and the English view of the Boer as an uncouth bully, ill-treating African natives. (R)*

In the beginning of October a force of South African Constabulary was recruited. General Baden-Powell, back in action after Mafeking, was given command of the force, which had duties extending over the two newly annexed republics. (C)

In October, the Household Cavalry, the whole of the C.I.V. regiment, the Royal Canadian regiment, and the Royal Canadian Dragoons, and other bodies of overseas colonials and South African volunteers were allowed to go home.

1st October 1900

The men paraded for road making but the Company Officer dismissed them. We even kept in readiness for turning out all the remainder of the week and everyone was confined to camp.

2nd October 1900

Usual duties. The band play to the troops each evening from 5.00 p.m. to 6.00 p.m.

3rd October 1900

Usual duties, mail arrived.

6th October 1900

Draft arrived, consisting mostly of men who had previously been invalided home from South Africa, and men who had been wounded. Some were young soldiers. About one hundred in all.

7th October 1900

Sunday in camp. Church parade.

9th October 1900

Usual parade and get the news that our two companies at Vlakfontein have been in an engagement.

10th October 1900

Received casualty list of 'G' and 'I' Companies. Two captains and one man killed, seven wounded and six taken prisoner. At 5.00 p.m. a special funeral service was held: the Battalion band played the Dead March and hymns.

Medical men attending to a wounded soldier in a field hospital, sited beneath the shade of a small copse. (A)

11th October 1900

We were ordered to prepare for a move at 4.00 p.m. The 1st Coldstream Guards, who had come from Pretoria by rail, relieved us. The Battalion (four companies only) and four companies of the King's Royal Rifles moved to Heidelberg Station and waited for the moon to rise. At 9.30 p.m. we moved off again and marched to Kraal Station, a distance of seven miles, and bivouacked for a few hours. My company was on outpost.

12th October 1900

We rolled our blankets and coats (all we have with us) into bundles and loaded the wagons at 5.00 a.m. We then made our own coffee for breakfast and started marching at 7.00 a.m.

After two hours marching, we arrived at Zuikerbosch and halted close by a stream. It was a scorching hot day and we had no shelter from the sun. We remained there until 3.00 p.m., when we moved off and marched to Vlakfontein, a distance of eight miles.

It was 7.00 p.m. and quite dark when we arrived. I walked to a farm about 300 yards away, where I found some water, though it wasn't very good. In the morning we discovered that it was the hole the cattle drank from. It was better than none, though admittedly it did have rather a funny taste. But what does a man care in this country when he is dry and thirsty? We made tea and afterwards received an issue of rum and had a good night's sleep. We were told to expect a good fight in the morning and an opportunity to have our revenge for our comrades who fell near this spot on 8 October.

As Tucker was making room for one hundred new recruits in Heidelberg, his old general, Buller, was bidding his men farewell in Lydenburg. Buller, who had always valued his mens' lives and their welfare very highly, was possibly the most popular general among the ranks. On 9 November he arrived at Southampton and was enthusiastically welcomed. His military mistakes were never wholly overlooked, however, and after a controversial Royal Commission enquiry he retired to the privacy of his manor in Downes, where, on 2 June 1908, he died.

The disaster of 8 October, which Tucker was so anxious to avenge, was practically a repeat of the earlier armoured train ambush at Chieveley, when, on 15 November 1899, Churchill and seventy men had been captured. On this occasion, a detachment of the Rifle Brigade were ambushed while reconnoitering the line towards Vlakfontein. A large force of Boers, led by Hans Botha, opened a terrific fire on the train, wounding seven and killing two before the British were compelled to surrender. It was generally believed that Boer sympathizers inside Heidelberg had tipped Botha off.

The ambush of the armoured train near Vlakfontein. The Boers blew up two culverts behind the train to cut off any support and tore the rails up in front of the engine, then they fired into the stranded carriages forcing the men to surrender. (F)

A group of Boers. Entering the second year of the war, the Boers had become more determined than ever to fight. (A)

13th October 1900

We were up by 6.00 a.m. and rolled up our blankets and coats, packed the wagons and then had a breakfast of salt bacon, coffee and biscuits. We marched off at 9.00 a.m. and joined General Clery with his troops, consisting of two infantry regiments, Thorneycroft's Mounted Infantry, one 5-inch gun, one howitzer battery and one field battery. When all was ready, we moved off again on the ridge of hills, towards Zuickerbosch and Heidelberg.

Breakfast time.
Bully beef for breakfast, bully beef for tea,
Biscuits as hard as bathbricks, a hundred
*   years at sea.*
Adam's knife and fork boys, Nature's
*   cutlery,*
But there's gun-fire tea for Kruger in the
*   morning. (E)*

About 11.00 a.m. Boers were sighted and our 5-inch gun opened fire on their laager. We continued the advance and passed by a Volunteer Sergeant of the Devons' who was being bandaged up. He had picked up a dynamite cartridge and half his face and two fingers on his left hand had been blown off.

About 1.00 p.m. we halted for half an hour. The Rifle Brigade then advanced to another kopje. The Mounted Infantry opened fire on the right of us. The Boers were retiring so we could not get near them and after a long march on the top of the kopje the pom-pom came up and opened fire. The 5-inch gun was also firing. The work of chasing the Boers was then finished for that day.

There were several small farms situated around and General Clery gave the order for all of the houses to be destroyed.

Rudyard Kipling, poet and writer, produced this sketch: his own satirical impression of the clumsy and blatant British pursuit of De Wet. His vehicle was designed to travel at walking pace and was preceded by a red flag of warning! (D)

In destroying the farms, General Clery was acting on the orders of Lord Roberts, who had conveyed his intentions to the Boer generals two months earlier. The following is an extract from a letter to Christian De Wet: 'Latterly, many of my soldiers have been shot from farmhouses over which the white flag has been flying, the railway and telegraph lines have been cut, and trains wrecked. I have therefore found it necessary, after warning Your Honour, to take such steps as are sanctioned by the customs of war to put an end to these and similar acts, and have burned down the farmhouses at or near which such deeds have been perpetrated. This I shall continue to do whenever I consider the occasion demands it.'

Clearing a Boer homestead.
The women were given ten minutes to pack their belongings before their homes were razed to the ground. (E)

British soldiers loading their loot on to a wagon. If the items they took for themselves were too large to transport, they simply commandeered a Boer wagon; after all, it was only going to be burned. (A)

Burning farms became a daily part of Tucker's military routine, but far from deterring the Boers, the outrage it inspired became their driving force.

This is an extract from General Smuts report to Mr Steyn, President of the Orange Free State. 'I feel altogether incapable of giving a description, even a mere sketch, of the devastation brought about by the enemy; of the pains and troubles caused to us, which have touched the hearts of our women and children as if they had been pierced by steel.

'Let me take as an example that part of the Krugersdorp district situated between the Magalies and Witwaters mountains; one of the most beautiful, most fertile, and best cultivated parts of South Africa, the so-called 'fillet'. When I came to these parts in July 1900, the land was green with an uninterrupted series of cultivated fields, gardens, and charming houses and farmsteads, a delight to the eye, and a proof of what our people had been able to do with respect to agriculture in half a score of years. And now? It is now a withered, barren waste; all the fields have been destroyed, the trees of the gardens cut down or pulled up by the roots; the homesteads burnt down, the houses in many cases not only destroyed by fire but blown up by dynamite, so that not a stone was left unturned; a refuge only for the night owl and carrion birds. Where, till lately, everything was life, prosperity and cheerfulness, death now reigns. No living animal, no woman, no child, not even a Kaffir woman is seen but with the traces of anxiety, misery, nay even with starvation, distinctly visible on their faces.'

My company was given the job of burning several small farms to the left and we moved off at once. Arriving at the farms, the women and children were ordered out and after every man had taken any article he thought fit, the furniture was broken up and the houses and all the goods were set on fire. Some men were busy killing fowls, ducks, geese and pigs and getting anything that was useful. It was good sport, but hard for the women and children. After all had been destroyed we returned to the remainder of the Battalion and shared all the loot equally among the company.

In addition to the twenty head of poultry, we also drove seventy head of cattle and horses back to camp. This was the best day's sport we had had, but our blankets didn't arrive until about 1.00 a.m. as all our baggage had been kept well in the rear.

A carriage—frail symbol of Boer family life before the war—is destroyed. (A)

14th October 1900

We were up about 5.00 a.m., loaded the wagons and marched back to the remainder of the column where our supply wagon was situated. The other troops had slept under canvas except for us and the King's Royal Rifles. We had none with us.

A rest day.

At 8.00 a.m. we moved to a commanding position on a high hill and bivouacked.

At 7.00 p.m. my section had a hearty supper of our loot, consisting of boiled chicken and ducks. An excellent meal, which we finished with an issue of rum.

Back in Britain another battle had been fought. On 25 September, Lord Salisbury had requested a dissolution of Parliament and the Election campaign had begun immediately.

Many Liberals had been campaigning against the war for some time; scenes of mob violence had greeted anti-war speakers such as Lloyd George and groups with names like the League of Liberals Against Aggression and Militarism and the Peace Society had sprung up. The British public were disappointed that the war, which was enormously costly, was not over and much of the campaigning had centred on this fact. The Unionists had implied that the Liberals were on Kruger's side in the war, and had even had posters printed showing Liberals helping Kruger to pull down the Union Jack and shoot British soldiers. The Liberals had made wild accusations against Chamberlain, suggesting that he was making a personal profit from armaments. In the event, the Unionists won the 'Khaki' Election on 14 October with a majority of 134 seats.

British troops bivouacking on the veldt. Often, if the baggage wagons were slow, the men had to sleep without tents. (A)

The war was, by now, costing the British taxpayer a phenomenal sum. Punch *came up with a suggestion:*

What shall we do with Kruger?
 What shall we do with Paul?
Then why not boom the old man 'Oom'
 At a leading Music Hall?
On show he would draw the shilling
 That heralds the popular star,
And if Kruger were only willing,
 He might nearly pay for the war.

All the comforts of home. Using brushwood and ingenuity these men have built their own dining room. (A)

Although Tucker was aware of the cold during the night, he does not appear to have worried overly about the fate of those he was making homeless. However, many men expressed their concern and doubt in letters home; one soldier assured his sister that he always fired into the air, another, Private H. Philpott, wrote: 'For the last four or five days we have been burning the farms of the men who are absent from home and who are suspected of being away fighting for the Boers. If the farmer was away, down the house had to come. No matter whatever the wife said to excuse her husband, the farm was destroyed. The farms burned well, there's no mistake. But we gave the wives time to get everything out of the houses they wanted before setting fire to them. I must say that I felt very sorry for the poor children who were turned out of their home.'

15th October 1900

I find it very cold during the night and early morning.

The regiment was employed nearly all day building walls. In the evening, my company was on outpost duty. The left half lined the walls and the right half remained some distance behind in support. It was a very quiet night.

16th October 1900

The left half of the company remained on outpost all day. The right half (which included myself) returned to the bivouacks at 6.30 a.m. We were on a ridge of hills between Vlakfontein and Zuickerbosch. The place is named Edens Kop Reitfontein. Our Colonel is keeping the men employed with his favourite amusement—stone wall building. We worked from 8.30 a.m. to 11.00 a.m. and from 3.00 p.m. to 5.00 p.m. daily, so you see it is not all honey to be a sweep as we are called.

Today I went out with an armed party to get wood from a farm we had destroyed.

17th October 1900

The battalion on wall building.

My section paraded at 12 noon for escort duty. The duty was to meet a train and collect the rations. The train also brought tents for us. On return to camp we pitched canvas. We also brought the mail with us. I got a letter from Jim.

18th October 1900

Wall building from 8.30 a.m. until 11.30 a.m. Our Maxim gun opened fire about 1.00 p.m. on a few Boers.

Washing parade at 4.00 p.m.

The 5-inch gun and pom-pom also fired several rounds in the afternoon.

A pom-pom gun in action. These Vickers-Maxim guns were also nicknamed ten-a-penny. The earliest type of machine gun had been used by the French in 1870 against the Prussians. A more refined version of this gun, used in World War I was described by Lloyd George as the most lethal modern weapon. (A)

Two men of the Rifle Brigade manning a machine gun in the line of defence on Eden's Kop. (H)

19th October 1900

Wall building from 8.30 a.m. to 11.30 a.m. and from 3.00 p.m. to 4.30 p.m. At 5.30 p.m. we were on outpost duty. At 7.00 p.m. we had just a little excitement: several rounds were fired by us at Boers walking about on a hill near us.

20th October 1900

My section remained on outpost as the observation post.
Band played to troops in the evening.

21st October 1900

Church parade at 8.15 a.m. At 9.00 a.m. we went to wash our clothing.
There was a severe storm in the afternoon.

22nd October 1900

Wall building in the afternoon. Severe storm. Band played to troops in evening.

One method of drying off after a bath. (A)

The Regimental Band preparing to play in the Rifle Brigade camp at Eden's Kop. The band represented one of the few sources of entertainment available to the men when camped on the open veldt and was very popular. (H)

A British sniper setting his sights. (A)

A group of Boers relaxing beside their bag after a day's bushbuck hunting. They killed not for sport but for food—a large commando could number several hundred men. (W)

23rd October 1900

Usual duties.

24th October 1900

Stormy weather. No work building. Sniping at Boers during the day.

25th October 1900

General French came near us. His scouts came into camp and we kept up communication by heliograph. He is making for Heidelberg.

26th October 1900

About noon the pom-pom and two companies went out and fired a few rounds. Usual duties.

27th October 1900

Usual duties. Very wet night.

28th October 1900

Church parade at 9.00 a.m.

It was a fine windy day and I did my usual weekly wash of clothing.

29th October 1900

Dull, foggy day. We received information that about 400 Boers with guns were near us. High fever in camp.

30th October 1900

At 4.00 a.m. we had to put our belts on and turn out in case of attack, but nothing came of it.

At 9.00 a.m. two companies went out ('A' and 'E'). We heard news that the Boers have been severely beaten in the Orange River Colony. The two companies returned with an immense quantity of mealies.

31st October 1900

Wet day again, but it cleared up in time for us to do some more stone wall building!

1st November 1900

Reported death of General De Wet.

A very wet night, company on outpost.

2nd November 1900

Company came off outpost looking like drowned rats. One section remained out. The rain poured down all day. Mail arrived.

3rd November 1900

Showery day. Usual duties.

At midnight one company attacked a farm.

4th November 1900

Church Parade and the usual Sunday spent washing and bathing.

6th November 1900

Usual duties, but stop to watch the pom-pom shelling. Boers tried to capture native scouts.

7th November 1900

Two companies ('A' and 'F') went to Vlakfontein to escort the 5-inch gun back.

8th November 1900

At 8.00 a.m. our Colonel took three companies, the Maxim, pom-pom and cavalry to attack the enemy who were in the vicinity and would not leave us. Several Boers were sighted and

'De Wet O' De Wisp.'
De Wet's uncanny ability to evade the British led Punch *to attribute him with magical powers. (B)*

The British employed large numbers of natives as transport drivers, labourers and guides. The Boers, too, used native guides. However, gradually the British had begun arming them and they were employed mostly in local defence (the Zululand Police, for example) and, later still, as nightwatchmen on blockhouse lines. The Boers, who had the horrors of the recent native wars fresh in their memories, deplored this practice and, if they caught a Kaffir, whom they suspected of aiding the British, they had no qualms about shooting him in cold blood. (E)

A heavily stylised illustration from the
Illustrated London News *of four men beside*
a damaged Vickers-Maxim gun. (D)

The truth about the farm burning was just
beginning to seep into British newspaper
reports, but, with the evidence on their
doorsteps, South African papers were filled
with distressing accounts. This extract is
from the Cape Times: *'Along the line of*
march General Campbell has practically
denuded the country of livestock and grain
stores, whilst the sight of burning
farmhouses and farm property is of daily
occurrence. A number of old men, many
sickly, who until recently held good-conduct
passes, have been made prisoners, and
accompany the column. These are cases
where women and children, the families of
prisoners of war either at Green Point or
Ceylon, have been subsisting upon the
charity of their neighbours, who, however,
are but little better off than themselves.'

heavy firing took place. The Maxim fired about 2,000 rounds,
our 5-inch gun fired nearly all day. We returned about 4.00 p.m.
Casualties were: the Captain of the cavalry and a native guide
wounded.

9th November 1900

The Battalion (three companies) moved off. Band and buglers
and one company left to garrison the hill. The regiment captured
one or two Boers, burnt several farms, and captured an immense
herd of cattle near Vlakfontein.

10th November 1900

We returned to the hill at about mid-day. Our 5-inch gun fired a
few shells at stray Boers.

11th November 1900

Usual church parade and washing.

12th November 1900

General Cooper visited us in the evening and stayed until the next
day.

13th November 1900

Battalion went out after Johnny Boer again, much firing, but
found the Boer post too strong. We returned about 4.00 p.m.

14th November 1900

Battalion went to Vlakfontein. Very wet day. Boers everywhere
round the hill. 5-inch gun drops seven shells into one farm.

This report in the Morning Leader *was*
written by E. W. Smith: 'Two white flags
were displayed over the house of Christian
Richter; a shot was fired at random.
'The first sight which met my gaze was
that of a score of men, some with their feet
on the necks of turkeys, ducks and fowls.
Quicker than it takes me to tell the story, the
women and children had been discovered in
an outhouse; several troopers were occupied
pouring paraffin about the flooring and walls
of the house. Within five minutes the
dwelling was ablaze. Still the womenfolk
rushed in and out, trying to save what they
could.'

15th November 1900

Battalion returned about 1.00 p.m.
   Lord Kitchener passed through by train. Wet night.

16th November 1900

Usual duties. Wet day.

17th November 1900

Rumours of a move. Wet day and night.

18th November 1900

Usual Church parade and washing.

19th November 1900

Very wet day. Four men struck by lightning.

20th November 1900

Usual duties.

21st November 1900

Battalion moved to Vlakfontein.

22nd November 1900

Battalion returned.

Lord Horatio Herbert Kitchener was born in 1850. After attending the Royal Military Academy at Woolwich, he entered the Royal Engineers and travelled to Palestine and Cyprus. In 1882 he commanded the Egyptian Cavalry and finally the whole army throughout the Sudan Campaign. He hated the press and made sure that they knew it, shouting, 'Get out of my way you drunken swabs,' to a group of journalists outside his tent. He never married. (C)

A more gentle use for bayonets. In the left of the picture there is a chair—General Buller had travelled with various items of furniture which included a grand piano. (E)

Roberts was appointed to the post of Commander-in-Chief in England, succeeding Lord Wolseley, whose term of office had expired, and before he handed over to Kitchener, he issued a further order on farm burning:
'As there appears to be some misunderstanding with reference to burning of farms and breaking of dams, Commander-in-Chief wishes following to be lines on which General Officers Commanding are to act: No farm is to be burnt except for act of treachery, or when troops have been fired on from premises, or as punishment for breaking of telegraph or railway line, or when they have been used as bases of operations for raids, and then only with direct consent of General Commanding, which is to be given in writing; the mere fact of a burgher being absent on commando is on no account to be used as reason for burning the house. All cattle, wagons, and food-stuffs are to be removed from all farms; if that is found to be impossible, they are to be destroyed, whether owner is present or not.'

A French propaganda illustration depicting the British soldiers revelling in the burning of a farm while the women and children watched hopelessly. True or false? (P)

23rd November 1900

Stormy day. Battalion went out again leaving the band to look after the hill.

24th November 1900

Looked for Boers.

25th November 1900

Returned to camp and prepared to move.

26th November 1900

Ready to move, but do not.

27th November 1900

Relieved by the Devon Regiment, encamp at the foot of Edens Kop. Spend the day washing clothes.

28th November 1900

Left Edens Kop at 8.15 a.m. Our field guns opened fire about one hour after the column moved out. Boers troublesome.

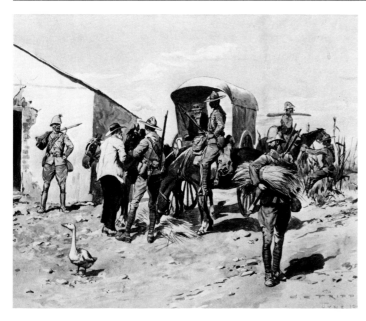

British troops searching a Boer farm for weapons or harboured fighting men. (A)

We had a hard day, fired plenty of rounds, captured thousands of cattle, brought some women and children in; they had a flag of truce, we burnt their farms. Rain came on, we were wet through. No tea. No rum. Pitched camp and slept in wet clothing all night.

29th November 1900

At rest on Vlakfontein Nek.

30th November 1900

Marched from Vlakfontein to Edens Kop.

1st December 1900

Reveille at 4.00 a.m. Parade at 5.00 a.m. to attack (I remained with the wagons as I had been appointed a new job) in conjunction with Ian Hamilton who started from Nigel. After much shelling the men advanced on the position, but there was nothing to fear, for the Boers had cleared out before we arrived. The farms had been destroyed and the women sent away. I had a good feed of fruit.

Hans Botha about here.

The camp was pitched on such a steep hill that the battalion had to be sent for to help pull the wagons up. Reached camp about 8.30 p.m.

2nd December 1900

Battalion in camp.

Me and the Quartermaster-Sergeant went with the wagon to collect the rations. We started out at 8.00 a.m. and returned at 5.00 p.m.

General Ian Hamilton was born in 1853. He was a soldier of great distinction, who collected medals and fame during the Afghan War, the Nile Expedition and in Burma. He was no stranger to South Africa—he had been wounded in the Battle of Majuba in 1881. (D)

Kruger, it will be remembered, had fled to Europe aboard the Dutch ship, Gelderland, on 19 October. His intention was to submit the case between the Boer and the British to International arbitration, and with this in mind, on 1 December, he docked in France, 'the home of freedom'.

Both in Marseilles and in Paris he was greeted by deafening cheers of Vive Kruger! Vive la liberté! Vive l'arbitrage! from admiring crowds, and during his brief speeches—delivered in Dutch—he vowed that, unless the Boers had justice, they would fight until their last breath.

A Boer farm burning. (A)

Another British soldier's point of view is provided by Lieutenant Morrison, who wrote:
'There were a number of very fine farms nearby, and we saw the Boers leaving them and making off. The provost-marshal came up from the main body, removed the Boer women and children with their bedding, and proceeded to burn or blow up the houses. From that time on during the rest of our trek, which lasted four days, our progress was like the old-time forages in the highlands of Scotland two centuries ago. . . We moved on from valley to valley 'lifting' cattle and sheep, burning, looting and turning out women and children to sit and cry beside the ruins of their once beautiful farmsteads. . . It was a terrible thing to see, and I don't know that I want to see another trip of this sort, but we could not help approving of the policy, though it rather revolted most of us to be the insurgents.'

3rd December 1900

In camp at Resquervad. Another journey for rations. Regiment digging trenches.

4th December 1900

Usual duties. One company went out looting a farm.

5th December 1900

Very wet morning, but we struck camp and marched into Heidelberg, leaving two companies of the Essex Regiment from Ian Hamilton's column, on the hill. We marched the eleven miles and arrived at Heidelberg about 5.00 p.m.

Our artillery opened fire on a farm close by the camping ground as soon as we arrived.

6th December 1900

Busy day collecting rations.

7th December 1900

Paraded at 2.00 a.m. My company led off. At daybreak Boers were sighted on a kopje just in front of us. I was with the baggage, and we didn't leave before 5.00 a.m. We heard the guns firing in front of us and we still kept on so as to catch up with the Battalion before dark.

A fine day we had looting farms, we found in nearly every farm the tables laid out for twelve or fourteen and the food consisted of mutton and goat and vegetables cooked over open fires. So you can guess how they lived. We had all we wanted and burnt the remainder. I know we made our mess up nicely with plates, knives, forks, spoons and mugs, and cooking pots, pails and cans. In fact, we had more than we wanted.

Wagon loads of furniture taken from Boer farms. Roberts' policy of destruction was rapidly undermining the whole fabric of the Boer community, introducing dissension into a climate of fear and distress. (A)

A chicken-looting party. From now on, it was open season on farmyard fowl. (A)

And chickens, all sorts of poultry and pork, as much as we could carry away. Me, being one of the lucky ones, having a place where I could keep it on our own wagon. I made sure of getting enough whilst I had a chance. And then I collected as many peaches and apricots as I could carry in a bag, so you see I didn't do bad.

We found the regiment at about 6.00 p.m. and then we kept walking on till we could find a suitable place to camp. It was 7.00 p.m. by the time camp was pitched and then I had a fine job of issuing rations for the next day. I think I finished for the day at 10.00 p.m. The men took their food with them for that day. The Colonel told us how lucky we had been. Apparently a large party of Boers had been sighted on our left, which means that they had been between us and the regiment. How they missed seeing us with all the wagons I'll never know. They would have given us a warm time of it, sure enough. We never saw any of the column from the time they left us at 2.00 a.m. until 6.00 p.m. All I knew was that they were in the hills somewhere and I could hear the big guns. It was a very anxious time.

The name of this place is Kaffir Kraal.

Following Robert's new order on farm burning, a soldier caught looting was liable to imprisonment. However, as Tucker was accompanied by officers he was not 'looting', he was 'annexing', while the authorities were even busier, 'comandeering' grain supplies and live stocks.

8th December 1900

Rested in the morning. So we amused ourselves watching the Engineers burning the farms and blowing them up. There were about twenty farms surrounding our camping site. Apparently the homes belonged, formerly, to English people before the war broke out. They were put over the border by the Boers who then possessed their property and used it as if they had owned it all their lives.

A remarkable sequence of photographs recording the destruction of a Boer farmhouse. (A)

We had thought we were stopping there all day but at 2.30 p.m. we moved off again taking several thousand head of cattle with us: sheep, goats, oxen and horses. After going about three miles we came across some more farms and my company ('A') were ordered to destroy them and 'make a good job of it, too', our Colonel said.

My friend told me how they marched off at once and set out to destroy one little farm, a nice little home it was. It seemed a shame to destroy it, There were two women and several children there. One of the women was not in a fit state to be moved so the Captain of the company refused to burn it, but he told the men to have a thorough search of the house and take anything they liked, so they only burnt the men's clothing. They then returned to us and found their tents had been pitched for them.

They were all well loaded up with ducks, poultry and numerous other articles. The remainder of my company had done well at the other houses in the vicinity especially one, a Parsee merchant's store. The men helped themselves to the best of everything in the way of silks and things. Afterwards they returned to camp with about a dozen Parsee prisoners with them. After they had had a good tea and a ration of rum they had a good night's sleep. As usual they had to sleep with their belts and boots on as they were the company on early picquet.

This place is called Blesbok Laagte.

9th December 1900

We were encamped near Elandfontein and in view of the Retz Kop camp. We are expected to remain here for a few days.

Some companies of the Battalion went out destroying farms with the Engineers. About 11.00 a.m. the alarm was sounded and every man had to parade.

We were soon told of a very disgraceful thing that had taken place during the night and early morning at one of the farmhouses. Two Dutch women walked round the ranks and looked hard at every man, but could not find the two men in my regiment.

Some of the thousands made homeless by the British. The refugees were transferred to the nearest of a score or so of concentration camps, where they remained for the duration of the war. (E)

The affair made the Colonel issue very strict orders to everyone. No one is allowed to leave camp in future whilst we are employed on this Mobile Column and picquets are kept all around the camp day and night to keep everyone in. The man who committed the disgraceful affair has been found out. He was a Colonial belonging to the ISB Company.

10th December 1900

Struck camp and marched off about 9.00 a.m. The Battalion went skirmishing over all the high hills they could find.

About 1.00 p.m. we were told that we were headed straight for Heidelberg. This was rather a surprise for we had not expected to go there. We arrived about 7.00 p.m., pitched camp and had a good night's rest after a hard day burning every farm we came across on the veldt.

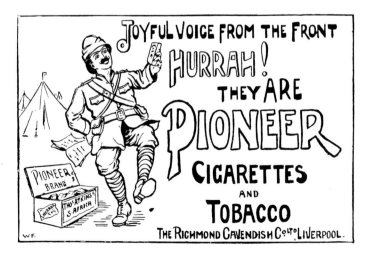

The sight of destitute and homeless women and children was becoming increasingly familiar throughout South Africa. (L)

Varying reports of Boer atrocities appeared in British publications, ranging from rape to murder, here the Globe correspondent attempts to put the record straight:
The Boers are by no means the undisciplined rabble which some people would have us believe. It is not too much to say that there was more indiscriminate looting done after the Modder River fight in a few days by the British than was done by the Boers in the whole six weeks before the fight. It is certainly worthy of remark that the Boers, who are not supposed to have any discipline at all, have, in this part of the country, apparently behaved with exemplary consideration for the rights of private property.
But above the clamour of blame and insinuation his voice was barely heard. The facts about farm burning and looting were gradually being made known, and the British public was eager to paint the Boers blacker than themselves. 'Pro-Boers' were not popular and Lloyd George was pelted with bricks—sold for the purpose at three-a-penny—when he tried to address a meeting in Chamberlain's political stronghold of Birmingham. He just managed to escape with his life by disguising himself as a policeman.

In the Continental Press the British troops were frequently accused of raping Boer women. There is little evidence to support or demolish these claims. In his book, With 'Bobs' and Kruger, Frederick Unger, an American correspondent who followed both the British columns and then the Boer commandos, reported the following conversation:
An old burgher was found crying bitterly. 'Why man,' said a friend, 'this is not the way to take defeat.'
'Ah,' was the reply, 'the English have destroyed my farms and taken my cattle; they have burned my home; and of my four sons, two are dead and two are prisoners; they have robbed us of our liberty, have taken our country and our capital; they have taken my house in the city, and, not content with all this, they have now robbed my daughters of their honour.'

The British soldier was perhaps the only person who did have anything to cheer about. For the commandos, life had become one long emergency, accentuated by the distressing plight of their families. (D)

Farm Burning and Concentration Camps

A British soldier's sketch of the 'trials' of looting. A stern Vrou is shown looking reprovingly down on the men's antics. (A)

In addition to their homes, most of the fighting burghers' clothing had been destroyed by the British and they were reduced either to rags or to stripping the khaki uniforms from dead troops, unaware that, if caught wearing the British uniform, they could be shot at once as rebels.

The British army moved across the veldt like a plague of locusts. Anything that could not be eaten or transported was destroyed. (A)

'When is a war not a war?
When it is carried on by methods of barbarism in South Africa.'
Henry Campbell-Bannerman, Liberal Leader.

As 1900 lurched fitfully to a close, Britain found herself more entangled than ever in South Africa. As has already been shown, Roberts' controversial policy of farm-burning had had little success in intimidating the Boers into surrender. Instead, it had driven more burghers back to their commandos, determined now to defend their country and exhibiting a resourcefulness and bravery which won them the admiration of the world. Following the annexation of the Transvaal and the Orange Free State, Roberts had issued a variety of proclamations, contradicting or reinforcing each other, all of which confirmed his persistent belief that the Boers were no longer regular combatants, but rebels, to be punished as such.

In the outlying districts many fighting burghers were completely unaware of the succession of proclamations and it was not until they came upon a ruined house or one of their number was shot for wearing a British uniform that the full horror of the situation came home to them.

'During the course of the morning,' wrote Deneys Reitz, 'pillars of smoke began to rise behind the English advance and to our astonishment we saw that they were burning the farmhouses as they came. Towards noon word spread that, not only were they destroying all before them, but were actually capturing and sending away the women and children.

'At first we could hardly credit this, but when one wild-eyed woman after another galloped by, it was borne in on us that a

Clearing a Boer farmstead. Any vehicle which could conceivably be of use to the commandos was destroyed along with the farm buildings, crops and forage. (A)

more terrible chapter of the war was opening. . . By now, the news had spread that the English were clearing the country, with the result that the entire civil population from the farms was moving. . . . The plain was alive with wagons, carts and vehicles of all descriptions, laden with women and children, while great numbers of horses, cattle and sheep were being hurried onward by native herdboys, homes and ricks going up in flames behind them.'

Some Boer women and children left their farms before the arrival of the British. Knowing that their homes would be destroyed and that they would be sent to camps, perhaps even split up from their children, they preferred to take their chances on the open veldt and struck out alone, hoping to reach the protection of a commando. Many of them perished, or were attacked by marauding bands of natives, or they were picked up by the British columns. (P)

The questioning faces of four Boer prisoners. As the women and children were shepherded into camps, so their menfolk, if captured, were being sent abroad to prisoner of war camps in their thousands. (S)

The truly tragic consequences of the concentration camp policy were revealed to the British public when the death-rate figures were published. These showed that in October 1901 the annual death-rate for all inmates of the camps was 344 per 1,000. The annual death-rate for children in that month was 629 per 1,000 in the Orange Free State camps and 585 per 1,000 in the Transvaal camps.

Emily Hobhouse, the daughter of a Cornish rector, was forty when she travelled to South Africa. During her visits to the various camps she noted everything she saw: 'Each woman tells me her story, a story which, from its similarity to all which have gone before, grows monotonous. But it is always interesting to note the various ways in which the great common trouble is met by divers characters. Some are scared, some paralysed and unable to realise their loss, some are dissolved in tears; some, mule and dry-eyed, seem only to think of the blank, penniless future; and some are glowing with pride at being prisoners for their country's sake.'

The British authorities were less than grateful to her for exposing their skeleton in the cupboard and when she returned to South Africa to resume her work, she was refused permission to land and deported much against her will.

The Boers appreciated her, however, and after her death General Smuts said this of her, 'amid the sufferings of war she represented the eternal human, the eternal woman, the simple feelings of pity and sympathy and comforting which the war spirit could not kill and which in the end have led to the rebirth of the larger South Africa.'

Razing the farms caused lasting bitterness among the Boers, fierce disapproval on the continent and posed for the British the problem of what to do with the women and children rendered homeless. Both for humanitarian reasons and to precipitate an end to the war, it was decided to set up camps to accommodate them and any surrendered burghers. The staffing and maintaining of these camps put an enormous strain on Britain's finances and also hindered military operations, while it freed the Boers from a weighty responsibility and allowed them to devote their energies to the fight. However, things went tragically awry. The humanitarian motive proved dubious and later embarrassing as the camps quickly became overcrowded and epidemics swept relentlessly through them. In the early months, 20,000 people died, 16,000 of them children. Measles, enteric, diptheria, typhoid, pneumonia, dysentry, malaria, bronchitis and whooping cough each played their fatal role. The overcrowded and unwholesome conditions of the camps ensured that once the epidemic had taken hold, nothing, and certainly not a single doctor with a few nurses, could halt its progress. Medical science had yet to come up with cures, antiseptics were little understood and hygiene often ignored.

The authorities, fundamentally well meaning, had based the camps' requirements upon military ones. The columns, however, were constantly mobile and therefore the satisfactory amount of men to a tent in transient conditions, proved unacceptable for whole families in stationary positions. Also the camps were not well-sited, often having no shade and little water. Camp superintendents had to order rations for constantly increasing populations, and women, who entered the camps voluntarily after trailing the Boer commandos, were often in a pitiful state and succumbed easily to the epidemics.

Emily Hobhouse, one of the leaders of the South African Conciliation Committee, travelled to South Africa in December 1900 and called the camp system 'wholesale cruelty'. During her six month visit, she travelled around the camps reporting her findings and distributing food, clothing, soap and other luxuries. She repeatedly lobbied Kitchener with requests for those women and children with secure friends and relatives to go to, to be allowed to leave; for more adequate medical attention in the camps; and for overall conditions to be alleviated. 'It can never,' she wrote, 'be wiped out of the memories of the people. It presses

A British concentration camp for Boer refugees. (J)

hardest on the children. They drop in the terrible heat, and with the insufficient, unsuitable food; whatever you do, whatever the authorities do, and they are, I believe, doing their best with very limited means, it is all only a miserable patch upon a great ill. Thousands, physically unfit, are placed in conditions of life which they have not the strength to endure. In front of them is blank ruin. There are cases, too, in which whole families are severed and scattered, they don't know where.'

Miss Hobhouse's report exposed the scandalous situation in South Africa and prompted the setting up of a Ladies' Commission.

At the end of 1901 the death rate steadied and then mercifully dropped a little, and camp life began to take on a more permanent style. Many camps were equipped with schools (an unaccustomed boon to some of the Boers) and the more enterprising set up drama societies, reading rooms and concert parties. The camps had shops, well-equipped with luxuries and the men were encouraged to go out to work, although many refused as they hoped to cripple the British Army with the added financial burden. The camps lasted well into 1903 and played a valuable part in repatriating the Boers after the end of the war.

Rations issued daily in an unprepared or raw state to each adult:
8 oz of meat (with bone and fat), 2 oz of coffee, 12 oz of wholemeal, 2 oz of sugar, $\frac{1}{4}$ oz of salt and one twelfth of a tin of condensed milk.
Soap was a luxury as was fuel—essential for boiling drinking water if one hoped to stave off the typhoid epidemic.

Extract from a report by Mr Scholz, Inspector of Camps for the Transvaal:

'Many of the children, when they first arrived at the camp, were little better than skin and bone and being in so emaciated a condition it was not surprising that, when they did catch measles, they could not cope with the disease. Many of the women would not open their tents to admit fresh air, and, instead of giving the children the proper medicines supplied by the military, preferred to give them home remedies . . . the mothers persist in giving their children meat and other indigestible foods, even when the doctors strictly prohibit it, dysentery resulting as a matter of course. In other respects the health of the camp is good, there being only one case of typhoid out of 5,000 residents in camp.'

Boer prisoners under guard, awaiting transportation to prisoner of war camps. Ironically, one of the camps was called Tucker's Island, Bermuda. (E)

On 11 December, Roberts telegraphed to Queen Victoria: 'I have just made over command of Your Majesty's Army in South Africa to Lord Kitchener, in whose judgement, discretion and valour I have the greatest confidence.'

The Queen obviously agreed with Roberts because she corresponded often with Kitchener during his period in South Africa.

Roberts sailed for England on the HMS Canada. The British public prematurely acknowledged his return as a sign that the war was finished. In gratitude for his services, he was awarded £100,000 and made an Earl and a Knight of the Garter.

A welcoming Punch cartoon quipped: 'Well done, indeed, Sir! You have had a tough job in South Africa; but Heaven help you when you get into the War Office!'

11th December 1900

A day at Heidelberg. The Battalion had a rest and a chance to wash up and get some things from the stores or canteen. The mail arrived.

Me and the Quartermaster-Sergeant had rather a busy day drawing three days' food and groceries from the Army Service Corps. I finished about 6.00 p.m.

The men of the Rifle Brigade form an excited crowd around the mailbag: impatient for their names to be called, disappointed if they were not. (H)

The Boers called the British columns 'caterpillar columns', because of the way they would extend, then halt to give the tail end (the baggage) time to catch up. Looping caterpillar columns were crawling all over South Africa.

12th December 1900

We left Heidelberg about 8.00 a.m. and were told we were to trek to Standerton. General Cooper was in charge of the Mobile Column. After a good day spent skirmishing over the hills, the Battalion pitched camp. A cavalry column was also working near us.

13th December 1900

The Battalion had another hard day of it skirmishing and leaving the baggage to follow after. We lost them during the night so they had to sleep without any blankets. The next morning they told us

'By his Own Noose.
Even the art of horse-stealing requires learning.'
A German cartoon from Kladderadatsch showing a plump John Bull having some difficulty reining in the emaciated horse of the Transvaal. (R)

how we had lost them: that evening, as they were making for the place where they had told us to meet them, they had seen a few Boers on a kopje nearby. The field guns and pom-pom had opened fire for we had seen the shells bursting. But as the Boers were so close, the Battalion had changed direction and made for another place where there was water. So that was how we had lost them. The men told me that, after changing course, they had marched for over three hours in the dark until they had come to a farm which had been destroyed during the day by the cavalry. There they had found plenty of water and a good fire as tons of mealies were burning.

As for us, when we discovered that we had lost touch with the column, at about 7.00 p.m., the officer in charge said that we had better form up in case we wandered into the Boer lines. We formed up until morning when we discovered that we were not more than half a mile from the column all the time, but we hadn't seen them because of the hills between us.

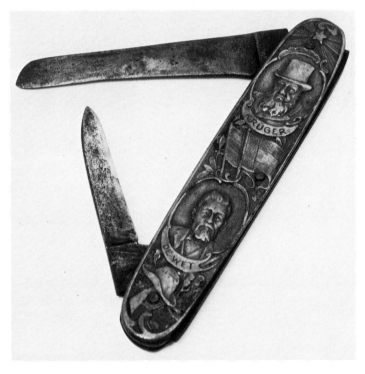

During the summer campaign of 1900–1901 (N.B. A South African summer coincides with a British winter) the Boers concentrated on destroying or paralyzing the communications of the British Army. De Wet was enjoying a measure of success in the Cape and Botha was preparing for a concerted attack on the railway lines to Delagoa Bay and through Natal; precisely where Tucker and his incendiary comrades were busy razing farms.

Kitchener had an imperious, self-reliant nature and was a great organizer The moment he took over as Commander-in-Chief he began revolutionizing the whole scale and system of operations in South Africa. From his headquarters in Pretoria he controlled everything. His mechanical web spread across the whole country and the Boers were methodically ground down by the sheer might and inevitability of the machine he had created; constantly supplemented with men and well supplied with artillery and ammunition. By the end of May 1901, the British Army in South Africa totalled 240,000 men. They were mostly needed to staff the 8,000 blockhouses and to participate in the sweeping 'drives', which Kitchener had devised. The Boer forces were hard to estimate, but of the 44,000 men and boys at large, it was thought that no more than 13,000 were capable of fighting at any one time.

He was acutely aware of the British public's impatience for an end to the war and so he pushed untrained men into battle too soon and consequently the columns proved non-productive, the Boers obstinate, and the war—seemingly—interminable.

A hand engraved pen knife, bearing two decorative portraits of Kruger and De Wet, which was taken from a captured Boer. (A)

14th December 1900

The baggage moved off at daybreak to join the Battalion and found they were anchored near a nice fruit garden and they were making a short job of it. There was all kinds of fruit in the garden but only the apples and peaches were fit for eating. You may be sure there were not many left on the trees!

After breakfast we moved off again.

Our first move was to see if there were any Boers on the same kopjes as there had been the evening before. We found they had cleared off. The remainder of the day was spent making a long

More ferocious than bargain hunters at the January sales, the men of the Rifle Brigade sorting through the belongings of a Boer family. The women are frantically trying to gather a few bundles together. (H)

sweep round and about. About 6.00 p.m. we halted and the column pitched camp. We were about 1,000 yards opposite the position we had left in the morning.

15th December 1900

We moved off again about 9.00 a.m. and trekked to Modderfontein, arriving there about 8.00 p.m. We halted at Botha's farm for about two hours for dinner and the usual burning and looting of farms. We discovered that the Boers who own the houses in this vicinity take the precaution of burying their valuable articles, for several boxes were unearthed by our men.

16th December 1900

Birthday.
A day's rest at Modderfontein. Church parade and washing.

17th December 1900

In December, having missed the troubles in China but determined not to be left out of any action which might be brewing in India, Kitchener resolved to bring the war to a head. He was supported in this endeavour by the British tax-payers, who were by now footing an enormous bill for the cost of the war on both sides, and by the men in the field, who were tired of the drudgery and demoralization of combating guerilla warfare.

Moved off about 7.00 a.m. We burned some stores at Malan's Kraal and several farmhouses. My company was afterwards sent to destroy a farm further on. They found all the furniture had already been removed and there was nothing left to burn.

Large parties of Boers were all around us and much firing took place.

One of the Hussars was wounded today.

We did not get to our camping ground till dark and it was pouring hard with rain. Camped at Beirlaagte.

18th December 1900

We expected an easy day in camp but at 10.00 a.m. my company went out with the Engineers to destroy some mealie stores. They rode out to them in wagons. Hundreds of Boers had been sighted on the hills and the sky line round the camp so the pom-pom went with them. Us that were left in camp had to turn out and quite a strong fight took place. We had three casualties and the Boers are known to have had twelve killed.

A couple of bushbuck before a Boer wagon. Wagonloads of women and children were joining the commandos and forming joint laagers. This imposed an added strain on the burghers who had to find extra food. The extra wagons also hampered their mobility considerably. (W)

British soldiers fighting off a surprise attack from superior Boer forces. (D)

NOTICE.

IT IS HEREBY NOTIFIED to all Burghers that if, after this date, they voluntarily surrender they will be allowed to live with their Families in Government Laagers until such time as the Guerilla Warfare now being carried on will admit of their returning safely to their homes. All stock and property brought in at the time of surrender by such Burghers will be respected, and paid for if requisitioned by Military Authorities.

KITCHENER,
Commander-in-Chief.

Pretoria. 20th December, 1900.

KENNISGEVING.

HET WORDT HIERMEDE aan alle Burgers bekend gemaakt dat indien zij na datum dezes zich vrijwillig overgeven zij toegelaten, zullen worden om met hunne families in Gouvernement's laagers te wonen tot tijd en wijle de Guerilla strijd welke nu voorgezet wordt zal toelaten dat zij veilig naar hunne huizen kunnen terugkeeren. Alle vee en eigendom door zulke Burgers tijdens hun overgave ingebracht, zullen worden gerespecteerd en uitbetaald worden indien verlangd door Militaire authoriteiten.

KITCHENER,
Opperbevelhebber.

Pretoria, 20 December 1900.

On 20 December the above proclamation was printed in both Dutch and English.

Peace committees were formed and emissaries appointed to carry the proclamation to the commandos. The hardened, fighting burghers were, however, unimpressed and the envoys met with taunts, violence and even death.

Generally regarded as cowards and traitors, these men, who had their country's welfare at heart as much as the commandos, found themselves divided from their own countrymen and so sided with the British in an attempt to bring the war to a speedy end. Kitchener, who believed that a divided nation would be easier to rule at the end of the war, was pleased by the split he had caused.

Seven of my section had to stop out with the Engineers burning mealies and furniture, they returned to camp at 6.00 p.m. with about sixty head of cattle.

19th December 1900

We moved off again about 8.00 a.m. and arrived at the next camping ground—Leeuwspruit—about 12 mid-day. We moved to this place for a better supply of water. We saw hundreds of Boers and the artillery and pom-pom had a lively time with them.

We have with us a large number of captured cattle and several Boer families.

Rain came on us as soon as camp was pitched and continued pouring down all night.

20th December 1900

Five companies went out early in the morning with some of the empty wagons to meet a convoy with rations from Vlakfontein. We arrived at the mine and loaded all the empty wagons with the mealies from the large mill that was there. During the six hour wait for the convoy bearing the rations we amused ourselves by catching fowl and going through the stores and houses but couldn't find anything good. After waiting all that time we were ordered to offload and return to camp again as the convoy could not come out to meet us on account of there being so many Boers in between them and us. We set fire to over 500 pounds worth of mealies and returned.

In the meantime, the remainder of the Battalion back at camp had been ordered to strike camp and pack up in readiness to lead and move off. When the wagons got back to camp we all moved off back to the mine with the Boers sniping at us all the way.

The mine is called South Rand Coal Mine, Leeuwspruit.

21st December 1900

At 3.00 a.m. we packed up. There were no rations for the troops. Every man was issued half a pint of Quaker Oats and told not to expect anything more before we get into Vlakfontein.

Making the most of half a pint of porridge. While attached to the mobile columns, the men were not always sure when their next square meal would be. (O)

We started off at 5.00 a.m. After going about four miles a large force of Boers was seen moving towards us. We had a few thousand oxen, sheep, horses and wagons with us, which we managed to drive over the nek of a hill to safety. The four field guns and two pom-poms remained to cover us. My company was the baggage escort and therefore placed at the rear of the column. Our guns opened fire and attacked the Boers for a time until the baggage got to Vlakfontein, or almost there. Then our guns retired and allowed the Boers to come on. My mate tells me that after the wagons were safe they used my company as an escort to the guns and soon a good fight was on, which lasted several hours.

We were too good for the Boers and they must have lost very heavily for several were seen to fall from their saddles and often man and horse fell together.

Five men in my Regiment were wounded. The Boers managed to reclaim a few goats that a Kaffir had been driving in; the Kaffir was shot. The Boers seemed very determined to do something brave but at the finish they ran for their lives.

The Battalion and the remainder of the column retired to camp having done a good day's work on nothing more than half a pint of shilly! They were given plenty of food when they returned to camp for me and the Quartermaster-Sergeant had been very busy getting food from the Army Service Corps whilst they were fighting.

The mail arrived.

In the Battalion Orders that night, General Cooper congratulated all ranks of the Mobile Column on their excellent work.

22nd December 1900

A day in camp at Vlakfontein, and rather a hard day it was for me to work from six in the morning till ten at night, and that is what they call at rest!

23rd December 1900

We left Vlakfontein and returned to the same mines we had left on Friday. We moved with little opposition. During the journey I saw a large number of the enemy but they did not try to attack us. We chased them out of sight and burned Commandant Buys' brother's furniture. Buys was too ill to be removed. The Boers had not expected us to return to the same place quite so quickly. They had got several head of cattle and a large flock of sheep together again. They fled, leaving livestock and also a quantity of potatoes behind for us. These the officers claimed for themselves.

We pitched camp about 5.00 p.m. (Grootvlei Rutfontien, Vlakfontein District).

24th December 1900

Five companies of the Battalion cavalry and guns went out at 7.00 a.m. to attack some kopjes four miles in front of the mine.

The rift between the 'hands-uppers' and the 'bitter-enders', as the two divided groups of Boers became known, widened steadily and in May 1901, Piet De Wet, a leading member of the Peace Committee, wrote to his brother, Christian:

'Which is better, for the Republics to continue the struggle and run the risk of total ruin as a nation, or to submit? Could we for a moment think of taking back the country, if it were offered to us, with thousands of people to be supported by a Government which has not a farthing? Put passionate feelings aside for a moment and use common sense, and you will agree with me that the best thing for the people and the country is to give in, to be loyal to the new Government and to get responsible government.'

The following day, Kitchener issued a much longer memorandum to his commanding officers outlining his plans for bringing in the women and children. 'This course,' he wrote, 'has been pointed out by surrendered burghers, who are anxious to finish the war, as the most effective method of limiting the endurance of the guerillas, as men and women left in farms, if disloyal, willingly supply burghers, if loyal, dare not refuse to do so.'

He planned to set up camps alongside the railway and divide the refugees into two categories: the first to include families of neutral burghers, non-combatants and surrendered burghers; the second composed of families whose husbands, fathers and sons were on commando. Preferences in food and accommodation were to be accorded to the first group.

Boers still in the field were to be assured that if they surrendered voluntarily they, too, would be allowed to live in the camps with their families and would not be sent abroad to one of the many prisoner of war camps.

French propaganda drawing. (F)

German cartoon from the Lustige Blätter.
Two British officers standing before
Raphael's painting, 'The Massacre of the
Innocents.'
First officer: 'He was a bungler at child
murder.'
Second officer: 'Yes, that sort of thing Mr
Rhodes does much better than Herod.' (F)

A home-made Christmas card showing six
different views, a portrait of Kruger and one
of White. Scrupulously fair and well
intentioned, it is impossible to say whether it
was made by a Boer or a British soldier. (A)

My company was positioned on the left flank of the column. I
stopped behind with the wagons and watched the fight in the
distance. They moved forward to within 1,400 yards of the
kopjes. The Boers were reported to be crawling through the grass

Tucker's shifting position along the railway
line was a critical one. At every moment his
garrison were liable to attack from the agile
bands of commandos which tagged them.
The men were forced to sleep in their boots
with their rifles loaded at their sides and
their equipment placed in regular order
outside the tents. The constant vigilance and
anticipation of attack imposed a severe
strain on the officers and the men.

Resting by the side of a wagon. The British
troops were on duty seven days a week and
were grateful for the occasional half an hour
spent relaxing over a game of chess or a cup
of tea. (J)

Bored Boers having tea in the prison yard of the camp at Cape Town. (L)

about six or eight hundred yards to the left of them. They at once got ready for them and the artillery commenced shelling the kopje in front. A large force of Boers had been there a day or two before but were reported to have trekked. After shelling the hills for some time, the cavalry advanced (about twenty-five men from the 13th Hussars, which is all the cavalry we have with us), and were within a hundred yards of the hill when the Boers opened fire. The cavalry had to retire faster than they advanced! The column immediately changed their front line from watching the left, and opened fire on the hills. At first the artillery had to be careful to let the cavalry get clear of their front. However, after they were clear, my section, who were leading, continued firing for about half an hour. Two other companies made a wide flank movement to the left of them with a pom-pom. When these companies were in front, they advanced and took the hill. When they reached the top they found the Boers had only been driven on to another, similar hill about a thousand yards in rear of the one they had just taken. Both parties opened a heavy fire on each other. Our gun, positioned on the left of the Boers, fired from the plain. The Boers had rather a warm time of it and after an hour, my company ('A') were ordered to retire to another hill to the right.

They got to the bottom of the hill safely, leaving one company behind to hold the position. There was one of our men lying at the bottom of the hill, dead. The company advanced in file to the next hill where there was already half of another company. They had to cross open ground, directly in the line of Boer fire. Despite that, they arrived safely.

When they reached the top of the second hill they found that they were in another warm show. Every man took as much cover as was possible behind the stones and opened fire on the hills in front.

They continued firing for about two or three hours. Firing over 200 rounds each.

The Boers quickly became adept at booby-trapping the railway line and every three miles or so a wrecked engine or the traces of burned trucks and carriages testified to their skill.

They had come a long way from such obvious ploys as the removal of rails or the loosening of bolts and their sophisticated traps were now all but invisible to even the most vigilant eye. Hidden under a heap of ballast there would be a sawn-off rifle, primed and surrounded by nitroglycerine cans or dynamite cartridges, all set to explode as the engine ran over, and depressed the trigger of the gun. (A)

The casualties following the attack on the Rietvlei Hills were one killed and two wounded. The Boers, led by Field-Cornet Buys, remained in the area and maintained a troublesome sniping fire.

A half bottle of Dagonet and Fils' Champagne. This was selected by the War Office for use in the hospitals and for the sick and wounded soldiers in the war. (A)

British soldiers preparing their Christmas dinner beneath the stars. The war, which was to have been over by the previous Christmas, showed no sign of an end. (D)

Meanwhile, the Engineers were busy burning a farm at the foot of the first hill.

The few cavalry and two companies, which were escorting the guns, made a sweep round and helped, but our force was not strong enough to take so many hills and hold them. As fast as we drove the Boers off one hill they started firing at us again from farther off. Finally, my company was ordered to retire from the hills and travel with the guns while another company took their place. They were with the guns for about half an hour when the Colonel asked their Captain to move them around and take the hill.

The Boers were still keeping up a heavy fire. It was almost 6.00 p.m.

The Captain said the men were not fit, as they had already had a hard day of it, and had not been able to get a drink of water all day. It was scorching hot. There was a farm under the hill and the Colonel was anxious to burn it, but our Captain gave the order to retire back to the mines where we were camped.

The men retired very quietly after their stiff day of fighting.

25th December 1900

Xmas day. Reveille at 3.30 a.m. Every man in camp had to get up and put his belt on. This is a daily occurrence while on the Mobile Column so as to be in readiness in case the Boers attack at

Back in Britain, Christmas was remembered with Kruger trinkets, pom-pom cigar lighters and silver flasks. (D)

Tucker's second Christmas passed off undisturbed. However, in Utrecht the Boers carried out a threatened attack.

On Christmas Eve the Boer commandant had sent a message into the town, demanding whiskey, cigars and other Christmas luxuries for his men, adding that if they were refused he would feel compelled to ride in and take them.

The garrison at Utrecht had mislaid their Christmas spirit, however, and sent no reply. At 2.00 a.m. on Christmas day the Boers attacked and were quickly sent packing minus two of their men.

OUT IN THE COLD
Dame Europa (to the Wails, Ex-President Kruger and Dr. Leyds). 'Go away! Go away! I've got nothing for you.' (B)

daybreak. At 7.30 a.m. we had a breakfast of biscuits, cheese, jam and coffee. At 9.00 a.m. we had Church parade. For dinner we had boiled mutton; the sheep had been killed and cooked in a very short time. in the evening we had the usual issue of rum.

Thus passed a second Xmas Day in Africa. At Grootvlei Rutfontein.

26th December 1900

(The day I will not forget for some time).

At 6.00 a.m. our Colonel took six companies of the Battalion, with four field guns and one pom-pom, also our small force of Hussars—about fifty all told—to do some more farm burning and to attack the Boers again. They left the other company ('F'), servants, grooms, cooks and store men—about 150 men in all— behind in camp, in charge of the convoy.

Captain Radclyffe was in command. There was also one pom-pom left in camp.

Well, the Battalion had been out for about five or six hours and we could see them from the mine. I was in charge of the wagons which carried the Battalion's food for the next day. I was sitting

The six companies, under Lieutenant-Colonel Colville, moved off in the direction of Roodewal, where they intended to burn several farms. The first, some five miles away, was cleared after a short skirmish during which three men were wounded. The second, Andrez Greyling's Farm in the Roodewal Hills, was spared because, at 1.00 p.m. Colville received a distress message from his camp. The baggage guard was under severe attack from a large force of Boers. He abandoned his advance on the farm and turned about at once.

Men of Colonel Colville's column, 1st Battalion Rifle Brigade. (H)

Tucker's camp at the Oceana Mine (ten miles from Vlakfontein) had been left in the hands of Captain's Radclyffe and Harvest. British intelligence reports were so poor that the proximity of Louis Trichardt's commando was quite unsuspected, which probably accounts for Tucker's uncharacteristic understating of the Boer numbers, (he estimated the force at around 300 when it was closer to 450).

As the Boers advanced, so the baggage retired, while Radclyffe and the infantry covered their retreat. But the Boers were in greater numbers and gradually they began to envelop the British position. The ammunition was all but finished so Radclyffe gave the order to retire but a Sergeant with eighteen men, cut off from the main group, was taken prisoner. At that moment the column arrived, firing blindly on the Boers and their own men for a few minutes before the Boers felt it prudent to retreat. They left their prisoners behind.

The Rifle Brigade Chronicle wrote of the incident: 'The splendid stand made by Captain Radclyffe with 'F' Company, is one that reflects the very greatest credit on him as well as on every Officer, Non-commissioned Officer, and Private Rifleman who took part in it, and affords a fine example of tenacity and courage under very adverse circumstances.'

The casualties, which included Radclyffe, had been heavy.

under one of the wagons, not thinking there was any danger, when all of a sudden, I heard someone shouting for the pom-pom to go out to the front. None knew that there were any Boers so close as that till the men began firing. Of course, it was every man for himself.

Well, all of a sudden, there were 300 or more Boers on the ridge about 200 yards off and they soon let us know they was there for they poured in a very heavy fire.

We hurriedly got ourselves together a bit and returned the fire.

Whilst we were firing, the black men were inspanning their oxen, and very cool they were too. They had sixteen oxen to yoke up each and you can be sure that took a few minutes to do well. While they were inspanning, we took cover behind the wagons and fired at the Boers. When they were ready to move, the black men started off with the wagons and we retired a short way to a small coal heap that ran along lengthways to the Boers. It did not give us much cover. We all stopped to see our wagons off. Three of them carried the stores, eight belonged to the Battalion, and two or three belonged to each of the other units. So you see there were a tidy few wagons there. If the Boers had managed to capture the convoy they would have had a tidy haul, for besides the convoy we had ten of the Army Service Corps wagons with us.

Well, as I was saying, after seeing our wagons off, we retired a little over an open piece of ground to this bit of a coal heap, and they didn't half let us have the brunt of their fire, because they could see that they had lost the convoy.

Well, we got behind this heap all right, and thought we were safe but they had got to the back of us and were letting us have it from the left, front and rear. Which meant we were getting it from three sides. We tried to catch the column up. In the meantime the pom-pom was retiring as hard as it could go. An officer and two men belonging to us were wounded, also three horses. The Boers were trying their hardest to get the pom-pom

A field surgeon attending to one of the wounded while under fire. In exposed situations like this one, the bravery of the medical men was indisputable. (F)

and they let us know it too. As it passed by me, and four of the chaps who were with the wagons, the shots were flying all round us like a swarm of bees let loose. There was a poor chap two files from me on the left, who got shot right through the heart. I can tell you, when he got hit, I thought it would be my turn, but it wasn't and I managed to get away safe.

At the same time the column were having a lively time. They were also being fired at from left, right and front and our Maxim gun was getting a lot of work to do. One man in the gun ditch was severely wounded as soon as the gun went into action. Two men were also wounded from 'I' Company. The Boers were forced to retire from the farm which they were defending. 'I' Company went forward and burnt everything. They could see hundreds of Boers about and their guns were shelling them in all directions.

This day's work has cast a dark shadow on the feelings of the Battalion. Our total casualties for the day were seventy-four; eleven of these killed. Two officers out of three were hit, also the Colour Sergeant and about three other Sergeants. The Boers, too, must have suffered severely and lost many men.

As the war progressed through its second year the Boers became more habituated to their roving existence. Discipline and organization had improved and the men had great confidence in their leaders. Their ranks had been pruned down by capture, death or surrender until only the strongest and most fanatical burghers remained in the field.

They made the country round Pietersburg and the south-eastern portion of the Transvaal, which had not been visited by the British, their base, and there they had a printing press, mills to grind flour and improvised workshops for the repair of damaged rifles and guns. Throughout the country they had set up heliograph stations and orders could be transmitted rapidly from Botha to De Wet. Their secret service, too, was excellent, drawing on information supplied by spies within the occupied towns and gleaning advance notice of the British plans by tapping the telegraph wires, which they always left unharmed when cutting the railway lines.

This cartoon from the Berlin based magazine, Kladderadatsch, shows the German view of the hunt after De Wet: John Bull, complete with a butterfly net, pinned down by small but sharp, wasps (Boers). (R)

One of the medals awarded to soldiers for bravery in South Africa. (Z)

The party that attacked the convoy were all Irish Americans.

Our Doctor and Adjutant went out with a white flag and an ambulance for our wounded. They found the Boers had collected them and treated them kindly, giving them water and dressing their wounds. Our wounded were brought back to camp and the wounded Boers were given the chance to return or to stay with us.

Both 'I' and 'A' Company went on outpost, as one company was not considered enough to protect the camp at night. We were told that we were to go to Greylingstad early in the morning.

Killed: 11. Wounded: 44. Prisoners: 19. Total: 74

27th December 1900

We started for Greylingstad early this morning. The convoy was well protected for we all expected to have to fight our way out of the hills, but there were only a few shots fired at us and they did no harm. We made it safely to Greylingstad by about 11.00 a.m. It was a hard march as we were in a hurry to get in with the wounded. We also brought in our eleven dead plus two more men who died on the road. As soon as we arrived in Greylingstad our wounded were sent by rail to Standerton, and a grave was dug opposite the railway station for the dead. There were already two or three graves on the spot. At 4.00 p.m. the dead were buried. All the officers of the regiment and a large number of the men attended the funeral. The Scottish Rifles, who were stationed in Greylingstad found one firing party, and a Major and Lieutenant and fifty men of the regiment also dug the graves. The dead were on a wagon. Their bodies sewn up in their blankets. It was an impressive sight to see them lifted off the wagon and laid in their last resting place. Just as we got to the grave side a severe thunderstorm came on and soon everyone was wet through, but we all stood silent while the Chaplain read the burial service. The dead were buried two in each grave and three in one. The rain continued to pour down for about three hours and we were all washed out. When it did stop it was a sight to see the men raking the mud out of the tents so as they could lay down and go to sleep after having their issue of rum.

A halt and a chance to relax for men of the Rifle Brigade, attached to the Mobile Column. (H)

28th December 1900

Today has been a holiday. A nice warm day and so it gave us a good chance to wash all our clothes and dry them. We heard today that some of the Devons had come to help us get to Vlakfontein yesterday. They had thought we were coming from the same direction as we had fought over on Friday, 21 December. It was lucky we had not gone that way as a large force of Boers had assembled there in readiness to receive us. The Devons had gone too far and had been attacked: three had been killed and several wounded. We heard that large forces of Boers are all around the district.

29th December 1900

Today we were going to move to another camping ground at 2.00 a.m. But just before then, four companies were marched off to Greylingstad station. Some time during the morning the Boers had held a train up about six miles away. The train was partly loaded with canteen goods, also forage and a quantity of bottled

beer, spirits and champagne. The Boers took all the liquors away on five ox wagons loaded with goods. They set fire to all the stuff they could not take away with them. Our men were going down by rail to the scene of the fire and to help some Mounted Infantry. (In the end they did not go but returned to camp.)

30th December 1900

I had to go by rail to Vlakfontein to collect stores. During the day the column shifted camp.

31st December 1900

We moved again, about six miles down the line to the spot where the Boers had held the train up. It was a scorching hot day. One man died on the march. We pitched camp two miles from Vaal Station.

And so the war moved on into another year—another century for some pedants—and, although the two republics had been conquered, the people most definitely had not! The commandos were aided by supposedly neutral burghers and the guerilla war was thriving. Generals Botha, De la Rey and De Wet were carrying out undaunted attacks on British positions, communications and railways in the Free State, the Transvaal and Cape Colony.

The constant plundering of supplies and destruction of rolling stock, which continued unabated along the vulnerable lengths of railway lines, made it obvious to Kitchener that some tighter means of protection were needed. Blockhouses—the solution he finally arrived at—proved slow to succeed and costly to maintain. (F)

On 30 December, Tucker and his comrades received a late telegram from H.R.H. the Duke of Connaught wishing them well at Christmas.

Chapter Six:
Enough To Make
A Bus Horse Laugh

Kitchener realized that he would not be able, after all, to intimidate the Boers into surrender (nor buy them off, if one of rumours that Botha and De la Rey were each offered £10,000 a year by the British government to lay down their arms, is to be believed), and therefore a new, more efficient system of defence was required. Chains of blockhouses (miniature forts built of stone or corrugated iron, linked by barbed wire) were erected at short intervals along the railways. Gradually they extended across the whole country, criss-crossing, intersecting and slicing the vast veldt into manageable sections. Into and against this armoured network, the commandos were then driven like game, hounded by huge columns of British infantry and cavalry. At first the Boers, more agile and swifter, succeeded in breaking through the barriers but as the chains spread it became more difficult and their numbers shrank. From the outset of the war, Kitchener had refused to exchange prisoners (a common and condoned practice in war) and now his policy was paying off. All captured Boers were sent to prisoner of war camps in British colonies. All captured British were, eventually, turned loose by the Boers who were unable to feed them. Before sending them back to their lines, the Boers made their prisoners sign declarations promising not to participate further in the war, then they stripped them of everything but their shirts and left them to stumble back to their regiments, demoralized and exhausted.

Lord Roberts was called 'the greatest soldier who ever lived'. He was certainly immensely popular with the public, a fact advertisers were quick to cash in on. (D)

1st January 1901

We had a day's rest but it was a very wet day.

2nd January 1901

In the afternoon we shifted camp to the top of the hill known as Bytel Plaatz, leaving the wagons at the bottom. We were told we will remain here for about ten days whilst they build a block house to protect the line. A very wet night.

3rd January 1901

Still raining. All of us nearly washed out.

4th January 1901

Still raining. My company went out to burn a farm, they rode in wagons.

5th January 1901

The mounted infantry, four companies, and the guns go out looking for Boers and to burn a farm. They had a slight engagement and fought a rear guard action coming back to camp.

Whilst we are encamped here my work is to go every morning to collect the Battalion rations from Vaal Station about two miles away. I have a strong escort.

6th January 1901

Church Parade. Chaplain was preaching to troops.

7th January 1901

Troops busy wall building.

8th January 1901

Usual camp duties. Same next day.

In England the return of Lord Roberts from South Africa was handled as enthusiastically and loyally by the press as his departure, the year before, had been. Punch *printed a long, sentimental poem (of which this is but a fraction) which seemed to imply that now Roberts was home the war was over. (D)*

> *Welcome, Welcome, long desired!*
> *Now the watching eyes astrain*
> *Over the misty-curtained main*
> *Have the sight that sets at rest*
> *Hearts the sport of hope and fear.*
> *Now the signal-lights are fired;*
> *Now with shattering thunder-shock*
> *Battleship and cannon'd rock,*
> *Booming out their iron cheer*
> *Greet you where your vessel rides*
> *Swinging on familiar tides*
> *Off the land you love the best!*

URGENT.

URGENT.
General Lord Kitchener (to Mr. John Bull).
'If you want this business quickly finished you must *give me more horses, and* men *to ride them. (B)*

Buller to Kitchener: 'You're a plagiarist. I used to say that.'
History repeating itself. The American paper, the Chicago Record *satirises the South African situation. (R)*

A bandolier taken from a captured Boer. (A)

10th January 1901

Mobile Column moved off at 6.00 a.m. We had an engagement with the enemy. Two of the mounted infantry were wounded. Pitched camp about 4.00 p.m.

11th January 1901

Moved off again, at 5.00 a.m.
Another slight skirmish but reached camp early.

12th January 1901

Five companies with guns and cavalry went out. We did not strike camp. They saw many Boers and had plenty of firing. They brought in three families—eighteen people in all—and cattle. They returned to camp about 3.00 p.m.

13th January 1901

Three companies—myself included—went to Vlaklaagte with our wagons for supplies, taking the Boer prisoners and their families with us. The remainder had Church Parade. We returned about 3.00 p.m.

14th January 1901

Column went out but did not take the convoy. They had a slight engagement and returned to camp about 3.00 p.m. Casualties were very slight.

15th January 1901

Struck camp and moved off.

We became more severely engaged as large forces of Boers opposed us.

We pitched camp about 2.00 p.m. We brought two Boer families of about twelve into camp. These were just trekking off to the Boers.

My Company on outpost at night.

The Column received orders to return to the nearest railway station as some changes had to take place. We received news of General French capturing 500 and wounding and killing 800 Boers at Elandfontein.

16th January 1901

We struck camp at 5.00 a.m. and marched off at 5.45 a.m. Captain Talbot took command of 'A', 'B', and 'C' Companies, with the baggage. 'A' Company leading. We marched off well prepared for a rear guard action. All went well for the first two hours and we expected to arrive at Vlaklaagte Station about 12 noon. The Standerton Police, about forty of them were scouting just in front of us. They held a ridge while the baggage closed up. Then we had to cross some very low ground with ridges on every side. We got about 500 yards across this dip. The police were on the ridge, on the right, and a sudden heavy fire was poured into them from about 500 Boers at very close quarters. The police did not have time to dismount but their horses took fright at the firing and threw several of the riders. At this time we could not see if they had been shot or thrown but the horses galloped back with empty saddles.

My company at once doubled round and faced the hill where the Boers were firing from and advanced towards them. When they were within a few hundred yards, they opened a very heavy fire

A group of Boer women and children, who had been leading a nomadic life on the open veldt. (F)

The duties of Tucker's column included the rounding up of all women and children in the area (often wandering, homeless, hoping to come upon a Boer commando). They were then sent on to the concentration camps. From the camps, the women repeatedly petitioned Lord Kitchener, but with no success. He disagreed violently with their allegations, believing all the women to be mere trouble-makers and largely responsible for the continuation of the war, yet he had never visited a camp himself.

During this period, Tucker's column moved camp almost daily, razing any farms they came across and fighting small skirmishes with the surrounding bands of Boers.

In January the Boer leaders held a conference at Ermelo. They debated whether they should continue the war or not and, plumping for the former, they decided to concentrate the great bulk of the Transvaal commandos in the south-eastern region. From there, they planned to invade and devastate Natal. They could hope to round up a force of 5,000 mounted men and a number of field guns.

British intelligence heard of the plans and reported them to Kitchener in Pretoria. Immediately, he travelled to Middelburg to settle the details of a movement against the Boers with General Smith-Dorrien.

At a point along the line near Balmoral, Boers were sighted and Kitchener, cautiously anticipating a trap, sent a pilot engine ahead of the train. It chugged over the suspect section of track without mishap and then returned. But Kitchener was not convinced. He gave orders that two heavily-laden trucks were to be attached to the engine. This time, the combined weight released the trigger of a Boer mine, which had not been affected by the engine alone, and the trucks were blown into the air. The Boers, hearing the explosion, hurried to the scene only to find Lord Kitchener's train quietly backing down the line.

on the Boers, taking care not to hit the police who had stopped in front of them.

Our fire soon made the Boers retire for we were firing at all ranges from 500 to 2,500 yards. The men could not see what they were firing at, but the fire had good effect. They soon reached the very top of the ridge and poured a heavy fire into the Boers, who, they could see, were retiring at the double now. We could hear the rear guard were having a busy time of it close by. The Boers were using a pom-pom and 3-pounder gun. 'D' Company and the Boers had a race to get on to one ridge. Ours got there first and a severe fight took place at the close range of about 300 yards. The Boers were driven off with heavy loss.

The enemy hung around on the skyline for hours but taking good care to keep out of our range. There seemed to be thousands of them. Our guns kept firing at any who came in range. This attack delayed us about six hours. We lay on the ridge all the time expecting another attack. At last we moved on again and camped in the same spot we had left the day before. Our casualties were eleven in the regiment, our guide killed and four of the cavalry wounded. We were lucky to get off so easy.

Our Medical Officer who went out afterwards and dressed the Boer wounded reported seventy-one wounded and thirteen killed. We buried one that they wouldn't take away with them. This was the same force that attacked us on the 26 December, at the S. Rand coal mine. They were after our convoy again.

A photograph showing an annotated group of Boers, taken from a British military intelligence report. (A)

*A Red Cross train preparing to move off.
(A)*

17th January 1901

Struck camp at 5.00 a.m. and marched to Vlaklaagte Station arriving there at 8.00 a.m. Our wounded were sent on by rail to Standerton.

18th January 1901

A day in camp.

19th January 1901

A very wet morning.

Four companies left early, by rail, for detachment by the line.

20th January 1901

Church parade.

21st January 1901

Our small column moved about four miles up the line and camped opposite Waterval.

22nd January 1901

The Battalion was employed entrenching this place: One hundred men to work about six hours daily until all trenches and gun pits are finished; a very good position.

23rd January 1901

Usual work entrenching and camp duties. Myself and the Quartermaster-Sergeant go with the wagons each morning early to the Vlaklaagte Station to draw rations.

No. 270.

Special Army Order.

SOUTH AFRICAN FIELD FORCE.

ARMY HEADQUARTERS,
PRETORIA
25th January, 1901

DEATH OF HER MAJESTY QUEEN VICTORIA –

The following telegram has been received from the Adjutant-General, War Office, dated London, 23rd January, 1901:—

"Commander-in-Chief deeply regrets to inform you of the death of Her Majesty Victoria, Queen of the United Kingdom of Great Britain and Ireland and of the Colonies and Dependencies thereof, Empress of India, who departed this life at 6-30 p.m., 22nd January, at Osborne House, Isle of Wight."

The following from Lord Kitchener has been sent in reply:—

"The news of the Queen's death has been received with the greatest grief by the Army in South Africa. In their name I beg to express our sincere condolences with the Royal Family on the great loss sustained by them and the Nation."

By Order.

W. F. KELLY, Major-General.
Adjutant-General

On the evening of Tuesday, 22 January 1901, Queen Victoria died at the age of eighty-two. She had been failing for a year but her serious condition, made worse by the news of the death of her favourite grandson, Prince Christian Victor of Schleswig-Holstein, who died of fever in a Pretoria hospital, was only made known to the public a few days before the end came. (F)

The station at Vlaklaagte. On the roof, several men have set up an observation post. (A)

The rounding up of stray families continued. Many of the Boer women argued with the British troops when they arrived to take them away. One woman, who claimed to be neutral, shouted at an officer: 'What do your proclamations mean? You have not kept to one of them. My husband obeyed your proclamation. What did he get for it? He was abused, robbed, half-starved, and now he is sent away.'

24th January 1901

Usual duties for the next three days.

27th January 1901

Struck camp at 2.00 p.m. for another move but it came on wet so the move was cancelled.

28th January 1901

We got ready to move at 5.30 a.m. but as it was a very wet and cold morning we did not move till 8.30 a.m. and then we all moved off riding in the wagons. We were taking a lot of empty wagons (which joined us this morning) to Greylingstad to be reloaded. Our journey was sixteen miles and if it had been a nice, fine day we should no doubt have enjoyed the ride but soon after we left camp, it came pouring down and continued for about five hours. None of us had our great coats so it didn't take long to wet us through to the skin; it was a cold day and miserable.

We arrived at Greylingstad about 6.00 p.m., shivering and wet. The tents were late in coming in so the Colonel gave all the men a run around the camp to warm them up and afterwards gave us all a double issue of rum.

29th January 1901

We moved off again about 8.00 a.m. to Witpoort.

General French with several larger columns was working by Bushman's Kop. We expected some of the Boers to be driven near us but did not see any. French got into action.

Our work was to escort a larger convoy from Greylingstad to General French's column.

General Sir John French was born in 1852. He served in the Nile Expedition in 1884–5 and accompanied Stewart's column in the attempt to rescue Gordon at Khartoum. He had become well respected and distinguished as a cavalry commander. (F)

Sheep driving. Several thousand sheep were captured from Botha near Piet Retief on 9 February. (F)

From now on Tucker's column worked in tandem with General French who, with 21,000 men, was advancing eastwards in a sweeping movement thirty miles in length, designed to net or push back the Boer forces in the area.

The massive operation—the first of Kitchener's 'drives'—bagged not only Boers but every single inhabitant young and old, male and female. Everything in the path of the advancing lines was destroyed, the ground was turned over in the hope of discovering caches of arms, and the inhabitants were sent on to concentration camps.

Generals French and Dartnell both had impressive records. After his victory at Elandslaagte in 1899 and his part in the relief of Kimberley in 1900, French was widely considered to be one of the best generals Kitchener had.

Dartnell, a Canadian, had served with the 'County Downs' in the Indian Mutiny, and had been head of the Natal Mounted Police for thirty years.

30th January 1901

Escorted a convoy of 150 wagons to French and Dartnell and brought back their empty wagons.

Thousands of cattle and sheep captured by the column were sent into Greylingstad.

31st January 1901

We moved camp about four miles.

1st February 1901

Reveille at 2.30 a.m. Breakfasted, packed up and moved off by daybreak. We had a very hard day's marching: it was a very hot day and we did not get to our camping ground till 5.00 p.m. having marched twenty-four miles. We halted close by New Denmark where we had been attacked on 16 January.

Very few Boers were seen during the march.

2nd February 1901

Marched off again at daybreak. About 6.30 a.m. a heavy mist came over. This caused us to halt and we all fixed our swords and closed up as we were in rather a dangerous place. One Boer lost himself in the mist and mistook us for his own party. He soon showed a white rag and gave up his arms. The mist did not last long and we soon went forward again and pitched camp at 9.00 o'clock.

Concerning the seven Generals and De Wet.

Now he cannot escape!

! ! !   *(R)*

An Engineer spinning cable from the back of his bicycle. (F)

Tucker refers to the 'late President Steyn' rather prematurely, or perhaps—taking into consideration his fierce denunciation of any peace that involved the forfeiture of Boer independence—wistfully. The President of the Orange Free State was most certainly alive although he had been ill for some time. The constantly vigilant and mobile life that he had been forced to lead as a fugitive leader was beginning to tell on him and when, in May 1902, he was shown the final peace agreements, he denounced them completely and resigned. He retired to his farm and was succeeded by Christian De Wet.

French's drive, the forerunner of many, was a painstakingly slow and enormously costly business which produced small returns in actual numbers of fighting Boers captured and put an enormous strain on the concentration camps.

On the whole the commandos fell back, as planned, before the advancing line, but some groups succeeded in storming weaker points and breaking through. On 6 February, Louis Botha, took advantage of the pitch darkness to stampede the British horses right through the camp of General Smith-Dorrien and escaped.

Kitchener was undaunted. Methodically he tackled each problem until he had perfected the 'drive'. Ever tighter and more impenetrable, his front lines extended forty, fifty, sixty miles; infantry were replaced by mounted men who could pursue the fleeing Boers; and the space between the mounted men was ever decreased. The advance became a mechanical operation with no room for human error.

Some Boers were seen on the skyline about 5,000 yards in front, so our guns opened fire. In the afternoon our mounted infantry came across some more Boers in a farm. Our guns were sent out and shelled them until it was dark. The telegraph section of the Engineers joined us here having laid a cable from Standerton, eighteen or twenty miles distance. Camped at Meiyersvlei.

3rd February 1901

Church Parade at 8.15 a.m. We had a day's rest. The mounted infantry had an engagement with Boers in a farm near camp.

4th February 1901

Ready again at 2.00 a.m. and marched off before daybreak. We had many empty wagons, sick and wounded men, extra cattle and prisoners from other columns to send on to Standerton.

On this march we came across Steyn's farm (brother of late President Steyn). My company had a busy time at the farm. First we had a walk around the garden, then a good feed of grapes, tomatoes, apples and peaches. Afterwards we put about 130 sacks of mealies on the wagons and a lot of bundles of corn. What we couldn't take away was burnt. Steyn and family were sent into Standerton under a small escort with the remainder of the empty convoy. Our force went onto Leeuwspruit but had to drive the Boers off before we could get there. No casualties.

5th February 1901

At 6.00 a.m. my company went out as covering party to a big convoy from Standerton. They got back to camp about 1.00 p.m.

At 3.00 p.m. our column, with the convoy of about 200 wagons, moved off again. About one hundred Boers gave us a little trouble but they were driven off. We marched about three miles and then pitched camp at Uitkek.

6th February 1901

A day in camp. A convoy of empty wagons and families were brought in from Dartnell's column. They had been attacked and lost 2,000 sheep. One woman had been shot through the head.

7th February 1901

Sudden order to move again at 8.00 p.m. We only went on to the next ridge, four miles distant. 'D' Company was left behind.

8th February 1901

Got ready to move early but rain delayed us. When we did move it took the convoy four hours to get over a drift. Today we only moved about two miles. Large convoys of families, wagons, sheep and horses came to us from the other three columns. The

*Butchering some of the captured sheep.
Kaffirs were employed to assist the camp
cooks. (E)*

last party arrived about 11.00 p.m. They had to fight their way in.
(A wet day.)

9th February 1901

We went on with the convoy and had a long hard day of
marching. Slight opposition on the road.

10th February 1901

We moved on again with the convoy but were delayed for four
hours getting over a deep drift (Kaffir's Drift); another long day

*In the camps congestion and rationing
reigned. Money helped, but few farming
families were wealthy. This extract from a
letter written by a woman in the Middelburg
camp is a pathetic reminder of their
hardships.
'Vegetables we seldom see here. For the
animals there is nothing in the veldt, and
with great trouble do we now and again get a
bag of mealies for £1. 7s. The Lord holds
His hand over us, otherwise we had long ago
perished. When shall there be peace? At
night when I sit lonely, then the tears roll
down my cheeks.'*

*The Rifle Brigade Convoy crossing Kaffir's
Drift. The long marches were hard on the
private soldiers. 'We went through water and
mud sometimes up to our knees,' wrote one
man. 'We were wet through to the skin.
Everytime we halted for a rest men would
fall down asleep. It was hard to wake them
up. Every now and then you would hear a
splash, which was someone falling over
asleep. They slept on their horses, and kept
falling off.' (H)*

*The strain imposed on the men involved in
the drives was obviously great, but here
Punch puts in a word for the under 'dog'.*

*Dear Friend of Animals, I write
To let you know my parlous plight;
Behold in me a living corse
That used to be a British horse.*

*At home they kept me sleek and fat,
And stroked me like a pussy-cat;
I never had to sit up late
Or carry any dreadful weight.*

*But here I hardly ever feel
Quite certain of a solid meal;
They make me march (this can't be right)
At any hour of day or night.*

*I barely have the breath to groan,
Beneath my two-and-twenty stone,
Including blanket, tent, and sack
Or ornamental bric-a-brac.*

*Sometimes to give the mules a change,
I wear a model kitchen range,
And count it lucky not to find
A grand piano up behind.*

*At times I sink my patriot pride
And wish I were the other side;
From all I hear, in point of feed
They do you very well indeed.*

*They ride at large with loosish rein
Which saves the neck from needless pain.
And lets you see the shocking pits
That break our prancers' legs to bits.*

*No doubt a Dutchman can't afford
Virtues that are their own reward,
But he has learned some little ways,
Of showing kindness where it pays.*

*Two envelopes bearing press censor stamps.
(Z)*

of marching, we arrived safely at Ermelo at 9.30 p.m. We pitched camp on the far side of town.

11th February 1901

Ermelo is a fair-sized town with a few large buildings and a well-built church. We did not stay long enough to see much of it. The mills were blown up before we left. At 2.00 p.m. we started back for Standerton, camping for the night at Kaffir's Drift.

12th February 1901

We have about 200 sick and wounded, about 200 Boer families and several Boer prisoners with us. Plus, thousands of sheep, horses, oxen and goats. The cattle are a great nuisance to get along. Today we did a long march and just as we arrived into camp, our rear guard saw some action: some Boers managed to get hold of the last flock of sheep and get away with them under cover of darkness.

13th February 1901

Boers started sniping at us very early from the surrounding ridges. We moved off about 8.00 a.m. fighting a rear guard action. We got safely onto another high ridge. After this ridge came a deep drift and the Boers did not intend us to cross this. They tried to surround us but were always kept at a respectable distance by our guns.

They kept up the firing all day but not one of us was hit. They only delayed us by six or eight hours and most of this time was taken up crossing the drift. Half of my company and half of 'I' Company had gone forward across the drift and taken up a position on high ground having a good view all round. The guns and remainder of us were busy guarding the rear. We camped by 'D' Company, the same company we had left behind on this ridge on Thursday, 17 February. They have been sniped at every day since we left them.

Kitchener's Web

In January 1901, Kitchener instituted his new system of blockhouses. These miniature forts, built less than a mile apart and linked by barbed wire, were designed originally to defend the lines of communications and the principle towns from commando attack, but gradually they spread to complete a network which embraced the whole country. By the end of the war they numbered 8,000 and covered a total distance of 4,000 miles.

For the men, blockhouse life was painfully demoralizing. Gone were the days of pitched battles and glowing praise in the papers at home. There was nothing glamorous or brave about sentry duty and minor fatigue work. They talked, smoked, gambled and became doubly downhearted when De Wet—who referred to Kitchener's labour-intensive scheme as the 'blockhead' system—managed several times to cut through the lines with apparent ease.

Some attempt was made by the Boers to combat the growth of the blockhouses. Home-made grenades were lobbed through the slim windows but the risks were high and, as Botha realized in 1902, there were just too many of them. The commandos' acecard—mobility—had been taken from them and this, together with the distressing condition of the women and children in the concentration camps and the deplorable state of the bare, wasted veldt which could no longer sustain the commandos, decided Botha finally on a call for peace.

A typical blockhouse had an internal diameter of twelve feet, a pair of walls sandwiched with shingle to check bullets and narrow slits in the walls through which the soldiers could fire. Around the outside of the blockhouse ran a ditch in which the night sentry—usually a native—could patrol in relative safety. (A)

Blockhouses varied in size and staff from a captain with one subaltern and twenty to thirty men under him, to a subaltern with ten men or an N.C.O. with six men. A captain was responsible for ten to twelve blockhouses, a subaltern for three to four, and each officer was linked by telephone. (A)

Botha's plans to invade Natal had now collapsed along with the morale of his men. On 13 February he received a message through his wife that Kitchener was prepared to meet him and discuss terms for peace. He accepted the offer and, brandishing a safe conduct, set out for Middelburg.

The scene in Standerton was one of chaos and distress. 'As far as the eye could reach— and it reaches far in South Africa,' wrote an eye-witness, 'is seen a never ending line of oxwagons. Women and children are arriving in hundreds. Their immediate resting place is on the high ground above the Vaal towards the south-east. Opposite them, at a distance, is a laager containing earlier arrivals, with horses, cows, sheep, goats and pigs innumerable, the stock of these unwilling emigrants from homes which, unhappily, have been harbours of refuge to the Boers.' The homeless groups awaiting re-settlement in the camps suffered cruelly from torrential rains.

Three captured Boers are brought before the commanding officers in Standerton. (A)

14th February 1901

We found ourselves surrounded by the enemy, so we did not move today but dug trenches instead. We were very short of rations. In the evening we prepared for a night action. At 9.00 p.m. some sniping into camp took place and some Boers made off with nearly all the sheep. Some volleys were sent into them. Afterwards all was quiet.

15th February 1901

We packed up at 3.00 a.m. and moved off at daybreak. The Boers tried hard to stop us but they were driven back and with heavy losses I think. A small convoy came out to meet us. We camped about eight miles from Standerton when all was clear and were supplied with rations from the convoy. The convoy which we brought from Ermelo, and the cattle, were driven into Standerton. The mail arrived this morning with the convoy.

16th February 1901

We moved to a kopje three miles north of Standerton and camped at Radameyer's farm. Mounted infantry went right in.
General Wynne came out to see the Colonel in the evening.

17th February 1901

Usual parades.

18th February 1901

Wet morning. Myself and the Quartermaster-Sergeant travelled with the wagons to Standerton where we drew a lot of stores from the ordnance.

19th February 1901

Wet day in camp.

20th February 1901

The column moved to Vlaklaagte in the afternoon.

21st February 1901

The column moved to Waterval. There were one and a half companies and head-quarters left there. They are to be relieved by the Scottish Rifles.

A very wet day.

22nd February 1901

The column moved off towards Greylingstad to pick up the remainder of the Scottish Rifles and to drop the remainder of 1st Rifle Brigade.

Same old routine till 10 September, when we moved to Greylingstad and took over the station from the Scottish Rifles.

Plenty of work.

It appears at this point that Tucker felt the tedium of his monotonous routine scarcely worth recording. The following chronological list of dates, from the **Rifle Brigade Chronicle**, covers the period which the diary misses. They serve only to underline Tucker's reasons for silence.

22 February. 'A' Company relieved by a Company of the Scottish Rifles at Vaal Station, and 'D' a Company at Grootpan.
Posts were also taken over as far as Greylingstad exclusive.
5 March. Major A. G. Ferguson re-joined from hospital and took over command of the Battalion.
4 April. 'G' Company left Vrischgewagd and moved part to Rietvlei Station and part to Greylingstad.
5 April. 'E' Company moved from Vrischgewagd to Greylingstad Station.
1 July. Captain C. E. Radclyffe, D.S.O., was appointed assistant Provost Marshal at Heidelberg.

Peace was in the air but, as a loyal Uitlander explained to a British correspondent, 'Your Government is trying to do the impossible. It is trying to run with the hare and hunt with the hounds. It is contemptuously ignoring the trials and sufferings of the loyalists in the vain attempt to gain the goodwill of an irreconcilable people who don't know what magnanimity means, and who will before long bite the hand that feeds them back to comfort and prosperity.'

The British troops in Greylingstad converted the railway station into a blockhouse by strengthening the outer walls with sandbags. (L)

Although it had been pre-arranged that independence would not be discussed, this was precisely the first point Botha raised with Kitchener when they met together in Middelburg on 28 February. Kitchener declined to discuss the point but was more amenable to the other questions and, between them, the two men succeeded in drafting out a set of terms that they hoped would bring about a lenient and immediate peace.

Kitchener sent Sir Alfred Milner a telegram outlining the results of the interview and the latter set to work with Chamberlain drafting out a set of final terms which would be offered to Botha in consideration of a complete military surrender.

They were: the Republics to be given representative government after a short period of Crown Colony government; prisoners to be returned at once; a general amnesty for Boers and Colonial rebels except for a temporary disenfranchisement of the rebels; Dutch and English languages to be taught equally in schools; one million pounds to be paid as an act of grace to meet the debt incurred by the Republican governments to their own people during the war; burghers to be allowed firearms for sporting purposes; African natives to be given the protection of the law, but not the vote; and no war tax.

It took Botha nine days to reach a decision, and, on 16 March, he wrote to Kitchener breaking off negotiations without giving any reasons. Kitchener was not anxious to go on with the war and the decision came as a blow to him. Lloyd George blamed Milner for presenting ungenerous terms, but the true reason lay in the Boers tenacious desire for independence.

CORNELIS BROEKSMA,
held en martelaar voor de barmhartigheid,
0 Sept. 1901 door de Engelschen gefusileerd, ómdat 1
niet zweeg van de wreede ellende in de vrouwenkampen.

A Dutch postcard of Cornelis Broeksma, who was reported to have been shot by the British on 30 September, 1901, because he refused to be silent concerning the suffering in the concentration camps. The proceeds from the sale of the card went to a fund, set up to aid homeless women. (F)

In December 1901, Kitchener gave orders that no more women and children were to be brought into the camps 'unless it was clear that they would starve on the veldt'. But as long as the methodical system of razing their farms and devastating the country continued unabated, they could hardly do otherwise! Whole families were left, abandoned, by the burning wreckage of their homes, a prey to the elements and to the roving bands of armed natives.

8 July. Major A. E. Jenkins arrived from England, on appointment as Second in Command, and took Command of the Battalion.
31 July. Two men serving with 13th Mounted Infantry were wounded near Van Reenan's Kop, Orange River Colony.
15 August. The Rifle Brigade Mounted Infantry, consisting of twenty-five men under Captain Power, was formed.
29 August. A draft of 206 Non-Commissioned Officers and men arrived from England.
9 September. The Head Quarters of the Battalion moved to Greylingstad. 'D' and 'F' Companies joined from North of Heidelberg, and the Battalion occupied the line from Waterval to Vlakfontein (thirty and a quarter miles).
17 September. Lieutenant C. O. B. Blewitt was killed in action at Blood River Poort, near Dundee, while serving with Gough's Mounted Infantry. Four men of the Battalion were wounded.
25 September. A party of Mounted Infantry surprised a Boer piquet South of Greylingstad. One Boer was wounded and taken prisoner; two more were wounded but got away.
27 September. A party of Mounted Infantry surprised some Boers North of Grootpan and took two prisoners.
2 October. 'A' Company, under Captain F. G. Talbot, occupied a Post, ten miles to the North, called Van Kolders Kop.
3 October. Some Mounted Infantry from Colonel Rawlinson's Column and the R. B. Mounted Infantry surrounded a farm in the Hex River District and took three prisoners.
23 October. The Battalion took over the posts to Eden Kop inclusive, and handed over Vlaklaagte, making the total length of line occupied forty miles, as well as Van Kolders Kop.
20 November. The R. B. Mounted Infantry and a few others went to the Vaal River to relieve some of the Railway Pioneer Regiment, who had been surrounded. They covered the thirty miles in five hours, but the Railway Pioneer Regiment had had to surrender in the morning, so the expedition was of no use, and the party returned to Greylingstad on the 21 November.
30 November. 'C' and 'G' Companies, with two sections of 'F' Company attached, joined Colonel Colville's column, Captain Bell in command, Lieutenants Harrison, Powell, Dick-Cunyngham and Sloggett with the detachment.

The approaching Christmas celebrations inspired Tucker to return to his diary. . . .

5th December 1901

Another move. The battalion moved back to our old and best camp, Waterval.

The Rifle Brigade's blockhouse at Waterval. Twenty experienced men could build three blockhouses in two days. Each fort was supplied with 8,000 rounds of ammunition, and fourteen days food and water supply. (H)

16th December 1901

Birthday
Another move. Battalion moved to Standerton.

We built blockhouses all the way from Waterval to Standerton and we find four blockhouses round Standerton and one over the Dutch Vrous on the refugee camp. Left about seventy men in head-quarters on Beacon Hill.

Two pro-Boer Flemish postcards sent home by a British soldier who wrote, patriotically, 'So much for the Belgian version of our position in South Africa. The British can be killed, they will die but they cannot be conquered.
'Long Live His Majesty the King—' (A)

25th December 1901

Xmas day. We spend a little finer one than last year.

I have just returned from going up the lines. There were eight of us in one mess in the Quartermaster Stores, so you can give a

A Christmas letter from the Orange River Colony, addressed to a prisoner of war in the Ceylon camp.
Letters from wives full of pitiful tales of the hardships of camp life and the loss of property could only make the powerless position of the imprisoned men more acute. (Z)

guess we didn't fare badly. We had a few poultry of our own and we had some Xmas pudding that some kind lady had sent to the Battalion. We were allowed a free pint of beer for dinner and an issue of rum at night and another pint if anyone liked to buy it, so it was not so bad after all.

We had a bit of a concert at night round a big log fire.

The relative luxuriousness of Tucker's third and last Christmas in South Africa was due in part to a collection which had been raised for the 1st Rifle Brigade during the year. A total of £1,300 was spent on comforts, warm clothing, socks, handkerchiefs, boot-laces, pipes, pencils, post-cards, dominoes and 400 lb of tobacco for the men.

By May 1902 most war-like efforts had all but ceased. Peace was in the air and the British officers, in holiday mood, took to hunting animals instead of Boers for a change.

The officers of the 2nd Battalion Rifle Brigade set up the Middelburg Hounds, which consisted of a 'bobbery' pack raised from Kaffir kraals in the district. They called themselves the Flat Hat Hunt and during their meets they killed fourteen steinbuck, one oribi and a number of hares. They closed the season, naturally, with a Hunt Dinner.

If hunting was too strenuous, officers could join in more leisurely games of cricket or polo, or simply spend the whole day out shooting duck and spur-wing geese.

Triumphal Arch celebrating peace, made from a portion of a blockhouse, in Newcastle. (A)

. . . But the prospect of another year of the same old routine sent his spirits and his pen underground once more:

1 January. Battalion Headquarters at Beacon Hill, Standerton, four companies on the line.
1 March. Draft of four Sergeants, six Corporals and 140 Riflemen left for India to join 3rd Battalion.
3 March. Draft of 150 N.C.O.'s and Riflemen joined from 3rd Battalion under Lieutenant M. H. Helyar.

The only event worthy of writing about now was peace, and on 1 June Tucker found he had something important to write. . . .

1st June 1902

Peace declared.

Great rejoicing all over South Africa. All surrendered Boers wearing red, white and blue rosettes on their hats and coats. We heard the news at 9.00 a.m. What Ho she Bumps!

2nd June 1902

Usual things: except making walls and trenches. We send seven men, one Sergeant and one Officer home as representatives of the 1st Battalion Rifle Brigade for the Coronation.

4th June 1902

Usual things. Just looking for Boers coming in to lay down their arms. Forty men go to Pretoria for the General Thanksgiving Service.

5th June 1902

Usual things. Saw Breyty bringing in his Commando to go to Leeuwspruit to give in their arms to Botha and Bruce Hamilton.

South African Campaign medal, inscribed: To the memory of those who gave their lives for Queen and Country. (A)

Peace: The Final Stages

In April 1902 there were approximately 23,000 armed Boers and rebels still in the field. They represented barely a fifth of the adult male white population and their numbers were dwindling fast. Many were starving, all were ill-equipped and fighting in tatters; the Boer army had never tried to rival the British when it came to orderly appearances, but now, treated by Kitchener as little more than bandits, and displaying the corresponding appearance, it was only a matter of time before their own people began to share Kitchener's view. In the last year their force had been halved and they now found themselves outnumbered ten to one by the British. Four thousand had been killed, many more thousands were prisoners of war or had surrendered voluntarily and joined their families in the concentration camps. Twenty thousand women and children had died in the camps, more were perishing hourly on the veldt. No help was forthcoming from Europe, the Cape Colony or from the sympathetic minority in England. Responding to the general pressure for peace, Schalk Burger, acting President of the Transvaal, and Marthinus Steyn, the Free State President, met at Kitchener's house in Pretoria for a preliminary discussion.

Kitchener welcomed the peace overtures, he was anxious for a clean end to the war and was prepared to make concessions to the Boer leaders. Here he differed from Alfred Milner (now Lord Milner) who believed that the Boers should admit defeat and give in, 'like other beaten people'. He wanted the Boer surrender to be completely crushing, believing then that the job of the future government would be made simpler. He had no time for concessions, appeasement or even diplomacy. Quite aside from Kitchener and Milner's differing views, there were those of the Boer leaders to be taken into consideration. Schalk Burger and Botha were firmly on the side of peace, whereas Steyn, supported by the charismatic De Wet, was staunchly opposed to any peace which necessitated the loss of independence. Peace then, if it was to be arrived at, would be a complicated decision and Kitchener, anxious to avoid jeopardizing the talks through any thoughtless speculation which might appear in the press, threw a blanket of secrecy over the proceedings.

Thirty Boer delegates, elected by secret ballot, from each Republic were authorized to travel unmolested across South Africa to attend a huge peace conference. The Boers, in sending their most talented generals to the conference, revealed their good faith in the British. However, despite absent leaders, the war continued and Kitchener dexterously combined his peace efforts with war-like ones.

On 15 May, the sixty delegates, together with their governments, met at Vereeniging. Their talks were held in a huge marquee which had been erected for the purpose by the British. As each delegate rose and spoke briefly of the situation in his district, a pessimistic picture appeared of the overall plight of the commandos. Because of the blockhouse lines, communications had been bad between the districts and many delegates were

Deneys Reitz travelled to the peace conference with J. C. Smuts and recorded his impressions in his book, Commando*: '. . . where the Commandant-General (Botha) was expecting us. Here about three hundred men were assembled. They were delegates from every commando in the eastern Transvaal, come to elect representatives to the Peace Congress to be held at Vereeniging, and nothing could have proved more clearly how nearly the Boer cause was spent than these starving, ragged men, clad in skins or sacking, their bodies covered with sores, from lack of salt and food, and their appearance was a great shock to us, who came from the better-conditioned forces in the Cape. Their spirit was undaunted, but they had reached their limit of physical endurance, and we realized that, if these haggard, emaciated men were the pick of the Transvaal commandos, then the war must be irretrievably lost.'*

Schalk Burger and Reitz surrounded by other peace delegates outside the main tent at Vereeniging. (A)

'HANDS UP!' (New Style).
Lord Kitchener was greeted with applause by
the Boer delegates when he said that if he
had been one of them, he would have been
proud to have done so well in the field. (B)

A NEW HERALDIC 'PIECE'.
The Royal Arms 'Disarmed' and Adapted to
a Very Special Occasion. (B)

Despite Kitchener's stringent precautions for
secrecy, the Daily Mail's *reporter, Edgar*
Wallace, managed throughout the peace
conference to supply his newspaper with
accurate reports of the proceedings.
Suspecting foul play, Kitchener admonished
him but Wallace feigned ignorance and
pointed out that, unlike the other pressmen,
he kept away from the barbed wire enclosed
camp at Vereeniging, spending most of his
time taking short pleasure trips by train. The
other correspondens grew daily more
annoyed as they floundered in a sea of wild
speculation and Wallace effortlessly
presented accurate facts.

His ace card was not a gift for
clairvoyance but an amenable sentry within
the camp with whom he was in league. As his
train passed the perimeters of the camp the
sentry would blow his nose on one of three
handkerchieves: red meant 'nothing doing';
blue, 'making progress'; white, 'treaty
definitely signed'. And so he scooped all the
other papers.

'We are good friends now,' said Kitchener as
he shook hands with the representatives of
the late Republics.

shocked to hear of the pitiful state of their fellow countrymen. The fact that the Kaffirs were now armed and taking part in the war against the Boers, together with multiple reports of cruelty and savagery, combined to shake the strong resolve of many of those Boers who had, formerly, been bent on continuing the fight.

Still, the Boers were a proud people and although there was an immediate prospect of utter ruin if the war continued, and even a probability of the whole nation dying out, they were not prepared to forfeit their independence. After almost three years of fighting, the British were not prepared to grant it. A deadlock had been reached but Kitchener averted a rupture by suggesting that a sub-committee of lawyers from both sides should be set up to establish the finer points of the peace.

The conference lasted from 15 to 31 May and, in the end, the Boers won nothing more from the British than they had been offered the year before. The one million pound promised 'free gift' designed to help towards paying off the promissory notes, debts, and to help toward rehabilitating the people and the country, was grudgingly raised to three million, although Botha estimated that nearly one hundred million was actually needed to set the country back up on its feet.

By a vote of fifty-four to six, the Boer delegates finally agreed to the terms and the treaty was signed at 11.05 p.m. on 31 May, 1902, two years and eight months after the beginning of the war.

Before the delegates dispersed, Schalk Burger addressed them: 'We are standing,' he said, 'here at the grave of the two Republics. Much yet remains to be done although we shall not be able to do it in the official capacities we have formerly occupied. Let us not draw our hands back from the work which it is our duty to accomplish. Let us ask God to guide us, and to show us how we shall be enabled to keep our nation together. We must be ready to forgive and forget whenever we meet our brethren. That part of our nation which has proved unfaithful we must not reject.'

Three cheers for peace at the Thanksgiving Service held at Pretoria on 8 June. (S)

6th June 1902

Standerton Commando came in from Leeuwspruit, about 1,200 in all, and a fine sight they looked in the distance. They were camped just by where we were before we had our last shift onto the kop.

7th June 1902

Usual things, still looking for Johnny coming in.

8th June 1902

Great Church Parade for all hands available on the Standerton square and a nice crowd there was there (Boers, Boer women, Tommies and Officers, English and all different nations) for the Great Thanksgiving Service.

8th July 1902

Usual routine. Received orders for England and I don't think there was one of us sorry.

A ration biscuit bearing the glad news 'The War is ended No more Biscuits required. Young Sam.', which was sent home to England, stamped and addressed! (A)

The men of the Rifle Brigade parading at Standerton. Home was now in sight. For many men, like Tucker, who had been away from their families for almost three years, this last delay was almost too much to bear. (H)

Boer prisoners, packed and ready to leave the camp on St. Helena and return to South Africa. 26 June, 1902. (A)

Boer and British united. (A)

18th July 1902

Parade about 10.00 a.m. to entrain for Durban. Arrived at Pietermaritzburg on 20 July, and stopped there nine days waiting for the ship. There were about 4,000 men waiting there for ships to carry them to Dear Old England once more.

29th July 1902

Entrained for Durban once more and reached there at daybreak on the 30 July. Immediately embarked on the *S.S Berwick Castle* and set sail at 3.00 p.m. for England.

3rd August 1902

Arrived at Capetown at 1.30 p.m. and left at 3.00 p.m. same day. Nothing of interest occurred during the voyage home.

22nd August 1902

Arrived at Las Palmas.

When Kitchener returned to England, six weeks after peace had been signed, he was rewarded for his services by being made a Viscount, a full general and being awarded the Order of Merit. At King Edward VII's coronation in August, his popularity was made evident by the loud cheers from the British public. Later in the year he was appointed to the post of Commander-in-Chief of the Indian army.

The S.S. Berwick Castle, with Tucker on board, arriving in the Solent towards evening. (V)

26th August 1902

Ran into a bank of fog; could hear steamers but could not see them. The fog cleared away and there was one of the Demfister line coming for us, straight for our centre. Both ships had to put their helms hard up or else there would have been a collision and very likely cut our ship in two and I am afraid I should have been no more.

28th August 1902

Arrived in the Solent at 5.00 p.m. but had to drop anchor off Netley Hospital till morning as the troops were not allowed in Southampton Docks after that time. You can be sure there were some prayers sent up.

29th August 1902

Hove up anchor and went in dock and entrained for Gosport, arriving there about 10.00 a.m. Busy all day giving in kits and drawing civilian clothes once more.

At 4.00 p.m. marched to the station and got into a train for home sweet home. Arrived home about 11.00 p.m. This ended my experiences and hardships of the South African Boer War of 1899, 1900, 1901 and 1902.

F G Tucker

The war had cost Britain a staggering £223,000,000, a sum which far exceeded even the most pessimistic forecasts. A total of 449,000 officers and men had taken part in the war: 256,000 of them British Regular soldiers, 109,000 volunteers, 31,000 men from the self-governing colonies, and 53,000 men recruited in South Africa.

Seven hundred and one officers and 7,091 other ranks had been killed or had died of wounds and 1,668 officers and 19,143 other ranks had been wounded. 13,000 officers and men had died of enteric fever and other diseases, and nearly 64,000 had been invalided home.

On the Boer side, 87,000 burghers—sixty per cent of them from the Transvaal—had fought against the British. Of this force 2,700 had been Regular soldiers, 2,100 foreign volunteers and 13,000 rebels from the Cape and Natal. At the end of the war over 40,000 were prisoners and 4,000 had been killed.